GW01057533

Critical Criminological Perspectives

The *Palgrave Critical Criminological Perspectives* book series aims to showcase the importance of critical criminological thinking when examining problems of crime, social harm and criminal and social justice. Critical perspectives have been instrumental in creating new research agendas and areas of criminological interest. By challenging state defined concepts of crime and rejecting positive analyses of criminality, critical criminological approaches continually push the boundaries and scope of criminology, creating new areas of focus and developing new ways of thinking about, and responding to, issues of social concern at local, national and global levels. Recent years have witnessed a flourishing of critical criminological narratives and this series seeks to capture the original and innovative ways in which these discourses are engaging with contemporary issues of crime and justice

Series editors:

Professor Reece Walters
Faculty of Law, Queensland University of Technology, Australia

Dr. Deborah Drake
Department of Social Policy and Criminology,
The Open University, UK

Titles include:

Kerry Carrington, Matthew Ball, Erin O'Brien and Juan Tauri
CRIME, JUSTICE AND SOCIAL DEMOCRACY
International Perspectives

Claire Cohen
MALE RAPE IS A FEMINIST ISSUE
Feminism, Governmentality and Male Rape

Melissa Dearey
MAKING SENSE OF EVIL
An Interdisciplinary Approach

Deborah Drake
PRISONS, PUNISHMENT AND THE PURSUIT OF SECURITY

Margaret Malloch and William Munro (*editors*)
CRIME, CRITIQUE AND UTOPIA

Erin O'Brien, Sharon Hayes and Belinda Carpenter
THE POLITICS OF SEX TRAFFICKING
A Moral Geography

Maggi O'Neill and Lizzie Seal (*editors*)
TRANSGRESSIVE IMAGINATIONS
Crime, Deviance and Culture

Diane Westerhuis, Reece Walters and Tanya Wyatt (*editors*)
EMERGING ISSUES IN GREEN CRIMINOLOGY
Exploring Power, Justice and Harm

Tanya Wyatt
WILDLIFE TRAFFICKING
A Deconstruction of the Crime, the Victims, and the Offenders

Critical Criminological Perspectives
Series Standing Order ISBN 9780–230–36045–7 hardback
(*outside North America only*)

You can receive future titles in this series as they are published by placing a standing order. Please contact your bookseller or, in case of difficulty, write to us at the address below with your name and address, the title of the series and the ISBN quoted above.

Customer Services Department, Macmillan Distribution Ltd, Houndmills, Basingstoke, Hampshire RG21 6XS, England

Making Sense of Evil
An Interdisciplinary Approach

Melissa Dearey
Faculty of Social Sciences, University of Hull, UK

First published 2014 by
PALGRAVE MACMILLAN

Palgrave Macmillan in the UK is an imprint of Macmillan Publishers Limited, registered in England, company number 785998, of Houndmills, Basingstoke, Hampshire RG21 6XS.

Palgrave Macmillan in the US is a division of St Martin's Press LLC, 175 Fifth Avenue, New York, NY 10010.

Palgrave Macmillan is the global academic imprint of the above companies and has companies and representatives throughout the world.

Palgrave® and Macmillan® are registered trademarks in the United States, the United Kingdom, Europe and other countries.

ISBN 978–1–137–30879–5

This book is printed on paper suitable for recycling and made from fully managed and sustained forest sources. Logging, pulping and manufacturing processes are expected to conform to the environmental regulations of the country of origin.

A catalogue record for this book is available from the British Library.

A catalog record for this book is available from the Library of Congress.

For my family and my students

Contents

Part I Evil in Philosophy, Theology and Religion

Part II Evil and Narrative

Part III Evil and the Social Sciences

Tables and Figures

Tables

Figures

Acknowledgements

Evil is a magnet for cliché. When I say many people contributed to this book, like all clichés, it is a cliché because it is for the most part true. Who are these people? Mainly, they are my students: past, present and undoubtedly future. I have been very fortunate to have come to the University of Hull and on my arrival here some six years ago, to be asked by my boss/Head of Department/fearless (more or less) leader, 'How would you like to give a class on evil?' It is a testament to Professor Peter Young's undeniable charm that I found myself answering with an enthusiastic, 'Yes! I'd love to.' And here we are.

Little did I know what precisely I was getting myself into, or how hard it would be—intellectually, emotionally and spiritually—for both me and my students. But over the years, this is what we have come up with, again more or less. These are my thoughts and my approaches to the subject. They are certainly not comprehensive, and by no means the last word, but the writers, thinkers, social scientists and other reprobates referenced here somehow got into the frame in the process of my engaging with my students about this vexed and fascinating topic. I hope readers will like it too, and I hope students—not just mine—will find it useful and, dare I say it, inspiring. If not, please to feel free to do better!

So, to my students, thank you. This is for you.

I would also like to thank Palgrave Macmillan for giving me the chance to write and publish this book, and special thanks go to Julia Willan and Harriet Barker for their kindness, generosity and patience in this endeavour. For all this and for your advice, I offer my sincere gratitude. I would also like to thank the two anonymous peer reviewers who offered advice on improving the original draft; again, thank you so much. I have tried to follow your guidance but, of course, any errors or shortcomings that still remain are attributable solely to me. I give thanks also to the generous and enthusiastic support of Professor Reese Walters who read the draft and very graciously suggested that the book be included in the Critical Criminology series. Looking at the other titles and authors in the series, I have to say I feel seriously outclassed! It is a wonderful thing to be included in such an auspicious group, and I cannot thank all of you enough.

Finally, in the spirit of cliché, I would be entirely remiss if I did not acknowledge the contribution of my family: Paul, Sam, Luke, Greta, our littlest vampire Genevieve and my dog/constant companion when writing, Stan. Anything worthwhile that might by chance come from me originates in them. Anything worth doing or having that I might conceive is, as always, for them.

Preface

The Palgrave Critical Criminology series of books is devoted to show-casing the importance of critical criminological thinking as applied to problems of crime, harm and justice from new or, we may venture, 'skewed' perspectives. Evil is not new, but it is definitely and deeply implicated in suffering, harm, wrongdoing and justice, and it is most resolutely skew-whiff. If you don't think so now, trust me, you will do when you get to the end of this book.

When we talk about evil, or identify something or someone as being evil, that is usually the end of the story: the moral conclusion. Think of those chats we have over the dinner table (or tray), at the bus stop or in the pub, sometimes with close friends or intimates, sometimes with strangers. The news is on, or there's a newspaper placard, some such, proclaiming with shrill indignation the latest horror *du jour*. The conversation begins. Why did that woman so callously torture and murder her own small child? Why did the nursery worker/broadcaster/priest/teacher/etc. use his (or sometimes her) position to sexually abuse those children? Why do people bully others online, often people they don't even know, to the point of pushing them to suicide? Why did the serial killer rape and kill all those people? The answer? Because they are *evil*. This is the moral and, hence, the end of the story. To continue, question, interrogate or go any deeper into the gory details, or to adopt the position of 'devil's advocate' or try to see both sides would be to make yourself look like a ghoulish voyeur, suspicious by association or just plain weird; not 'normal', like the rest of us dishing out the label of 'evil' and then stepping back alongside our comrades to shake our heads collectively in dismay at this latest incarnation of the 'other' sect. While society exists on a diet of evil, and regularly dines out on it, it is for the most part an exercise in binging and purgation, not a wholesome fulfilling meal. This book seeks to put some fibre and meat (or non-animal-based protein) back into this meal, which while it may not make it necessarily more palatable, will I hope add substance.

In his book on evil, Terry Eagleton uses the metaphor of violence to illustrate his viewpoint:

> The word 'evil' is generally a way of bringing arguments to an end, like a fist in the solar plexus... Either human actions are explicable, in which case they cannot be evil; or they are evil, in which case there is nothing more to be said about them. The argument of this book is that neither of these viewpoints is true.
>
> Eagleton (2010: 8)

The social sciences have historically concentrated on the question of the social 'good', treating evil as a residual, empty or negative category of human experience. Accordingly, evil has been conceptualized in social and criminological theory as the privation of 'the good'; a consequence of social processes that deny the legitimacy of human existence, survival, freedom, dignity and choice.

In the wake of twentieth- and early twenty-first-century horrors and atrocities, however, evil is increasingly construed more 'positively' as a category of social life in its own right: an active and dynamic phenomenon; something that human agents *do* to each other and the natural world and also *have done to them* by other human moral actors (the possibility of evil by non-human animals or natural evil is not part of the remit of this book). This book is designed to introduce readers and students of disciplines like criminology to the main themes and interdisciplinary theoretical approaches within this burgeoning field of study in the social and human sciences.

In the words of the twentieth-century French philosopher Paul Ricoeur (1913–2005), evil presents a challenge to human understanding that is not like any other (Ricoeur, 1984). It has, thus, been approached throughout history in a number of diverse and, at least to contemporary ways of thinking, bizarre, outrageous or even morally indefensible ways. Part of the challenge of evil that Ricoeur identified a generation ago was the need for us to make some fundamental decisions about how we want to think about evil and deal with it from now on. Because let's face it, the fact is that evil has always been with us and it always will be. It traverses time, distance and space, and impacts the lives of individual subjects as well as every conceivable type of group collective regardless of social variables such as class, gender, race, sexuality, ethnicity, age and so forth. To varying degrees, every person and all cultures and societies of all times have in some way or another had to grapple not just with the experience of evil but also with the age-old 'problem of evil', a term for which in the philosophical-theological tradition is known as *theodicy*. Everyone experiences evil at some point in their lives, usually in the form of suffering and wrongdoing, and it is generally believed that we all know it when we see it. But is the problem of evil really so simple? In light of those undeniable and compelling facts, the question now, as Ricoeur sees it, is how we deal with evil on *our* terms, in late modernity, and from now on: should we think about it more, less or approach it differently than before? And can reflections on philosophical and theological resolutions of the problem of evil in theodicy help us in this process?

Until quite recently, academics and others in the scholarly communities for the most part have chosen the second option, pretty much ignoring evil as an embarrassment or irrelevance to the serious work of critical reflection on just about any subject. My discipline, criminology, has been at the vanguard of such an approach, tending to regard evil as a kind of sentimental or residual category that has nothing to do with the work of contemporary social-science research and, thus, has had its day. Evil has been perceived as the type of concept that the founders of the social sciences, such as Emile Durkheim or Karl Marx, regarded as a sort of catch-all category under which bad things that happened but where poorly understood (no science) people, things and/or events were placed. The preference was to construe evil as the diversity of 'social evils' that are traceable to a range of societal factors pertaining to various social demographics as the result of structural causes such as poverty, famine, disease, marginalization, violence, war or other external forms of inequality, crisis and/or deprivation. Since then, evil has been widely regarded by many as merely a sentimental if archaic notion of religious groups, tabloids and other quotidian discourses of moral outrage in response to trauma, suffering and harm with tangential links to the individual subject (a highly prized constituent of the modern moral and legal landscape), and as such really has no legitimate place in the scientific study of crime, punishment or criminal justice.

But maybe it's time for these attitudes and approaches to evil to undergo something of a radical rethink. Why? Because for one thing, there are many indications that the more we ignore evil, by assuming that it's an outdated concept or just stupid and the credo of brainwashed zealots, the more vulnerable to its most pernicious damage we seem to become and the more it tends to proliferate and expand, to happen again and again, and to become much worse either by getting more extreme (e.g. child sexual abuse, genocide) or pervasive (e.g. anxiety, depression). When we, in modern secular and so-called civil society, decide that evil is just not the topic for us, the sort of intellectual vacuum created seems to serve the interests of other moral and social

entrepreneurs who would make great capital out of the widespread igno-
rance of the notion and the distaste for it, thereby ensuring only that
they are unhampered by the need to respond to any substantive external
rational or temperate debate. And I am not talking about just the obvious bad guys of contemporary society like terrorists or serial killers who
openly trade in evil, but increasingly other more 'legitimate' or enfranchised agents who often are empowered or backed up by the state, such
as governmental regimes (e.g. the Bush administration, the Mugabe
regime, the BBC), corporate actors (e.g. bankers, the military, the police)
or members of the criminal justice system (e.g. judges who cite evil as
an explanatory factor in their sentencing reports)—all of whom either
rely upon or take recourse to evil as an explanatory or causal factor, or
in some cases actually make their livings and advance their careers by
doing it so well! Maybe it's time, as the philosopher Hannah Arendt
argued sagely in the wake of the Holocaust, to face up to evil as a problem for *our* times, as a question and challenge for *our* world and our
possible futures; something to take seriously and try to better understand, and thereby minimize in what is a complex institutional and
diverse modern social and moral framework. If we take this approach,
as I suggest we do, then where do we start? Ricoeur poses an important
question, and however we choose to answer it, the way the question
has been articulated presupposes that we first have a sufficiently robust
knowledge of how evil has been thought about and dealt with before,
throughout history and across different societies and cultures. This is
so that we can learn from the past, and not repeat the same mistakes
or at least not in the same disastrous ways, thereby helping to ensure a
better response in the future. That is what this book is fundamentally
about.

This book addresses current trends in the study of evil, arranged over
three main themes or sections:

- Theodicy and the origins of an onto-theological concept of evil in
  theology, rationalist epistemology and moral philosophy—in these
  chapters, we will concentrate on the language and experience of evil
  as conceived within various religious, theological and philosophical
  traditions.
- Evil as symbol, myth and literary trope in the narrative approaches of
  psychoanalysis, hermeneutics and cultural studies—in this section of
  the book, we will concentrate on how we tell stories about evil; that
  is, how we use narrative to make sense of it, castigate it and even
  enjoy it.

- Evil as a product of collective and individual experience—as shaped by the body, gender, everyday life, the family and the state—as represented in 'post-metaphysical' theories of evil in sociology, anthropology, feminism, politics and criminology; in other words, we will examine how evil is finally being recognized within contemporary scholarship, and how these ways of discussing it help us to make sense of our own experiences of evil as embedded within these seminal social institutions.

This book is organized into ten chapters, each concentrating on a different theoretical approach and/or topic:

- Theodicy—the problem of evil in a world created by a benevolent God
- Enter the Evil Genius—encountering metaphysical evil
- Radical freedom, radical evil? The problem of evil as one for modern moral science
- Telling evil stories—understanding cultural narratives and symbols of evil in the phenomenological hermeneutics of Paul Ricoeur
- 'Something to be scared of'—evil, myth and psychoanalytic theory
- Evil and literature—romanticism and after
- Doing evil—what makes evil a compulsion
- Genocide, slavery, holocaust and war—atrocity and the banality of evil
- Axes of evil—the war on terror, the 'enemy within' and the politics of evil and the state
- Touching the void or through a glass darkly? Rethinking evil in criminology

But at the outset, what we must try to avoid assuming that these three 'phases' of study, theory and/or analysis are in any way a comprehensive representation of evil—that is, covering all the ways of dealing with the subject of evil—or that they somehow represent a kind of logical progression, if not of history, then of thought, whereby one 'phase' is distinct from or follows on from and supersedes its predecessor. What I mean here is that just because religious conceptions of evil tend to come first historically, this does not necessarily mean that they are cancelled out by subsequent philosophical or postmodern thinking on the subject; previous language about evil has a nasty tendency to pop up in the most unexpected places, so keep a look out. As the cultural and literary theorist Terry Eagleton (among others whose work will be examined here) argues in his book *Holy Terror* (2005), love, fear, sacrifice, martyr-dom, scapegoating, the sublime and death are just as relevant to the functioning of the modern nation state today as they ever were to any social assemblage across cultures and throughout history. And when you drill down into them, they are jolly interesting too.

Will this book solve the problem of evil? I could be evasive and say that the answer to this question is 'unlikely', but I know that it is 'no'. But the odd thing is that when you look at all these theories and theses together, that's OK. In fact, it's probably a good thing, because if there's anything that seems to get evil people on the rampage or evil events underway, it's thinking that we've got it all sussed and sorted out: 'no problemo'. As we will see, the notional application of rationality and the plain old job of making sense out of evil can end up being really and truly horrendously awful. The task is, then, to try to make sense of the darkly inexplicable without making too much sense, if you see what I mean. Or to try to maintain a healthy distrust in our *faith* (because that is what it is) in the institutional, bureaucratic and scientific sys-tems we devise to deal with these evil bastards who do such terrible things—no system will ever completely stop them but, of course, that doesn't mean we shouldn't try. To deal effectively with evil, we need science, we need society, but we also need more (or sometimes possi-bly something else or less). What both the study and experience of evil reveals perhaps better than any other topic is just how messy and disrup-tive it is to any intellectual efforts to put order on it, and also just how durable older and more traditional, mythical and even highly personal and subjective ways of perceiving it are, even in the most modern and rationalized areas of our lives. So, although we might be ultra-moderns, even the most ancient ways of dealing with and understanding evil still have something to say to us, if only because we share with our ancestors the trait of being human.

Finally, with respect to the aim of the Critical Criminology series to highlight and advance innovative thinking and intellectual entrepreneurship in academic scholarship in criminology (and any other genre of thought, for that matter), the general aims of this book converge on using a range of interdisciplinary approaches (e.g. theo-logical, philosophical, cultural, social-scientific and postmodern) to this distinctive area of human experience in order to enable readers to reflect upon the 'problem' of evil as a concept previously considered beyond the limits of social theory. This is not to pillory social theory, but to add to it, as I hope my readers and students will do, and do it better and with more courage and honesty than I have been able to do. This is to further develop the critical capacity to utilize interdisciplinary theory in a criminological context in order to address this important area of contemporary social experience. I have chosen a number of examples in the book, such as the Rodney King beating and the *Fifty Shades of Grey* phenomenon, to illustrate and try out the different theories. I hope you will choose your own examples from your own personal experience to do the same, and I encourage you to do so—your experiences of evil are significant and important. Don't be afraid to contribute your thoughts and to improve and further develop our discipline. I encourage you to be compassionate and thoughtful in your analysis, but also to be bold and brave. In an age dominated by the media and challenged by the scandals of victimization and the ideals of human rights, the study of evil could and should help us to understand and cope with these pressures and problems better. I do hope so anyway.

So, welcome, my new apprentices. Let our study of evil begin.

Part I
Evil in Philosophy, Theology and Religion

1
Theodicy: Understanding the Problem of Evil

The first way of making sense of evil that we will consider is distinguished by its attempt to adapt study of evil as much as possible to the classic philosophical principles of rational/logical knowledge and coherence, known as *theodicy*. More precisely we will look at what the philosopher Paul Ricoeur called the onto-theological problem of theodicy, drawing as it does upon the ancient and classical domains of *ontology*, the philosophical study of being (including metaphysical realities and entities), and *theology* (the study of God, faith and religious beliefs). From a contemporary modern and secular (or perhaps more properly 'laicized') perspective, theodicy can appear to be confounding and archaic. For some, even considering such a theory of evil feels like a recursive step backward to a bygone and primitive age where myth and superstition as opposed to scientific knowledge and reason ruled. In modern times, it seems odd and counterproductive to try to reconcile the basic elements of theodicy together in a coherent whole—God, other transcendent worlds and their (possible) inhabitants and faith on the one hand, with human rationality and knowledge of our physical world with its real-life suffering on the other—but this is precisely what theodicy attempts to do, utilizing the core principles of modern rational thought. But rather than being what is '...a pale version of itself, a boutique topic' (Fuller, 2011: 93), theodicy still has much to offer in terms of revealing aspects of the phenomenology of evil in a (post)modern contemporary world. As the sociologist Steve Fuller (2011: 93) puts it, by 'sociologising' theodicy we can increase our understanding of evil and learn how to 'suffer smart' in the twenty-first century. In a global world that continues to be beset by many and persistent evils, the problems of distributive and social justice, competition for scarce resources and the management and dispersal of risk between and across the human

3

and non-human animal and natural environments, such an engagement with evil becomes a moral and practical imperative. Being able to 'make sense' of evil in this regard is all the more pressing in such a complex global world in which the future consequences of our actions and inactions are ever more difficult to regulate, control and predict.

The types of rationality utilized in the panoply of theodicies are themselves hugely diverse, covering a wide range of philosophical, theological and latterly sociological theories and concepts, so for reasons of space we can examine but a few. In this chapter, I will try to provide an overview or map of theodicy as a way of thinking about and trying to make sense of and in many ways 'discipline' evil from the perspective of human cognition. This is a mode or model of thinking about evil that has been used in very different and creative ways by some of the greatest minds of the past to test and develop methods of thinking about evil and how we should deal with it as something that is intrinsic to and revelatory of the human condition; evil as something elemental to being human as created and fallible beings. In accordance with the aim of this book, I will explore theodicy from a criminological perspective, that is to say, how it helps explain evils of a criminal type, things that criminal/deviant actors do that cause suffering and harm to victims, and what the implications of theodicy is for the criminal justice system as well as notions of wrongdoing, innocence, culpability, justice and reform more generally. Drawing mainly from Paul Ricoeur's essay on theodicy (1984), but also considering some of the classic theodicies of Leibniz, Bayle, Saint Augustine and Malthus, this chapter traces theodicy primarily from the rational but also Gnostic and mythic traditions. I will conclude this chapter by taking into consideration other more recent commentaries on theodicy and reflecting upon its potential as a way of analysing the challenge of evil for criminology today.

What is theodicy?

Theodicy or 'the problem of evil' has this basic and simple structure:

> God is omnipotent, omniscient and all good (and exists!)
> God created the universe
> Yet evil exists.

How are we to make the first two premises consistent with the last? How are these basic truths to be reconciled? Why would a benevolent, loving God allow the pain and suffering that accrue from evil to exist in the world? And if He is all powerful, all knowing and benevolent, then why didn't He create us to be all good? Or why doesn't He do something to prevent it? These are the sorts of questions that have both inspired and dogged theodicy arguments.

The term 'theodicy' is probably most commonly associated with the seventeenth-century German philosopher Gottfried Leibniz (1646–1716), presumably because his book on the subject of evil was entitled *Theodicy* (1709), although the term has been traced back as far as the ancient Greeks and treated by far too many theologians and philosophers to list here. Actually, Leibniz's interest in evil spanned the whole of his intellectual life, being the subject of his very first and last published works (Murray, 2005). Among his other contributions to the study of evil and philosophy as a whole, which we are really only able to sketch here (there are a wealth of critical commentaries available for further research, some of which are listed in the References), Leibniz is probably most famous for his declaration that this is the 'best of all possible worlds', and this basically sums up his argument in relation to the fundamental premises of theodicy outlined above. The philosopher Susan Neiman (2002) describes Leibniz's theodicy rather cleverly as portraying God to be like a diligent housewife in a market, carefully weighing up the options before choosing only the best for (in this scenario) His cosmic brood (this being us, you and me and everyone who ever did and ever will exist). The main problem with this image is that it implicitly depicts God as somewhat limited in His capacities (what philosophers have labelled the 'underachiever problem' (Murray, 2005)) whereby God is for some reason unable or possibly even unwilling to create a world without evil, but is nevertheless caring and compassionate by at least trying to do His best by the creatures He created and (possibly also) creation.

So on this reading, God is possibly not so powerful or putatively benevolent after all. While the implied denial of the perfect attributes of omnipotence or goodness to God here may seem a bit harsh, possibly even heretical or contradictory, a brief consideration of the alternatives might show Leibniz's theodicy in a better light. Consider, for example, the resolution of the theodicy from other perspectives such as that provided by the seventeenth-century French philosopher Pierre Bayle (for a more detailed sketch of which I would refer readers to Neiman, 2002: 34–35). Philosophers have labelled this the 'holiness problem' (Murray, 2005), but we may put it another way, drawing upon a common phrase drawn from contemporary popular culture, 'It's all good'. What Bayle means by this is that whatever evil there is in the world, it's all OK because it is part of God's plan and, therefore, by definition, good, and it will all be resolved in the end (e.g. by way of messiah appearance, apocalypse, final judgement, eternal reward, whatever). Instead of sidelining the divine attribute of God's omnipotence in favour of His well-intentioned (if imperfect) benevolence, as Leibniz does, theodicies like Bayle's rather emphasize God's eternal power and His inscrutable (from the perspective of human reason) knowledge and will. God is God after all; He can do what He wants for whatever reason He wants, even breaking His own moral laws and allowing, even making, people suffer if that's what He chooses to do. But in the end, it's all 'good' because the rules don't apply to God and it will all make sense according to His final purpose, and at the end of the day, that's all that really matters. Hence, the holiness problem: the God who is, by 'virtue' of His own divine powers, actually quite wicked and monstrous, possibly even evil, by condoning or sanctioning human suffering while being able to prevent it but choosing not to do so because He has other purposes in mind. And so, we have our first set of dualities in relation to theodicy reasoning, in this case, about God Himself: is God an underachiever or a power freak? Is this the best of all possible worlds or is it a divine moral free-for-all? Is God a loving if imperfect carer or a wicked monster?

Ricoeur's (1984) seminal essay on the onto-theological problem of evil may shine some light on what will be a familiar theme in the study of evil as the questions above suggest. As Ricoeur astutely notes, the first thing that we can see in the constitution of the problem of theodicy is the construction of a stark and recurring *duality*, that is to say, a polarization of good and evil into two main strands: (1) the power and goodness of God on the one hand; and (2) the persistence of evil and humanity on the other, each in apparent contradistinction to each other. The problem of evil as modelled on theodicy is to make these fit into a single, coherent argument, but nevertheless these dualities persist, often with God on one side and the realities of human wrongdoing and suffering on the other. Ricoeur argues that this approach is consistent with a particularly Western and rationalist view of the nature of the problem of evil: i.e. situating the mutually exclusive and oppositional categories of good and evil. And, indeed, in general cultural discourse we are all familiar with such dualisms and dichotomies regarding the good versus evil binary to this day: black/white; this/that; either/or; one or the other; and ne'er the twain shall meet sort of thing. But while this may be logical, rational and in some respects comforting, it ignores aspects of feeling, action and everyday real-life experiences that are central to both the unfolding, understanding, dealing with, struggling against and seeking to prevent and come to terms with evil. The reality is that such binaries of absolute good on one hand and completely dastardly evil on the other, while certainly not unknown, are relatively speaking quite rare—regardless of whether or not the actors involved or divine, demonic, human or some combination thereof. Usually, there is some contamination by one of the other, some diabolically vexing mix of goodness and wickedness that makes the issue of separating the good wheat from the evil chaff downright consternating to try to sort out and clean up. The reality is that we are often victims and perpetrators in the acts of evil that cause suffering, trauma and harm. And it would seem that this is becoming more the case with the further development of global capitalism and its complex web of technologies and market economies that implicate us in the unintentional commission of human suffering and damage to the natural environment, often on a grand scale, affecting people and places far removed from us geographically as a result of our everyday activities as consumers at home. Consider also the numerous and polarized arguments on social phenomena such as the London riots of 2011, where it is difficult if not impossible to establish clear and stable boundaries in terms of who precisely are the victims and who are the victimized, even in close proximity, despite it being generally agreed that some of what happened was very bad indeed, and is symptomatic of an unfolding moral and social crisis. Somehow just labelling those caught on CCTV as 'evil' does not help solve or prevent such instances of crime and harm.

When it comes to trying to make sense of evil in terms of identifying the 'facts' and setting out the 'real story' of what has happened, this kind of fundamental disagreement and polarization of views is often observable, especially in explanations put forth via the print, broadcast and social media. This is not just a consternating anachronism or conundrum of rational, syllogistic logic that leaves us feeling at our wits' end and bemused by things that don't go together and won't make sense; this is what in philosophical terms is an 'aporia'—something that requires a new way of perceiving things and of thinking about them. But the issues at stake are not just abstractly philosophical; when evil has occurred, they are deeply emotional and often passionately felt. So who gets to say, who decides what is what and who is who in these axial debates, or is it all destined to descend into a cacophony of conflicting, arguing voices in which one side demonizes the other and exonerates itself from moral responsibility and hence the need for action, punishment or change? Do we accept things as they are as the best that they can possibly be, or resign ourselves to the ethos that in the end it's 'all good'?

There are currently many books and articles available that analyse the nature and meaning of evil from philosophical and cultural/media perspectives; rather than restate these, I will turn my attention to evil from the viewpoint of criminology. We take recourse to the kind of thinking and modelling enshrined in the theodicy to underpin and provide a foundation for some very important sociopolitical discourses and also systems and institutions that many millions of people come into contact with and in some ways rely upon, their lives either healed or destroyed as a result: possibly the most important example being the criminal justice system. This dualism at the heart of theodicy accords with a particularly logical-rational and also juridical (and thereby criminological) articulation of the problem of evil. According to these accounts, as Ricoeur (1984) explains, evil in the form of experiences of things like sin, suffering and harm is further bifurcated in other dualisms, this time in evil as:

- *wrongdoing* (actions that are blameworthy and actor(s) who are prone to guilt); and
- *suffering* (those acted against who are blameless, those left crying out for justice).

This derivative duality belongs to what Ricoeur calls two further heterogeneous categories that are particularly amenable to and familiar from the prospect of criminology: that of *blame* and *lament*. Something bad has happened, someone has been harmed, someone or some group is/are guilty and to blame, and they must be identified, accused, found guilty and punished to express remorse and made not to do it again. And not coincidentally, this is basically the remit of the criminal justice system from the police to the courts to prison and after—to take notice of, find and separate the criminals from the rest of us and deal with them appropriately, punishing first and rehabilitating them after so that they offend no more. Penal law is, as noted by the eminent criminologist Nils Christie (2001), ' ... oriented towards finding responsibility of guilt ... '; penal law is built

> ... upon dichotomies, either guilty or not guilty. A decision of 'half guilty' does not count. Truth-Commissions, they are in a way relieved from the dichotomies. They can think in continuums; it was bad what he did, awful, but certain acts were OK. If the total picture was of a character that made him 'guilty', that is not central in the description.

Within penal law it has also to be a personalized guilt.

Christie (2001: online)

Aside from newer developments like Truth Commissions, that's the central idea that more or less shapes the institutional plan of the modern criminal justice system, however that is articulated and put into practice, and it is one fundamentally based on theodicy as a philosophical model and the individual as a culpable (and potentially redeemable) moral agent.

To briefly summarize then, in theodicy, evil first distinguishes itself as the opposite of absolute goodness (personified by God) and second manifests itself in human reality as suffering, further dividing into what Ricoeur calls the heterogeneous categories of blame and lament, guilt and punishment, reform and healing, each pair of which are two sides of the same coin, as it were, different and discordant but deeply interconnected in the delivery of *justice* (as discussed below). A consequence of these derivative dualities that spin off from the original theodicy duality of good and evil is that the focal point is very much on moral evil or the evil that is or pertains to the *human* as a primary source—as offender and victim. The effect of theodicy is that God starts to fade into the background a bit, and becomes distanced from His creation in many respects, and certainly from the evil that humans experience and are responsible for—a feature of theodicy that will be even more in evidence in the rationalist theodicy of Rene Descartes (discussed in the next chapter). And in many ways, this is understandable from a common-sense perspective, if only because the task of trying to understand God's role and purpose in this whole problem is frustratingly speculative, and a matter that over the course of modernity will become more recalcitrantly theological and removed from the other scholarly disciplines. So, while 'the God question' doesn't totally disappear, it does become somewhat devolved into the realm of religion, theology and (occasionally) metaphysics, distanced from the evil that humans are morally responsible for and that human beings *do*.

As God recedes into the background, any reliable absolutes that can help anchor and orient the system of (modern) rationalist ethics go with Him. What we then get is a proliferation of new and increasingly unstable dualisms founded in world of human agency and morality—the choices we make and the things that we do—originating, as we have seen, with the dualism of blame and lament.

- *Blame* is specifically linked to the realm of human *action*, being a violation of a prevailing code of conduct and thus attracting the declaration of guilt and the assignment of punishment. In the face of human suffering, blame is the beginning of how we assign culpability to one or more (human) agents who are responsible and ultimately answerable for the evil that has taken place.

- *Lament* takes place where *suffering* has been endured by a person or group upon which evil has befallen, where they were not responsible for making it happen—whether through the intentional or unintentional actions of someone else, natural disaster, accident, illness, death or some other affliction.

Lament is where we typically expect to find *victims*. Throughout this book we are interested primarily in human (as opposed to natural) evil, that which takes place as a result of the intentional action of one or more actors; but it is important, nevertheless, to note that evil is not solely the preserve of human activity. Certainly, the issue of natural disasters, as a genre of human evil, which result from human activities that can be traced to things like climate change puts the distinction between natural and human evil into a new and challenging light. But for now, we will mark and generally observe the distinction between natural and moral evils as more or less distinct.

The point being made here by Ricoeur (1984) in his discussion of blame and lament is that both philosophy and theology have tended to think of evil as the common and singular root of both wrongdoing and suffering. Hence, the polarity of wrongdoing and suffering, and of blame and lament have become in our way of thinking intimately linked. This is epitomized in the notion of *guilt*, which in most Western societies bridges the gap existing between the dualisms of blame and lament, wrongdoing and suffering, the evil that is committed and the evil that is undergone. The apportionment of guilt (to one or more human agents), therefore, becomes the key dynamic in making sense of and dealing with evil, and in many ways, the sole factor, from a practical standpoint and from the subjective point of view of many victims and other bystanders.

This bridging of guilt can be observed in the intentional infliction of pain in the form of *punishment* (e.g. deprivation of liberty, shame, humiliation) on the wrongdoer, which is in itself *not* evil. To reiterate, the intentional infliction of pain by one or more human beings upon another and the production of lament (remorse) is not in itself evil, not according to theodicy. In fact, based on this model, it is good, because (depending upon your point of view) it mollifies the rest of the community, makes the wrongdoer remorseful, instigates personal change and ultimately ensures that such evil doesn't transpire again. Or that's the idea. To reiterate, pain and suffering can be good. While evil is often the result of an offence committed by one person against another, in the context of punishment, the production of that secondary dyad of *blame* and *lament* (in the form of remorse) absolves the pain inflicted on the wrongdoer of the designation of evil in the name of one thing:

Justice

What is more, Ricoeur argues, despite their polarities, this deep unity of sin/wrongdoing and suffering, and subsequently blame and lament, guilt and punishment, healing and justice, witnessed in or around the phenomenon of evil reveals to us something about the 'deepest unity' (1984: 636) at the heart of the human condition. It certainly underpins a seminal principle of modern civil society under the systematic organization of the modern nation state as central arbiter of power and authority.

This is the mapping of moral evil as distinctively human in the classic rationalist theodicy. It is, like human beings themselves, deeply divided and intricately intertwined; pertaining to the individual and the collective; deeply emotional and intimate and at the same time enshrined in public institutions and hierarchies of bureaucratic authority. Figure 1.1

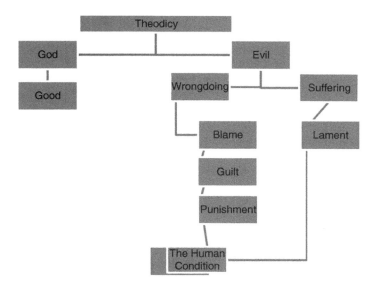

Figure 1.1 Ricoeur's model of theodicy
Source: Adapted from Ricoeur, 1984.

sets out in the form of a diagram how I understand Ricoeur's argument concerning the layout of these different factors comprising the classic theodicy.

While this diagram is a distillation of what are some very complex ideas, basically, in visual form, what this image immediately conveys is where the action was deflected to and has more or less remained until quite recently: on the *offender*. Based on this model, as previously noted, God in His absolute goodness becomes fairly removed from the action, i.e. there is not much happening on that side of the diagram; neither is there a lot happening, it has to be said, on the far side, where we find the suffering and lament of the victims. And, indeed, this is reflected in the criminal justice system itself to this day, whereby God acts as place holder, a kind of symbolic guarantor of the rationality and at least commitment to absolute good (manifest in the principle of truth) anchoring the whole system, and while victims are slightly more in evidence, their involvement is still subsidiary to the wrongdoer in the classical model. With respect to this marginalization of victims, challenges in recent years have been posed, and this view of justice modelled on theodicy is changing, and victims and their advocates are becoming increasingly vocal in their demands for a transformation of the criminal justice system and cultural attitudes to victims and justice in general. This in itself constitutes a major critique of a view of evil modelled on theodicy that goes back to the inauguration of the age of Enlightenment to which we can trace this fundamental institutional model and cultural principle, and how it sought to resolve the problem of evil from an onto-theological-philosophical standpoint. In what is now a largely secular Western modernity, most people don't ordinarily think of the criminal justice system and its foundations and origins in this way, and it does pose a certain challenge to those in the legal-judicial and academic communities who presume that evil has nothing to do with criminology but is a primitive and residual aspect of pre-Enlightenment religious doctrine. As can be seen by the theodicy model of the 'problem of evil', our criminal justice system still owes a great deal to this basic principal philosophical structure. Hence, understanding it is a key element in its present and future development and reform, not a backward or retrograde step.

The resolution of the problem of evil in theodicy presumes that the phenomenon of evil in the face of the existence of an all-good and all-powerful God is one which is not and cannot be God's fault, by definition. Evil is, therefore, somehow the fault (if not necessarily the unique experience) of human beings:

- God cannot be evil (or can He? Can God suffer evil? These are questions we will return to presently).
- Hence, God is not culpable or responsible for evil in our world.

This means that theodicy is by its nature an apologetic for God in the face of the reality of evil in the world. God (whether underachiever or power mad) is off the hook. Human beings, it would seem, are the guilty parties in the frame, as well as the victims, though both of these are debatable, not least as represented in sacred scripture, theology and religious traditions. This is where Gnostic, mythical and wisdom traditions are key, as ways of knowing that try to help us make sense of who God is, and how we can endure the evils we continually face. We will turn our attention briefly to these shortly.

In the meantime, it is worth pointing out that this raises questions about the nature of human guilt and by implication what would appear to be the inherent faultiness of the human condition. God made us; we are creatures created by an all-good and all-powerful Being—so how is it possible that we can we be actively or positively evil? How can a blameless, absolutely good entity like God be responsible for the reality of evil indirectly by creating us, who are evil? Also, why does evil happen, and more to the point, why does it happen to *me*? And why does it seem to happen so much to 'innocent' people, like children and other blameless or vulnerable people, who are not responsible for the actions that cause their suffering?

As Ricoeur explains, the experience of guilt based on such an understanding of evil entails that the 'fault' at the core of evil (and thus human nature) is its *historical* (and thus pre-existing and human) and also essentially *passive* nature. In other words, moral evil is (or feels like it is) the result of the 'seduction' of the overwhelming power of the 'dark side' of human nature and, thus, is the manifestation of nothing more substantial than human weakness, what we lack as creatures in comparison with God. In addition, evil is the outcome of something that precedes us all, the history of the whole of human wrongdoing and its consequences for subsequent generations, something which God does not really share in because He exists outside of human history in a timeless eternity. And, indeed, a great deal of human suffering befalling blameless victims is the direct result of those who lived previously, even long ago, and whose actions have exerted sometimes extremely negative and deeply pernicious consequences for those living in the present, as for example in the notorious cases of the international slave trade and colonialism, and the legacies of racism in modern global societies (such evils and their possible resolutions will be discussed further in subsequent chapters). These and many other such historical evils raise serious questions about the culpability of living people or agencies to say sorry or make restitution (as, for instance, in the case of governments apologizing for the actions of previous administrations or historical policies that were deemed acceptable at the time), an issue again which will be returned to in due course. For the moment, this historical perspective on the 'phenomenology of the experience of evil' (Ricoeur, 1984: 635) should direct our attention to a range of issues pertaining to the possible, probable or predictable impacts of our actions as moral agents now on future generations, such as in the cases of cybercrime, organized crime, terrorism, corporate crime, human trafficking, global warming and climate change, to name a few. Here, again, we see the focus on human agency and the moral legacy of things that happen in the social world in the here and now, but also how these impact on human and the natural worlds, and the links that are (currently) known and unknown. It also throws light on our bizarre and persistent passivity or apathy when it comes to taking the necessary steps to understand, reverse or at least ameliorate such evils for ourselves as well as distant other and/or future generations. Again, theodicy can help us to understand these enigmas pertaining to evil, and explain why we are typically so apathetic and enervated when it comes to trying to effect change.

The problem of evil, its proliferation and the apocalyptic suffering it causes are, in the wake of the 'long' twentieth century and its multiple atrocities, more pressing than ever. 'In 1945, [the philosopher Hannah] Arendt declared: "The problem of evil will be the fundamental question of postwar intellectual life in Europe" ' (Arendt in Bernstein, 1996: 137). Sadly, how wrong she was; if anything, the evidence suggests just the opposite. Ricoeur identifies these two factors—God's blamelessness and human fault at the core of the theodicy problem—as underpinning the strange kind of passivity on our part fundamental to this view of evil and the human condition. Evil is not God's fault, but ours because we are so weak and susceptible to its seductive lure. But God created us as limited and imperfect creatures who have free will and are prone to evil acts. So, then, is evil really our fault if we were made this way? What is more, the quality of temptation that pervades evil suggests the presence of a 'seducer'—a person or entity doing the luring, a demonic or devil figure, if you like (one of which appears in the next chapter), who busies himself with the tempting of us poor weak mortals. Poor us, whatever are we to do? I know: nothing!

The outcome of this aspect of theodicy is that instead of feeling empowered to deal with evil in our midst, we rather feel ourselves to be victims in the same acts that make us guilty. And it would seem that the more power we get, the more prone we are to this weakness to temptation and playing the victim, or simply just surrendering to inaction in the wake of the complexity of evil as we moderns frequently experience it. The more potent human action becomes on the natural and social worlds with the development of science and technology, the more damage—as opposed to benefit—we (often unintentionally) seem to cause. This is the opposite of the optimism characteristic of Enlightenment thinking as a remedy to pre-modern, 'dark' ages. Or, as the sociologist Zygmunt Bauman (1989) argues, this proliferation of evil in ever more brutal and diverse forms and the victimization of ever more and less deserving victims are very much complicit in the project of modernity itself. The manufacture on a global industrial scale of suffering and harm is well underway, a process overseen by powerful elites who are less apologetic and answerable for their crimes and the harm they do as time goes on. The fact of the matter is that we live in a world where it is 'less risky to steal the bank than rob the cashier' (Christie, 2001: online). The polarity of the luxurious comforts of consumer society and the unequal distribution of atrocious suffering emanate from the perverse and unequal construction of desire and need. This is enshrined in that most essential component in the industrial production of apathy and passivity: the phenomenon of *denial* (Cohen, 2001). The separation of science and technology from the realms of morality and aesthetics (i.e. goodness, creativity and beauty) epitomize what Bauman calls the 'rationality of evil' (in Welzer, 2002) and goes some way to explain the way things are and why we feel so helpless in changing this.

This strange and paradoxical mixture of passivity and agency, victimization and guilt, is what gives evil its *enigmatic* and *ambiguous* character.

'The devil made me do it ... I was just following orders ... It wasn't really my fault ... ?'

In the classic syllogism of the theodicy in its pre-modern versions, God is (in the first instance) accorded the attribute of existence as part of His list of perfections (*apropos* Thomas Aquinas's ontological argument). While human beings it is assumed also exist, the same cannot be said for evil. There is a strong and vibrant tradition of theological and philosophical thought that posits just the opposite: that evil does not exist, and that is what it is (or more to the point what 'is not'). This is a conception of evil within the Gnostic tradition, from the Greek *gnosis* meaning 'to know'. Basically, what this posits is that there is a difference between physical (bodily) reality and the reality of the mind or spirit, and it is the latter which is 'good' and the former that is 'bad' and responsible for much of what is in essence the venal temptation to do and enact evil. This is the basis of what has become known as the mind/body split, associated with the Gnostic tradition generally and Cartesian philosophy more particularly.

In the Christian tradition, following the theology of Saint Augustine and the Neo-Platonists, all evil is viewed as essentially negative, that is, non-existent. It is an absence, a lack. This means that it consists not in the positive manifestation of anything 'real' or actual, but in the loss or deprivation of something necessary for the real manifestation of perfection, including the perfection of being/existence. According to Neo-Platonism, this must be the case, otherwise there would be an 'ideal form' of evil 'out there' somewhere against which all manifest forms of evil deeds in the world of perceptions are to be measured. Such a thing is unthinkable, not least because God created everything that exists, and He is not the author of evil. So it would seem that a 'seducer' or some form of ideal evil is a fiction or figment of human imagination. This is the source of the devil character, which according to this view, is a ruse we use to try to absolve ourselves of responsibility and make evil someone or something else's fault: 'The devil made me do it' type of argument, or perhaps more precisely, excuse.

Saint Augustine was one of the first thinkers to reject the notion of the reality or substantiality of evil, reversing one of the central principles of a doctrine called Manichaeism, of which Augustine, prior to his conversion to Christianity, was a major proponent, which acknowledged the reality of evil as the battle of the forces of good against evil, darkness against the light. Augustine's notion of evil as a negative category—a state of privation of the good—still persists as the basis for Christian and rationalist conceptualizations of evil today. Remember this—we will encounter it again in our discussions of the war on terror and the axis of evil. It's not just the stuff of fairy tales, sadly. This is very, very 'real', as a designator of evil, and one with real political and adversarial bite in late modernity (again, something that will be turned to again, specifically in relation to the 'axis of evil' argument explored in Chapter 9).

This take on evil as non-existence does not then necessarily mean that there are no manifest or 'positive' aspects of evil. Clearly, pain and suffering exist in a 'positive' (albeit sometimes subjective) sense, as at least by-products of injury, trauma and harm. And, indeed, moral evil depends on more than simply refraining from doing good (although it consists in this too) but also in actively choosing to do evil. The point here is twofold: first, that evil in itself exists as a kind of *relative category*, whether as the privation of good or the perversion of (rational) human action; and second, that evil exists as an outcome of human action separate from our experience of God, that is, as an outcome of human agency or *free will*. Whether or not doing evil is essentially down to a fault in rational decision-making is a question we will return to again in Chapter 3 on radical evil and the thinking of Immanuel Kant, whose philosophical ethics and writings on evil continue to expand upon the challenges and problematics of theodicy.

For now, evil based on the Augustinian/Neo-Platonic model is conceptualized as something which is not real, but only relative. Only God is absolute, and by extension only the good is 'real' (presaging Hannah Arendt's thesis and its roots in Augustinian thought regarding the substantial nature of the good versus the 'banal' and 'superfluous' characteristics of evil (Bernstein, 1996)). So, this inherent relativity means, in effect, that what is evil in some circumstances may be good in others; and probably there is no form of existence which is exclusively evil in all its possible contexts, or indeed entirely 'good' (the latter of which with the (possible) exception of God). For example, think of the 'good' of Christ's scourging and crucifixion in the context of what Christians call the 'good news' of the gospels, and also the goodness of intentionally inflicting the pains of punishment in the greater good of rehabilitation, or the putative virtue of telling the truth when it could cause someone else pain. Once again, evil is construed as something that humans are responsible for as a result of their own actions through the exercise of their free will. And freedom is by its nature fundamentally good (or at least better than the alternative), and from a theological standpoint, human freedom is inherently an expression of God's infinite love, that as His creatures we are free to return this love, choose to be good, kind or compassionate, or not, as we choose. God created human beings to be free, and by implication this means we are free to choose to disobey His divine will and/or the moral law, that is, free to do evil. Evil exists in the world because for some reason or other, we choose to do it, as we are free to do. And, hence, we are to the ones to suffer (although again, in the mythic tradition of scripture, it would appear that God suffers too as a result of our bad deeds, and indeed is capable of inflicting pain and suffering on His creation). Ultimately, evil is our fault, although there are times in the Hebrew Bible when God/Yahweh appears to act in an evil manner and later show remorse, such as in the story of the flood. This leads us again to the resurgence of funda-mental tensions that haunt the theodicy, such as the notion of the evil God who, for His own inexplicable (from our point of view) purposes allows or wills our suffering. But as Richard Swinburne argues, the point here is that evil in relation to the divine will and/or perfect goodness must always be viewed in context, as a direct result of evil's relativistic nature:

> I accept that an omnipotent being can prevent any evil he chooses, but I deny that a perfectly good being will always try to do so. If a perfectly good being is to allow evil to occur, he must have the right to do so, and there must be some good which is brought about by allowing the evil to occur and could not be brought about by him in any better way, and so great that it is worth allowing evil to occur. If the perfectly good being is also omnipotent (i.e., can do anything logically possible), then it must be logically impossible for him to bring about the greater good in any better way.
>
> Swinburne (1996: 30–31)

While some readers may balk at the religious ideology from which theodicy arguments are derived, they have the distinct advantage of eliding the trap of situational versus dispositional arguments about evil, such as those put forward by contemporary social scientists such as Milgram and Zimbardo (considered later in this book) and others such as Simon Baron Cohen.[1] What a contemporary philosopher like Swinburne finds among the goods thus generated from a divinely con-doned phenomenology of evil are the freely given and selfless virtues of compassion, sacrifice, responsibility and care. He argues that in the face of evil, simply being 'of use' or at least trying to be by the expres-sion of these goods, even when there is little hope of success, is itself a very good thing (e.g. offering sympathy or opportunities to talk, more practical things like cooking meals, helping out with cleaning, trans-portation or bills when someone is in pain following the death of a beloved child). The illness or sudden death of a loved one is the sort of deeply inscrutable and seemingly 'pointless' evil that, while horrendous in terms of suffering, can ultimately elicit the best in human nature. Does this make it all OK? No, not to me it doesn't, not as someone who has coincidentally during the writing of this book witnessed such agonizing pain unfold in the lives of others. But such responses can make what is completely unbearable slightly less catastrophically atrocious through opportunities to be compassionate and useful; in the face of evil, these should not be neglected or rejected. In the end, it is this truth, this overriding reality about the human condition that puts the dualities, reversals and ambiguities of evil as an intellectual puzzle and efforts to solve it in the shade. That in doing what seem to be small or insignificant acts of kindness or compassion, we don't know the impact of the good that may accrue. And what is more, according to Swinburne, these experiences of compassion in the face of overwhelming evil transform and change our essences as moral subjects in ways that help ensure greater benevolence and thoughtfulness in our future dealings with ourselves, others and our world. When viewed in the context of Hannah Arendt's banality of evil thesis (Chapter 8), such a boon to the virtue of *thoughtfulness* (as opposed to the evil of thoughtlessness) constitutes a significant advantage, for individuals and communities, especially in an age of social diversity, secular postmodernity and hyper moral relativity in which so many things are interconnected. If anything, this renders evil and theodicy as objects of study more relevant than ever. However, as Swineburne acknowledges, there is a tendency within theodicy to construe the suffering of evil and the depth of the pain inflicted as the result of losing a loved one to illness, for instance, as a matter of luck and random chance or alternatively as 'just deserts'—that life is basically and fundamentally a lottery or that we deserve the pain we get; this is what evil tells us. We will return to this issue of the severing of evil from deserts and the serendipitous nature of suffering in the next chapter when we consider the story of Job.

For now, the thing to note is that theodicy demonstrates that evil is thus not absolute, i.e. it does not share any attributes with a perfect and absolute God; hence, it is something that can be dealt with or potentially explained away within the context of a broader historical, theological or philosophical narrative. To put it another way, this most rational approach to evil concludes with a recognition that it cannot be rationalized; evil is not rational, it eludes with astonishing ease our attempts as rational beings to deal with it in this manner, to the extent that such attempts can sometimes exacerbate the original suffering and make things worse. But this is what we 'know'; this is the legacy of the Gnostic tradition. Fortunately, for us, it is not all we have in our armoury against evil.

Let's finally (and briefly) turn our attention to the mythic and narrative traditions identified by Ricoeur in his essay (1984), and conclude with some remarks on the social-scientific encounters with theodicy.

Mythic, narrative and social-scientific theodicies

Thus far, this chapter has mapped some of the most classic and sophisticated examples of the onto-theological theodicy and how this conundrum of the problem of evil has been 'solved' by various philosophers and theologians. What we come up against in the end is theodicy's limits, as a rational or Gnostic question, and this tells us many things about the dichotomous and circular language we still use about evil and its explanations and remedies. Now, let us turn to the other traditions of theodicy, rooted in the ancient and spiritual/religious traditions of storytelling to see what we find there by way of explicating evil. Let us also ask: how do we, as social scientists, read and interpret sacred texts?

First, consider these famous stories from Genesis 3: 8–11:

> Then the man and his wife heard the sound of the LORD God as he was walking in the garden in the cool of the day, and they hid from the LORD God among the trees of the garden.[9] But the LORD God called to the man, 'Where are you?'
>
> [10]He answered, 'I heard you in the garden, and I was afraid because I was naked; so I hid.'
>
> [11]And he said, 'Who told you that you were naked? Have you eaten from the tree that I commanded you not to eat from?'
>
> Genesis 4: 8–15

> Cain spoke to Abel his brother. And when they were in the field, Cain rose up against his brother Abel and killed him. Then the LORD said to Cain, 'Where is Abel your brother?' He said, 'I do not know; am I my brother's keeper?'[10] And the LORD said, 'What have you done? The voice of your brother's blood is crying to me from the ground.[11] And now you are cursed from the ground, which has opened its mouth to receive your brother's blood from your hand.[12] When you work the ground, it shall no longer yield to you its strength. You shall be a fugitive and a wanderer on the earth.'[13] Cain said to the LORD, 'My punishment is greater than I can bear.[14] Behold, you have driven me today away from the ground, and from your face I shall be hidden. I shall be a fugitive and a wanderer on the earth, and whoever finds me will kill me.'[15] Then the LORD said to him, 'Not so! If anyone kills Cain, vengeance shall be taken on him sevenfold.' And the LORD put a mark on Cain, lest any who found him should attack him.

Religious myths concerning the origins of evil like this taken from Genesis have a distinctly different 'feel' than those like Malthus's and Calvin's resolution of the theodicy (cited below). Narratives like Genesis from religious myth represent evil as something emerging from living in a community and in dialogue with God in a kind of ordinary everyday way, and the consequences of getting on God's bad side. What comes out of this is the emergence of the *law* as an expression of God having to be more explicit about his demands on human beings who have proven themselves to be so fickle and open to persuasion (and, indeed, seduction, as Ricoeur states in his analysis of the theodicy) and the attempt to distance themselves from punishment and blame for their evil actions (as in the case of Adam and Eve and Cain). But at the heart of these encounters with evil is still communion with God and with the community in the course of ordinary everyday life, modelled on intimate interpersonal relationships like the family and the centrality in dealing with these consequences of things like unconditional parental love. Significantly, such a representation of God in the mythic tradition accords with the view of God in Leibniz's theodicy, whereby His role as benevolent Father takes priority over his attribute of omnipotence, omniscience and judgement (although these figure to some if partial extent). Also, we observe, especially in the story of Cain, what today we would recognize in many respects as a very contemporary communitarian response to crime, inscribed in an ancient biblical story about unjust and murderous evil that is dealt with by God in a humane, compassionate and pragmatic way, focusing on the safety of the offender (Cain) and the need for his inclusion back into the community, and for those who are angry to not react in the spirit of vigilantism but with restraint.

Now, let us consider two examples from the Protestant Christian and Muslim mythic traditions:

Calvin

Adam was denied the tree of the knowledge of good and evil to test his obedience and prove that he was willingly under god's command. They very name of the tree shows the sole purpose of the precept was to keep him content with his lot and to prevent him from becoming puffed up with wicked lust … Augustine speaks rightly when he declares that pride was the beginning of all evils. For if ambition had not raised man higher than was meet and right, he could have remained in his original state … Adam so corrupted himself that infection spread from him to all his descendants. Christ himself, our heavenly judge, clearly enough proclaims that all men are born wicked and depraved when he says that 'whatever is born of flesh is flesh' and therefore the door of life is closed to all until they have been reborn.

Abu Hamid Al-Ghazali

Indeed, all poverty and loss in this world is a diminution in this world but an increase in the next. Every lack in the next world in relation to one individual is a boon in relation to someone else. For were it not for night, the value of day would be unknown. Were it not for illness, the healthy would not enjoy death... Behind this sea is the mystery of predestination where the many wander in perplexity and which those who have been illuminated are forbidden to divulge. The gist is that good and evil are foreordained... No one can rebel against God's judgement.

(both of the above extracts cited in Rorty,
2001: 188–122 and 54–55)

These offerings from what Ricoeur calls the wisdom tradition by those such as Al-Ghazali and Calvin illustrate the difference between these and myth: 'Myth narrates, Wisdom argues' (Ricoeur, 1984: 638). Calvin and Al-Ghazali focus on the dualistic nature of evil highlighted by theodicy, its dichotomous relationship with the good as an oppositional object, and increasingly on the dictates of the law, more or less in the absence of a present, benevolent and loving Father-type God as described in the Genesis stories above. What is more, in these examples, evil is determined and defined increasingly from the perspective of the individual, specifically with reference to the intrinsic evil of the *body*, drawing very much from the Gnostic/Neo-Platonist traditions. What's more, in the Calvin excerpt, we see what is still the predominance of the biological language of 'contagion' to define and deal with evil, that it can be biologically identified (as, for example, in our times by way of an 'evil' gene) and surgically excised from the otherwise healthy, good organism of the body politic. In each of these contexts, evil becomes something that is experienced and talked about as wholly 'other', characterized by its very alterity in relation to the normative construction of goodness, and the almost species-level distinction between 'us' and 'them'. This approach may result in a Durkheimian social consensus emanating from the collective denunciation of the (criminal/deviant) evil act or person(s) among us, but it also generates considerable fear and anxiety among the general population for fear of falling foul of the seductions and contagions of evil as a failure on the part of (individual) humans to abide by God's law, as noted in the work of Foucault. Such concepts are foundational to the tradition of social-scientific and criminological reasoning as the basis of social critique.

As implied in the story of Adam and Eve, an engaged and community-based God can't be watching all the time, but a distant and omnipotent God in the tradition of predestination represents the ultimate in full-spectrum surveillance—God as the ultimate in CCTV technology, who does nothing to prevent evil, but simply records and later uses this to condemn and punish. Compare this with the God of the early books of the Hebrew Bible/Old Testament who dealt with evil in the present moment in a loving and protective way of punishment (much like a committed if frustrated father); this other God tots up infractions for final reward and/or punishment in the afterlife—a much more cold and calculating sort of entity, less interested in relationship, love and care, or the daily work of managing the evils that do and are going to happen within the community when you are dealing with imperfect beings. These latter narratives of evil relate more to the 'holiness problem' described above, whereby God knows and could prevent evil but not only chooses not to, but punishes us for doing what He predestined to happen in the first place; once again, bringing our culpability as responsible, or even free, moral agents into dispute. The temporality of evil is significant here, relating solely to God's time as opposed to human history, that is, eternity; God is not 'with us', not as in other mythic Hebrew traditions, sharing the human realm much in the same way as we do, e.g. walking, looking around, asking what's up and so forth. The only time that matters in these latter stories is eternity—history as eschatology—and even this is cold comfort, when the upshot is that we are dealing with a God who created us and the cosmos with the intention of rewarding few and punishing many, for all time—not very rational or consoling.

The social sciences: Malthus's theodicy and beyond

The notion of the relativity of evil within a broader moral (and, indeed, social-scientific) narrative context is central to one of the most infamous of all theodicies, that of the economist Thomas Malthus (1766–1834) whose resolution of the theodicy focused primarily not on the concept of justice but rather on the notion of *scarcity*. Basically, Malthus tried to reconcile these in the chilling implications of his infamous population theory (where the human population varies in direct proportion to the scarcity of resources) with the goodness and benevolence of God.

Malthus's theodicy begins with a critical analysis of human nature, drawing on Aristotle's theory, that the natural state of humanity is rest or indolence, not action or activity. ' "Men" [sic] are inert, sluggish, and averse from labour' (Malthus in LeMahieu, 1979: 469). They are also prone to the desire to procreate, thus leading to another evil: overpopulation. Hence, 'men' require a positive impetus to get to work and avoid fornication. God, Malthus argues, provides such an impetus in the form of hunger, scarcity and want. In response to this 'positive' impetus toward rectifying man's indolence in the form of hunger and want, 'man' must work to get food to satisfy hunger; if there is too much procreation/fornication, then great, and it has to be said indiscriminate, suffering and starvation will result, thereby providing positive sanctions against what Malthus considers an excessive amount of sexual activity.

Thus, while things such as pain, hunger and starvation are in themselves evils, in the context of forcing lazy fornicating 'men' off their backsides and back to work so that they refrain from too much sex, they serve as 'goods' in the sense that they divert man from his idle and sinful nature, and put him on the correct path—which is, conveniently enough for Malthus, the industrial-age economist, to work to the point of exhaustion for subsistence wages and to reproduce in accordance with such external market constraints. Similarly, Malthus argued that God allows moral and physical 'flaws' in the universe because ' ... the constant effort to dispel this darkness, even it [sic] fail of success, invigorates and improves the mind' (Malthus in LeMahieu, 1979: 470). Thus, according to the Malthusian theodicy, moral and natural evils together help 'men' to achieve their full potential, to develop and to succeed in a purposely inhospitable world. Malthus declared that 'moral evil is absolutely necessary for the production of moral excellence' (ibid.: 471).

The teleological character of this argument and its hyper moralism modelled on the Protestant work ethic and implicit ethos of anti-Catholicism sometimes found in Scottish Enlightenment thinking are more than evident in this particular theodicy. Malthus's theodicy has been attacked vigorously from a number of quarters (not least by theologians) as at once implicating God in the production of some of the most dire and indiscriminate acts of evil and experiences of human suffering on a colossal scale (famine, war, disease, and so forth) as somehow 'good', making the designation of 'good' and 'evil' in the event utterly meaningless. In addition, it is noteworthy that this thesis, strongly influenced by what was then the dominance of Darwinian evolutionary theory, has obvious ideological connotations, the first of which is its function as a shameless apologetic for the Protestant work ethic which, as Max Weber famously argued, was particularly amenable to a high modern industrial capitalist political economic framework and colonialism. The Malthusian theodicy was also socially and ideologically conducive as a justification for denying the need for the equal distribution of resources to the poorest and most needy (near and far) and seeing their 'salvation' in the form of work, not simply absolving people from their duty to act in a compassionate and socially responsible way, but *actively prohibiting them from doing so*. What is more, we observe in Malthus's theodicy the focus on the (unruly) body and sexuality of the 'other' (women and those of non-WASP ethnicities) as significant sites for exerting unequal institutional powers of exploitation and social control upon entire populations in the rationalization of 'evil' in modern post-industrial capitalist societies, again evocative of the Gnostic tradition and his narrow and rigorous prejudice against the body in favour of the spirit/mind. We will return to the role of the body, gender and sexuality and evil again, most explicitly (in all senses of the word) in Chapter 5.

Conclusion

How is evil made sense of and dealt with within the different and diverse theodicies, and what are the implications and legacies for us moderns, and social scientists, of these explanations?

The sort of language about evil as relating to the criminal, deviant, marginalized or otherwise deserving (and preferably conveniently distant) 'other' is still very much in evidence today, as is the insistence about how to deal with the real and present deeds of evil or evil people on an ongoing basis. This is represented, for instance, in what are commonplace media discourses about petty criminals, terrorists, welfare scroungers, young/single/prolific parents, paedophiles, refugees, famine 'victims', the poor, disabled people etc.—as diverse and in many ways atomized members of society. As Durkheim argued, while even in (post)modern, diverse societies we rely upon the denunciation and separation of such 'evils' and evildoers to create a viable ethos of social consensus, we also require workable strategies for dealing with these individuals within the remit of the law and in accordance with principles of human rights. So, we need workable structures pertaining to institutional arrangements such as community punishment (formal and informal), protection and reintegration in the here and now; we can't just wait for the end of time for the final judgement as the ultimate and highly anticipated punitive opportunity. The problem with the language of alterity and evil as non-being or relating to eternity or the enigmatic plan of some abstract, imperfect, power-crazed, omniscient, transcendent and/or hapless God is that it makes it very difficult to engage fruitfully with the subject of evil today, in the here and now, or to be able to countenance it and discuss it meaningfully and maybe even solve (at least some of) the problems behind it and prevent or reduce it. At the same time, however, the capacity to refer to a priori (deontological) principles as the basis for these fundamental decisions regarding norms of good and evil has advantages that the relative nature of (consequentialist) situational-dispositional approaches might lack. This does not always mean the decisions will be easy or palatable. But they may be more philosophically informed and reflective, one would hope.

How, then, do we, as social scientists, read and interpret discussions of evil contained within or attached to such sacred texts and onto-theological/mythic/wisdom traditions?

Theodicies like the one produced by Malthus accord to very human, rational discourses like economics and biological evolution, which often produce resolutions that are horrific in their spiritual and ethical consequences. Among other things, this exposes the limitations of purely rational discourse at the heart of theodicy: that attempts to 'make sense' of evil on a rational human model not only don't work, they often end up making the original situation or crisis even worse. In effect, attempts to rationalize the existence of an all-good, all-loving and benevolent God with the existence of evil in theodicy renders a dichotomous view of good and evil that is so polarized that it often results in the collapse of the boundaries between good and evil itself; either God becomes wicked by allowing or even planning our downfall, or human suffering is presented as good, or the notion of human freedom or agency itself disappears. On the other hand, something like evil as encountered in the mythic and narrative traditions with the emphasis on care, compassion and reform can, even within secular modernity, prove much more humane in their real life moral implications. While the latter may not resolve the issue of evil by leaving it open to mystery, at least it doesn't end in the justification of human suffering and the image of the vindictive God or a heartless colonial social order as implicated within the Malthusian theodicy or the implied apathy condoned by Bayle.

By reconsidering the explanations and resolutions of evil from a variety of mythical and religious texts, social scientists can get a much more diverse and nuanced picture emerging of what is, after all, an ancient and universal human experience. Hence, as social scientists and criminologists, we see from explanations offered by economists like Malthus how limited but also revealing they can be about the ideologically motivated values and presumptions of their own age on the prevailing moral code. At the same time, other more culturally and historically diverse texts are perhaps a way of encountering the 'problem of evil' in a fresh and possibly more meaningful if challenging way, that deals not only with difference and the present moment, but also recognizes the complexities of communities and everyday life as in the mythic and narrative traditions can be extremely effective in communicating their messages about the persistence of evil.

While criminologists have thus far had little to say on the subject of evil (we will return to this in the final chapter), sociologists are engaging more fully with this vexed topic. In essence, what do they have to say on the notion of theodicy?

Contemporary sociologists such as Ian Wilkinson argue that we should begin by viewing suffering (the outcome of evil) in a new way. In his book *Suffering: A Sociological Introduction* (2005), he reviews the contemporary critical social-scientific research to conclude that this 'new' vision of evil and suffering must start by rejecting a number of presumptions attached to or emanating from the traditional Gnostic-based theodicy. This first relates to a rejection of the (Cartesian) mind/body split: it is not the case that the body is evil, and neither is the 'spirit' or mind wholly good; we need a more robustly holistic and embodied approach in contemporary studies of evil (as will be explored in subsequent chapters). Second, as classic rationalist theodicy so aptly demonstrates, we must acknowledge the inadequacy of human reason in this area; while reason may be regarded as a distinctively human characteristic, rendering us morally responsible for our actions, this is in itself not our only trait nor does it sufficiently arm us to deal effectively with something as deeply pernicious and evasive as real evil. In our world, this means it is important to recognize the impotence of scientific discourses such as psychology, biology and even sociology to in any way adequately capture the true nature of pain and suffering at the heart of evil. The real meanings of suffering and evil are not reducible to an intellectual puzzle modelled on the theodicy, but rather inextricably bound to the 'flow' of the everyday experiences of those who live through and with them in a way that always eludes any abstract rationalization or institutional control. In addition, as we have seen, such theodicy-type explanations of evil are by their nature manifestly functionalist or in other ways exclusionary; someone or some group is always marginalized and subsequently, and disproportionately, expected to pay (Wilkinson, 2005: 27). As contemporary sociologists caution, to devise or become overly reliant upon such explanations is to itself add additional 'symbolic violence' (ibid.: 27) to the suffering of the other. There is always something about evil that is not only elusive but 'unspeakable' (Wilkinson, 2005: 28), and in many important ways, theodicy can contribute to and amplify these socially over-determined silences, thereby increasing their distress and leading to further ethical detachment on the part of those responsible. Any such dichotomous representations of good/evil as putative stable binaries are already innately and profoundly culturally biased and bound (ibid.: 29). On the other hand, what theodicy does is establish beyond doubt

> ... the brute fact of suffering in historical experience. Accordingly, whereas the documentary evidence of our intellectual history records a constant struggle to account for the apparent 'disproportion' between what happens 'in' human suffering and the normative assumptions of theodicy, it is only in modern times that this aporia is deemed to expose the intellectual bankruptcy of any recourse to speculative metaphysics.
>
> Wilkinson (2005: 36)

Wilkinson's solution? To focus more on *experience* as a bridge between real-life suffering and the realities of cultural history. This sort of post-metaphysical and phenomenological approach will be further explored in the third and fourth chapters, following a more intensive examination of the metaphysical view of evil and speculative reason in Chapter 2.

Philosopher and sociologist Steve Fuller (2011) is inclined to take a more positive view of the potential for sociologizing of theodicy. Echoing Ricoeur's (1984) opening question, he asks, should evil and human suffering today be 'tolerated, minimised, redressed or somehow transcended?' (Fuller, 2011: 93). In a post-metaphysical age of science, technology, secularism and globalization, we as global citizens and moral agents are in a (historically) unique position to take a 'godlike' (ibid.: 93) stance on such questions based on a theodicy point of view. Rather than resulting in the distancing of God emanating from the classic theodicies, after the scientific and a number of social revolutions, our critical knowledge of normative order and collective experience could actually draw us closer as moral actors and powerful—even quasi-omnipotent/omniscient/benevolent—agents. 'Thus, we may be entering an era of "moral entrepreneurship"' (Fuller, 2011: 93). Such optimism is deeply embedded in the foundations of the social-science disciplines in the notion

'of social rationality or *sociodicy* in Jon Elster's (1983) evocative term. It has been common in the history of philosophy that reciprocal inequalities (*à la* complementarities) among people living together are necessary to hold society together. This thesis has been often expressed in terms of hierarchy as the university social glue. (Brown, 1988)'

(Fuller, 2011: 95 [original emphasis])

From our distinctive historical, moral, and technological perspective, we are in a hitherto unique position to be free to adopt alternate normative actions and views, as indeed theodicy advocates in its view of human responsibility for evil and the need for human action to counter its negative effects. These need not be tied to any particular cosmic or religious world view, but neither do they have to be divorced from any number of such ideologies as versions of the wisdom and/or mythic traditions with their enduring and powerful narratives of consolation and healing. What is necessary, and what the social-science disciplines should be in a fortuitous position to bring, is a critical and reflexive awareness of the sociocultural norms that have implicated theodicy reasoning in the very worst excesses of social injustice.

In a modern world dominated by increasing and widespread suffering as the result of human violence and exploitation, these and other social scientists argue that theodicy should not be abandoned, but rather revised as a mechanism for addressing as opposed to simply documenting or excusing the pernicious evils of our times (Morgan and Wilkinson, 2001). In a capitalist global social-economic order that facilitates new evils on such a colossal scale, the challenge is to embrace an ethos of 'moral entrepreneurship [that] normalises evil by recycling it into good' (Fuller, 2011: 113). In the twenty-first century, this will 'demand from social theorists unprecedented levels of realism, imagination and will' (Fuller, 2011: 113). The most inclusive and informed study of evil can help, not hinder, such imaginative and entrepreneurial enterprises. In the next chapter, we will continue our investigations into the philosophical and specifically metaphysical treatment of evil in the history of modern philosophy and popular culture.

Note

1. I reference this book with the proviso that Baron Cohen's thesis regarding evil as an 'absence' construed as 'erosion of empathy' (Baron Cohen, 2013) and in particular his alliance of this with autism is controversial at best, in any case highly problematic. I write this as a parent with two children on the autistic spectrum; like many such parents and others who have experience of autism (e.g. Rachel Cohen-Rottenberg, 2012), I have to say I am not convinced nor do I recognize the links Baron Cohen makes. However, I leave readers to weigh the evidence and decide for themselves, including the reference but acknowledging its controversial nature, a not uncommon theme in the study of evil.

2
Enter the Evil Genius: Encountering Metaphysical Evil

In the previous chapter, we examined the problem of evil as represented in the theodicy, or how to reconcile the reality of evil in the world with the existence of God who is all powerful(ish) and absolutely good (ish, or possibly wicked). As we saw there, evil in theodicy is regarded as diametrically (if not also diabolically) opposed to the good, or a privation of the good from a rational point of view, whether conceived of in terms of logic, knowledge or power—very much prized and very human attributes in modernity. The somewhat paradoxical result is that evil in theodicy often turns out to be indistinguishable from the good, or else what becomes to be regarded as 'the good' takes evil to previously unknown levels of excess, whereby some theodicies (e.g. the Malthusian theodicy) advocate a perverse rationalization of human suffering on a massive scale. On this logic, something like pre-marital sex is regarded as evil and sinful because it violates God's law whereas the deaths of millions from starvation, war and genocide should be condoned as 'good'. As Max Weber noted in his landmark analysis of the Protestant work ethic, such rationalizations of evil serve potent ideological functions in terms of legitimating the oppression and exploitation (if not actual destruction) of whole populations in modern global capitalism, as well as striking fear in the hearts of believers about evil and the destiny of their eternal souls.

But many modern readers will say, hey wait a minute, we (or many of us) aren't really that scared anymore about evil on the eternal theological-eschatological timescale; we are more worried about evil in the here and now, in this life! And, of course, this is an important point. Then again, while the ideological threat of the onto-theological theodicy might make some of us toe the line and accept our lot for fear of damnation in the next life or exposure as sinful in this one might

31

have faded, at the same time, fear of the transcendental presence and influence of evil as a malicious, diabolical presence in newly emerging domains of virtual reality remains. We may think of the so-called Internet trolls and others who use these new spheres of virtual reality solely for the purpose of finding others to intimidate, manipulate, harass and control, sometimes with devastating consequences, as the highly publicized suicides of some young and other vulnerable people who have been on the receiving end of this sort of abuse attests. I will argue in this chapter that what this vexatious and purely villainous type of evil hides is an equally powerful ideology underpinning theodicy that encourages ordinary people to accept their lot as, if not preordained by God, then predicated upon what are portrayed as the equally irresistible forces of socio-economic chance that are also ultimately for our 'benefit' and outside of our control. This arguably constitutes a variation, if not exaggeration, of the previous excesses of evil as exploitation, abuse and control exerted by some corrupt institutional regimes and malevolent individuals, outside and beyond religious institutions to more fully incorporate individuals and the state.

This chapter continues our examination of the treatment of evil in the modern philosophical tradition, focusing this time as a starting point on a story of one man's encounter with another type of transcendent evil being. This is the 'fiction' or 'fable' of the Evil Genius in Cartesian philosophy, specifically his role in Descartes' version of the theodicy developed in his seminal and landmark work in rationalist philosophy *Meditations on First Philosophy* (1641). Through this fable of evil, I will try to make sense of the notion and ongoing problem of the human encounter with metaphysical evil; specifically, how this relates to the meaning of transcendental evil in contemporary thought and cultural discourses. What I propose in this chapter is that, despite Descartes' valiant attempt to deal with it decisively from a rational point of view (and perhaps because of it), the problem of metaphysical evil has not gone away, nor can it simply be discarded or dismissed in the rejection or revision, as some social scientists have proposed, of theodicy (or indeed religion). The resilience of evil in the guise of the Evil Genius as such a prevalent and influential character in contemporary popular culture is itself indicative of the endurance of the notion that there are dark forces from beyond our material world that are responsible for causing the trouble we encounter and do, or for just making us fail to get things right and know the 'truth'. In this chapter, I will concentrate on the Evil Genius, beginning with Descartes' famous fable, tracing the philosophical and cultural reflections upon its meanings and implications for interdisciplinary social science.

Rene Descartes (1596–1650) was a French philosopher writing in the early seventeenth century, and one of the prime architects of what has now come to be known collectively as the Enlightenment. In his most celebrated work, *Meditations on First Philosophy* first published in 1641, Descartes set out his classic and most developed argument for what we now consider the basis of modern rationalism and scientific method. To briefly summarize, what Descartes was primarily interested in doing in this work was to wipe the philosophical slate clean insofar as that was possible, and to start the whole task of thinking again, this time on distinctively modern terms. Descartes considered that medieval philosophy had become stale and increasingly irrelevant for people living in the seventeenth century—too busy doing things like counting angels dancing on the heads of pins, and even more worryingly concentrating on the faults and limitations of being human as opposed to the strengths and speculating about the nature of (divine) metaphysics. Descartes thought that we should rather concentrate on the world as we *are* capable of knowing it with the powers of human cogitation, *our* world, from *our* viewpoint, on *our* terms. Chief among his targets in his endeavour was what he considered to be the overly powerful influence on philosophy by the classical thought of Aristotle. In this regard, he was especially keen to bring to an end the project of scholasticism in medieval philosophy over which Thomas Aquinas (who developed Aristotelian thought in Christian theology and medieval philosophy) stood like a colossus.

A major part of Descartes' project to unseat Aristotle as the main influence on philosophy was to reject the *senses* as the primary source of knowledge, and also the appeal to nature as the source of empirical evidence as a principal method of knowledge and proof. Descartes' major shift in focus was rather to the power of the mind, specifically human rationality and cognition modelled not on empiricism, but on a more conceptually reliable resource—mathematics (specifically geometry)—rather than looking to nature and the senses as the foundational sources and models of acquiring that most elusive sort of knowledge: *certainty*.

So how does Descartes go about doing this? He starts off in the *Meditations* by establishing two things:

1. A proof for the existence of God—Descartes' ontological proof (so far, so good—in the wake of the trials of Copernicus, this would go a long way to keeping him out of trouble with the Church; it also allowed him to display his genius by inventing a new and original ontological proof)
2. Establishment of the separation of the body from the mind

Some readers will recognize both of these from the previous chapter, and even if they don't, will probably know that neither was new in the seventeenth century nor exclusive to Descartes. And they would be right. Despite the proposed novelty of Descartes' project as he brands it, both of these have their roots in ancient and indeed medieval philosophy. They have also historically attracted a great deal of attention by philosophers and others, but these will not be the main area of our attention here, just worth mentioning.

It would be the next stage of his argument that would allow Descartes to finally make the conceptual break from pre-modern to modern philosophy, transforming metaphysics from a science founded in ontology (the study of being) to one based on epistemology (the knowledge of individual self-reflection) (Gasche, 1986). Basically, Descartes achieves this by putting forth the notion that it is easier for humans to know what is in their minds—what can be thought according to the principles of their reason—than to know what they can perceive about God, knowledge in consensus with others or more importantly from observation of the natural world around them that they perceive with their senses. Descartes points out how our senses regularly lie to us—he uses the example of the stick that looks bent when put in the water as an example (again, an old philosophical trick borrowed from the very traditions he is seeking to unseat, both ancient and medieval). As humans, in contrast to God, we are unfortunately prone to error, mainly because we tend to or are compelled to rely on our senses as the primary source of evidence for our knowledge. Error is, by its very nature, bad because it leads us astray and is ultimately responsible for untold amounts of human misery. Here, we start to get the imaging of evil not as the result of moral sinfulness or frailty, but rather as simply going wrong due to making mistakes or being inaccurate or misleading. Zbigniew Janowski (2002) interprets Descartes' emphasis on human weakness to the evil of error as a sort of Cartesian construal of the theodicy—i.e. how can human beings as creatures created in the image of an all-good perfect God still get things wrong and stray from (in this instance) omniscience? How does this happen? More to the point, how do we resolve this new theodicy that shifts the spotlight onto the evil of human error?

Descartes suggested that we begin by trying a thought experiment. It's easy and anyone can do it at any time. Pretend we're together, and I'm standing here now, talking to you. I can see that I am wearing shoes, and that the walls are blue, and that you, my readers, are there with a book or some such item in your hands, etc. However, how do I know that I am not dreaming all this, or that any of you aren't dreaming it and none of it is actually real? Alternatively, how do I know that some alien or transcendent being is not simply manipulating areas of my brain to give me the impression of witnessing these things when in fact I am nothing more than a brain in a vat of liquid with electrodes attached to it, stimulating the necessary neural pathways to simply give me the impression that all of this is real? Finally, how do I know that I'm not mad, and that my insanity isn't responsible for this wonderful illusion taking place right now?

Again, as Descartes was fully aware, posing this question was nothing new; this is another oldie but goodie like the eponymous bent stick, and certainly one that was well known in ancient Greece. But his use of this thought experiment and its repercussions within the fable of the Evil Genius and as a prelude to his *Meditations* put a somewhat different spin on an old tune. In order to fully appreciate Descartes' philosophical 'mash-up', and also make it more fun to reflect on what he was doing, let's use an example from more contemporary times and popular culture to explore these ideas. For this, I will refer to the 1999 film *The Matrix*.

Try this thought experiment: the blue pill or the red pill (from *The Matrix* (1999), scene 8, if readers are interested in watching).

How do we know that what we experience as the real world is actually real? In the past, people were compelled to answer such questions by admitting that they couldn't ever really know that any of these things wasn't actually the case. In ancient Greece, the sceptics were particularly keen to make their presence known in the vanguard of such displays of well, scepticism—forever pointing out how we can never be completely certain not just of these kinds of things but of anything, and that we must always doubt even what we think we think we know. To paraphrase a well-known modern sceptic (or maybe just famously confused or misguided person, depending upon your politics), former US Defense Secretary Donald Rumsfeld, we must acknowledge that we don't even really know what we think we know. Even our grasp of known unknowns is pretty dodgy. This sort of deliberate undermining of what was hitherto regarded as more or less reliable knowledge by sceptics had, in the view of thinkers like Descartes, held back the cause of human cognition in general (and, in particular, the advance of scientific knowledge) for centuries, and it was time to call time on scepticism as something that prevented advances in scientific knowledge and the improvement of the human condition. But in the face of the pernicious and persuasive powers of scepticism, Descartes was resourceful and clever, and determined to demonstrate once and for all that the human mind can know some things, and with complete and absolute certainty.

He set out to beat the sceptics at their own game. For this, he needed help. For assistance, Descartes sought not God's help, as had been the usual course of action for his philosophical predecessors, but the help of another similarly transcendent being, and one moreover who was up to no good as part of his job description. Enter the Evil Genius, or the Evil Demon, or deceiving 'God, or whatever I may call him' (AT 7: 24) in Descartes' words.

So okay, Descartes put it to the sceptics, I must by the nature of my limited understanding subject what I know to doubt. So I doubt my previous knowledge, my opinions, everything based on hearsay, habit or tradition. But let's not stop there. Let's take it up a gear. I can doubt that anyone else really exists, and that I am alone in the world. I can doubt even myself, that I exist or have a real body or shoes, etc. I might even really be made of glass.

'My hand, this paper, this fire . . . ': Descartes, the Evil Genius, *The Matrix* and the Glass Delusion

> But it may be said, perhaps, that, although the senses occasionally mislead us respecting minute objects, and such as are so far removed from us as to be beyond the reach of close observation, there are yet many other of their informations (presentations), of the truth of which it is manifestly impossible to doubt; as for example, that I am in this place, seated by the fire, clothed in a winter dressing gown, that I hold in my hands this piece of paper, with other intimations of the same nature. But how could I deny that I possess these hands and this body, and withal escape being classed with persons in a state of insanity, whose brains are so disordered and clouded by dark bilious vapors as to cause them pertinaciously to assert that they are monarchs when they are in the greatest poverty; or clothed [in gold] and purple when destitute of any covering; or that their head is made of clay, their body of glass, or that they are gourds? I should certainly be not less insane than they, were I to regulate my procedure according to examples so extravagant.
>
> Descartes ((1641), from the First Meditation)

A great deal has been written and debated with respect to this seminal text and its meanings in Cartesian scholarship and the history of philosophy more generally. But for obvious reasons of space—and also because we are not 'doing' formal philosophy here, but just peeking in for our own purposes as nosey and curious social scientists and/or students of evil—we will focus on how this story may or may not relate to the project in hand to do with evil, and its metaphysical character in contemporary society and culture. And there are plenty of good-quality secondary resources available on this topic (many of which are listed in the References).

For now, let us concentrate on Descartes' questioning of whether or not what we take to be reality is actually real, or if we are, in fact, mad or dreaming; an issue that Foucault and Derrida (see Foucault (2006); Melehy (1998)) argued over quite heatedly (more about this later). But he interjects that I might not just be dreaming or crazy; I may actually be made of glass. What an odd thing to say, especially for a philosopher who was so known for his commitment to reason, not the fanciful embellishment of his writing. But, in fact, there was a malady or what we would call a mental health condition in the seventeenth century that was widely known as 'the glass delusion' in which the sufferer thought he (as it mainly seems to have been) was made not of flesh but of glass. Descartes would have known this, and, given his mentioning of it, let us look at it in a bit more detail as perhaps revealing interesting aspects of this text pertaining to the nature of human cognition, the philosophical subject (one of Descartes' most important inventions) and the nature of its encounter with and subsequent shaping of metaphysical evil. In particular, I want to focus on evil in relation to the mind/body split and the 'reflective/reflexive' nature of modern philosophy and the self.

Descartes was not only interested in and contributed to the study of mathematics, but was also interested in optics, and it is one of those odd things from history that so many of the great thinkers of the early modern period (not just Descartes but also Galileo, Gassendi, etc.) were similarly keen on and even, like Descartes, indulged in a bit of optics experimentation and lens grinding themselves. And in many ways this is not surprising, as the development of these sciences and mathematical theories was intimately linked; in addition, as Gasche (1986) remarks, the optic metaphor predominates in reflective modern philosophy, emphasizing its transparent and reflexive character (most significantly the active and transformative power of human cognition as opposed to simple observation of the material world now providing the 'mirror' of nature). This metaphorical image for the new science is one that would promise (like the new technologies such as the telescope and microscope developed in the early modern period) to bring other worlds closer to us and potentially placing them in our burgeoning power utilizing science and technology to enhance our knowledge, thereby bypassing God. However, these endeavours and technological developments also threatened to make us more 'transparent' to ourselves and others, thus rendering us vulnerable to the knowledge of others and their potential external power and control. This latter prospect posed for many people, especially those who had considerable social-cultural-political-economic interests vested in their public image as opposed to their real selves, posed a very real worry. So just as the new science promised to reveal novel and exciting frontiers of knowledge, it also risked exposing those 'darker' or obscure areas of privacy many preferred to remain hidden, or to reveal sources of temptation that led people to do what was considered evil or wrong (and not just 'mistaken' wrong, but the moral deviance that folks deeply desire to do, secret or private behaviours that depart from the public persona people want to put forth and promote). For those whose power base related to the preservation of a public image, this was no small matter; this sort of knowledge could 'shatter' their identities and their worlds. In this context, the metaphor of glass expresses the transparency and fragility of the self as emerging from early modern ideas of rationalism and science even as it is born as the subject and crucible of modern philosophy. It also reveals insights into one of the most persistently dark sides of modernity and its impact on the living subject that has become endemic if not epidemic in contemporary social life: anxiety and depression (Kristeva, 1992).

In what is a rare commentary on the glass delusion, Speak (1990) identifies this as a historical psychiatric disorder that is linked to the culture of early modern Europe and what was, and in many respects remains, the unresolved problem of the mind/body duality. It is a form of melancholia; again, a type of mental illness that Julia Kristeva (whose work will be discussed again in Chapter 5) identifies with evil in modernity. 'Two quite distinctive symptoms, however, set the Glass Man apart from other melancholics: an irrational fear that he was fragile and therefore likely to shatter into pieces, and an aversion to sunlight' (Speak, 1990: 192). The aversion to light with respect to the age of Enlightenment is instructive, ironic and paradoxical. This sense of fragility and revelation/exposure regarding the new science contrasts quite starkly to what many of us now perceive in hindsight as what was the overwhelmingly optimistic spirit of the age, as enshrined, for example, in Enlightenment philosophy and the faith in science and technology, and what they could achieve in terms of changing and improving us and our world(s). Here, again, we come to the critical issue of the mind in relation to the body (and other bodies, and the natural world). While there has been much made of the mind/body dualism in terms of its relegation of goodness to mind/spirit and evil to the body/material as encapsulated in the Gnostic tradition (Chapter 1), the reasoning behind this may not quite be what it seems. Certainly, Speak finds evidence in the biblical and folk traditions of the time that locate the inferiority of the body in its venal and sexual linkage to the moral codes of chastity, and, in particular, the fragility of women and their bodies, and the dangers of femininity that lie in this erotic context. Such cultural encoding of sexuality and femininity in modern morality continues. However, she also notes the elements of purity and fortune present in early modern discussions of the glass delusion that draw attention to the fragility and proneness of the body to breakage; that the problem is generated by even the most optimistic visions of Enlightenment is that the body is or might be insufficient to encase what in modern terms is the newly confident, independent and expansive modern mind/soul. Even then, the thinking might have been that we need better, more technological, automated or cybernetic bodies. Our bodies—and by extension the natural world as a whole—much as we are attached to them, might not be able to accommodate or even survive what our minds and technologies can dream of and possibly make real. While this opens up the prospect of new and brighter horizons for what it is to be human, or simply to be, it also unleashes deep-seated anxieties regarding the collateral destruction, mourning and loss with respect to the decaying body (as explored, for instance, by Donna Haraway in her landmark 'Cyborg Manifesto' (1991)).

What the glass delusion connotes, and also Descartes' passing mention of it, is the underlying anxiety concerning the impact and possible consequences of all that goes under the banner of 'Enlightenment', in terms of its risks and promises. While the 'dark ages' had its drawbacks, and many (though not all) would be happy to see the back of it, it could—as they say in some popular magazines marketed toward women—also usefully hide a multitude of sins. If we were to embrace this new science and all it promises, would it expose us to heaven knows what? Asking questions and expanding your subjectivity is an empowering but also dangerous business. In addition to the above anxieties, the former reigns on human imagination itself are under threat. The deterioration of tradition and stable social roles initiated by Enlightenment could furthermore threaten the now fragile boundary separating imagination from mind/reality. In other words, science and the optimism of Enlightenment and the possibilities of science could make us all deluded to the point of actually being insane; as with hysteria, much of the anxiety pervading this fear is about the ironically feminizing aspects of modern science, with those in charge ceasing to be 'real men' (sic).

But at the same time, the curiosity underpinning the modern project promised to be potentially healing:

> Given this prevailing spirit of inquiry, it is likely that the melancholic's photophobia was related to a fear of self-revelation. Yet ironically, the very source of this apprehension also exerted a strong attraction on its victim. Walkington explained this paradox using a traditional biblical emblem: although the soul was not completely blind like a bat, it was, like an owl, dazzled by sunlight, seeing as if through a latticed window, the body casting a sable night over the understanding.
>
> Speak (1990: 199)

I might make myself more powerful and audacious than ever, but also find myself abject; I might expose myself as an object of surveillance to God and my enemies, but I might acquire a better self-understanding; I might achieve enlightenment, but then again, I may actually find out that I am not 'real' in the sense of being 'human', that I'm actually quite deranged, or that I don't have a soul. Sufferers of the glass delusion were obsessive/compulsive, driven by anxiety and irrational fears. Glass lends itself to speculation—a transparent membrane that separates and connects, magnifies and shrinks, reflects and distorts; a barrier as well as a window onto this and other worlds. The symbolism here relates to evil as mirror images, apparatuses to other realms, alter egos, the doppelgänger, split personality—playing on the dualities and oppositions as proposed in theodicy but also reliant on how their meaning is fundamentally about their connectedness.

Let us return to Descartes' fable. In fact, not only might all that I consider to be real not actually exist, I can suppose that there really is some higher being manipulating me, making me think I know these things when, in fact, none of them are really true. Clearly, it is a contradiction in terms to say that God would do this, being the source of all truth and goodness, and not a deceiver. But let's say for the sake of argument that there is such an evil deceiver:

> I will suppose therefore that not God, who is supremely good and the source of truth, but rather some malicious demon of the utmost power and cunning has employed all his energies in order to deceive me. I shall think that the sky, the air, the earth, colours, shapes, sounds and all external things are merely the delusions of dreams which he has devised to ensnare my judgment. I shall consider myself

as not having hands or eyes, or flesh, or blood or senses, but as falsely believing that I have all these things. I shall stubbornly and firmly persist in this meditation; and, even if it is not in my power to know any truth, I shall at least do what is in my power, that is, resolutely guard against assenting to any falsehoods, so that the deceiver, however powerful and cunning he may be, will be unable to impose on me in the slightest degree.

Descartes (1984: 15)

Descartes is here not just tolerating uncertainty (as mere mortals who lack omniscience are compelled to do), he is *actively courting disbelief.* Again, this places him in opposition to pre-modern thinkers such as Saint Augustine who foregrounded the virtues of belief in the act of knowing: 'Understand so that you may believe; believe so that you may understand.' The traditions of the past and our position in the cosmos as beings created by God are being significantly altered if not overturned here. This is an important and revolutionary moment in what makes us *moderns.*

At the conclusion of the First Meditation, we find ourselves in the presence of something extraordinary: a true, authentic example of metaphysical evil. As the philosopher and Descartes scholar Stephen Gaukroger points out, this is not what we might call epistemological evil, or simply a malevolence to do with human knowledge in the form of a fault in the reasoning process. It's not that sort of problem. Descartes isn't presenting us with a puzzle that needs working out in the way that the traditional theodicy does. We are not going down the more conventional route as advocated by the likes of Augustine, Leibniz, Calvin or Malthus to try to divine the nature of being (ontology) or mind of God derived through human rationality, nor to deploy other theological principles with respect to temporal shifts of time vis-à-vis eternity or the divine plan for humanity as encapsulated in something like predestination. None of these principles or devices are used to create a narrative that makes (logical) sense, that approaches the problematic of theodicy and seeks to resolve it via something like a traditional syllogism, as for example in the classic theodicy.

From a certain perspective, this is not surprising, given that part of Descartes' stated mission is to unseat Aristotle, it is thus consistent that he would subsequently reject the syllogistic rationality that applies deductive reason to a pair of premises that results in a clear, logically consistent conclusion, as in Aristotelian method. But the premises of the theodicy, i.e. the absolute goodness and omnipotence etc. of God and the fact that God made us and we are prone to evil, are not necessarily inconsistent; we might just *think* they are, or fail to conceive their true relationship. Likewise, Descartes finds no logical contradiction in the fact that it is conceivable that I might have no body, that no one else might exist, that my body might be made of glass, or even that my understanding of the world could be wrong. I might think these things because I am dreaming, or insane, or for some other reason. It might be the case that all of these things are true, and that an evil demon is responsible for making me think otherwise.

The point Gaukroger is making here is that the evil demon or evil genius is, like God, a transcendent or metaphysical being, outside of and beyond this world. He is not an epistemological or knowledge-bound demon, a representation of human cognition—as Descartes notes, he might make me think that I live in a world where $2+3 \neq 5$, but he cannot impose the sort of logical contradiction that makes me believe that $2+3=5$ and $2+3 \neq 5$ at the same time, i.e. the law of non-contradiction or 'the excluded middle'. His transcendence makes him extremely mysterious as his motivations will be essentially unknowable (at least to us), a matter of pure speculation. But what such an evil being cannot do is change the perfection of the world as God made it. To put it another way, an evil genius can deceive me and lead me to make erroneous conclusions, but he cannot alter the laws of philosophical-mathematical logic. Why he would do this, I cannot know. This is metaphysical evil. The nature of this type of 'pure' malevolence without any evident purpose coupled with unfathomable motives will be a common feature of discourses about evil and also about (some) crime. The lesson here is that we still use the language of metaphysical evil about the real worldly evil in our midst, done by non-metaphysical very corporeal and human actors who are motivated by evil in a 'pure' yet purportedly inconceivable, unfathomable and motiveless way.

But as Gaukroger says, even the evil genius cannot make $2+3=5$ and *not* equal five at the same time. Either we are deceived or we are not; in error, or correct. The logical consistency of the world as God made it remains intact—even the evil genius cannot disrupt the perfection of the world as the real perfect God created it; all he can do is make it seem to be something it is not. Here we can compare Descartes' evil genius/deceiving god to the real God: Descartes clearly indicates that the evil genius is, like us, a flawed being, differing from the real God by his imperfection (again, like us). There is also the fact that he doesn't really exist but is simply one of any possible number of mnemonic devices for demonstrating that (a) our cognitive 'hard wiring' may be faulty, and

(b) helping us to make way for a new way of subjecting everything we know to the strongest possible scrutiny, according to Newman (2005). So what the evil genius *can* do is lead me into error when thinking about the world by observing it with my faulty senses and/or brain. Descartes imagines that this would be the result of our having been created by another less-than-perfect God, or alternatively being created by ourselves (equally scary). So again, the source of the trouble is this strange transcendent and malevolent being somehow implicated in the propensity to error for human beings who are or have thus far been happy to rely upon their senses. Whatever we can deduce about such a transcendently evil being is that it is probably more like us than like God, again bringing the concept of evil closer to the human as opposed to metaphysical realm.

Satan in Job

Before moving on to see how Descartes deals with this problem, let us consider this type of purely evil presence in another context, in the form of transcendent or metaphysical evil. We might ask if and where else have we encountered such a being before, the presence of such pure transcendent malice? Such an encounter can be said to have taken place in the Western Judeo-Christian tradition in the biblical book of Job. Here, God is challenged by Satan to test the virtue and loyalty of one of His favourite and most faithful believers. God agrees to the challenge and allows Satan to visit all kinds of undeserved evil and suffering on poor Job (and his family).

In the Christian tradition, this fable is interpreted as being about ultimate redemption and even as pre-figuring the story of the suffering of the innocent Jesus as saviour/messiah. But in the Jewish tradition, the meaning of this story is not so consoling, but is much more ambivalent. As Levinas (in Nemo (1998)) argues, evil in Job is just the opposite of consolation—it is a disruptive narrative revealing the excessive nature of evil and human suffering. It is anti-consolation *writ large*. Such a view of the unaccountable, motiveless, excessive and transcendent nature of evil that is not pre-empted by God is intrinsic to the historical narrative of Jewish suffering, and contrasts to the ultimately reassuring cultural and religious narratives of evil developed within the Christian tradition (consider the resolutions of the theodicy such as those proposed by Malthus, which simply makes human suffering relative to other greater goods). Not only does the Hebrew God not pre-empt Job's suffering, he actually condones it.

On this reading, metaphysical evil is something to be really worried about because:

(a) it situates a man (here exemplified by Job) rather helplessly 'between two worlds' (Alexander, 1990) or rather between two Gods; and
(b) such transcendent evil threatens to disrupt the connection between sin and suffering, guilt and punishment by exposing the evil of suffering visited on those who are blameless (Sia, 1985).

But these aspects of the story pertaining to such an evil genius-type character don't bother thinkers like Descartes (for the moment), as he proceeds to engage in the *Meditations* with evil himself on his own terms (thus by-passing God), and so dealing with problem (a); problem (b) is less easily dispelled, but we'll return to this in a moment. In this sense, Descartes' resolution of the first problem he sets himself is very much like the traditional theodicy in the fact that God becomes increasingly distant from the action, even more so than in traditional theodicy.

While the Christian tradition tends to view Job as a portent of the suffering of Christ, with its messianic and salvific conclusion, Jewish exegesis has tended to be more sensitive to the ambivalence and anxieties incorporated within this story. In his analysis of centuries of Jewish debates and interpretations of evil in Job, Mittleman (2009) breaks it down into two basic positions: Job the patient and Job the rebel, with each interpretation having prominence at different socio-historical times. Job the rebel exhibits the sort of self-consciousness and autonomy put forth in Cartesian philosophy and underpinning modern individualistic cultures: 'Job the rebel becomes a model of sincerity or authenticity, a chief value of modernity' (Mittleman, 2009: 25). However, Job the patient is a much more ambivalent, negative and difficult character, celebrated in antiquity and in the rabbinic tradition. This interpretation rejects the theodicies of Leibniz and Descartes, and their reliance on the individual and ultimate redemption; in this reading of Job, all the characters (Job's friends but also Job himself and even God) are flawed and, in different ways, mistaken in their views. In seeking to explain Job's suffering by way of something he must have done wrong and thus be to blame, his friends were wrong: the reality is that suffering comes to many innocent people who don't deserve it. In denouncing God, Job is to blame for his blasphemy and infidelity. For exposing Job to the evils of the demonic Satan and for forgetting his covenant with his people, God is to blame. The only character to come out of this parable unscathed is Satan, by exposing God's favouritism to Job over Abraham, which in a legalistic sense violates the terms of the original covenant (Mittleman, 2009). Here, we encounter not only the vexed figure of the wicked God (as in Chapter 1) but also even more challenging and interesting, the good Satan, the devil's advocate and ours too.

So, what is the upshot of these stories? Then and now, what many people seek to discover in the wake of evil is the motive for evildoing. In Coleridge's famous phrase, the 'motive-hunting of motiveless malignity' is perennial, usually resulting in the conclusion that the perpetrator is evil and that's it. But when the villain in question is Satan, this explanation really falls on shallow ground, as by definition we know that he is evil (. . . or do we?). In such instances, the next port of call is often to try to establish desert in the sufferer, that the predations of the demonic figure were somehow justified because only a God-like transcendent figure was in a position to know about the victim's true sinful character because, like God, Satan could see Job (and us) all the time, i.e. there is no place to hide from this surveillance. But what the story of Job tells us is that this is also mistaken; sometimes, evil happens to people who simply don't deserve it. And that exposes the most terrifying thing of all in the face of evil: the disruption of the link between wrongdoing and punishment established and codified in the theodicy and by extension in the law. In addition, we see that evil of a certain magnitude visited on good or innocent victims still draws on the fabular encounter with pure, disinterested metaphysical evil as a source of deep concern, still evoking fear, dread, self-doubt, error and chaos—all things that sabotage confidence in our ability to achieve justice, for instance, via the criminal justice system. So what are we to do? Disbelieve everything we perceive, leave it to God to judge in His own time and forgive willynilly? Rely on ourselves, our boundless powers of self-confidence, take recourse to our tools of reason, science and technology by covering the world in CCTV cameras or taking surplus of everyone's DNA? Create and escape to new virtual worlds which are completely human-made and then patently fail to make safe from predatory and motiveless evil? Wait for things to work themselves out in the course of time? Or, as advocated by the rabbis, should we recognize evil for what it is in our midst and suffer, but regard our suffering in this world as ' . . . opportunities for greater heavenly blessedness' (Mittleman, 2009: 32)? How? By doing what we can to accept our lot and to try to help each other when in trouble, to be morally authentic and sincere (e.g. Levinas in Davies, 1998) or simply to try to be of use (Swinburne, 1996). This involves recognizing that in many ways good and evil are random and shifting, and that suffering evil is often merely the result of bad luck—being in the wrong place at the wrong time with the wrong person or people. As argued within the rabbinic tradition, what the story of Job tells us is that we shouldn't really take too much heed of what people say when they are in pain. In other words, we should try not to be too hard on ourselves or each other, especially when evil befalls. Because the truth is that often neither reward nor punishment in this life are deserved; they cannot be taken as signs of culpability or desert. And, anticipating Kant, when Job chastises God for creating him as the flawed creature he is, God also gave us freedom and the law, and the capacity to act for the good despite such dispositional constraints. Instead, we need to be reserved in our rush to judge, to be pragmatic and realistic, and to strive to do the best that we can with the tools and information we have, without overreacting as a result of fear or being self-righteous or vindictive. For now, what the search for order and rationality implicated in theodicy and metaphysics exposes more than anything is the chaos and suffering in the face of evil that belies such a philosophical project:

> The diminution of metaphysical theodicy gives expression to the dynamic, 'disordered' world of modernity. In a world without an ultimate purpose that bridges the physical and the metaphysical, the natural and the divine, humans are thrown back onto their own resources. The virtue of authenticity, of being true to oneself, replaces the rational project of understanding the universe as given in reason and revelation. Rather than seek certitude in God, moderns seek honesty, or at least clarity, about their own experience. Job becomes a paradigm of this search. God becomes an accessory to the human project of self-creation. It is difficult to see how, without the indulgence of a second naivete, theodicy can be restored as a respectable intellectual project. But it is also difficult to see why, given the horrors of our time, it should be. The problem of evil cannot be solved by profound contemplation about the problem of evil.
>
> Mittleman (2009: 50)

Neither is it feasible that the problem of evil can be solved by flamboyant declarations of self-confidence and certainty, however elegantly and rationally put by even the most enchanting of French geniuses.

Having recalled this brush with Satan, let's return to Descartes' fable. In this story, the evil genius is not engaging directly or even indirectly with God, but with Descartes himself. In fact, Descartes summons the evil genius up out of his own imagination—he is a fictional or fabular presence, but one with a purpose. This malicious demon doesn't challenge God to the detriment of a single symbolic human being (like Job)—just the opposite. Descartes' summoning of the evil genius makes God more distant from his worshippers and His created world than ever before. What's more, Descartes is the one human being who is only too willing and able to take him on. Not only is he happy to take on this role, there is also a strong implication that there is no need for anyone to repeat his experiment (Maritain, 1969). In a quasi-Christ-like gesture, Descartes accomplishes the task for us all, and for all time to come.

First, Descartes allows the evil genius to place everything possible into doubt. He inaugurates a unique moment in the history of philosophy: *hyperbolic doubt*. This is not your ordinary doubt; this is super doubt. If ordinary doubt is like light armoury, hyperbolic doubt is like an armoured tank. Newman (2010) uses the metaphor of a bulldozer, the biggest one you can get! This is, after all, a ground-clearing exercise; an act of wilful demolition, prior to building a new philosophical edifice on newly cleared ground. Hyperbolic doubt is extreme and universal. If I doubt everything, I can even doubt my own existence. But wait a minute—if I doubt that I exist, then who is this thing doing the doubting? I might be able to doubt all things, but I can't doubt that I doubt. If I am doubting, I am thinking—so I *must* exist. *Cogito ergo sum*: I think, therefore, I am.

This is true and certain knowledge; the Archimedean point that enables Descartes to defeat the evil genius and also to defeat the sceptics—to use doubt to beat them at their own game. It also provides the paradigm for a new modern kind of thinking; one that relies on the powers of rationality for its certainty, not on things like the senses, nature, tradition, etc., which are now still under the shadow of doubt (at least until we can clear them up with science). The model of the new modern scientific way of thinking is mathematics, specifically geometry, which does away with the messy business of sensory observation, but here we will leave Descartes.

What Descartes does in the *Meditations* is to establish that it is our reason—particularly, when thinking about certain kinds of things that are not reliant on our senses or observation of nature—that is, in contrast, reliable and credible. Human beings can achieve not only knowledge but also certainty. And what is more, it turns out that we don't, strictly speaking, need God to do it, but can rely on the power of our own reason, even if it means fighting a transcendent demonic being of pure evil in the process. No problem!

This is a revolutionary moment in philosophy: in many ways, the birth of modernity, if it is possible to pinpoint such a thing. It is, according to Gasche (1986), the birth of the modern subject and the inauguration of philosophy as one modelled on reflection, reflexivity and a constellation of other conceptual metaphors involving mirrors, replicas and doubles. While such imaginaries and images can be disrupting and disturbing, they also provide important and (occasionally) potent conceptual sites for imagining alternatives and other possible worlds, as for example in the tropes of replicants and 'other' as alter ego, doppelgänger or the 'evil twin' in popular cultural genres such as soap operas and science fiction (TV Tropes, online: undated). These are other versions of ourselves in which the darker, secret malevolence that we practice to disguise or deny in our ordinary real lives are let out to play; this image of the evil reverse reflection of ourselves is a potent and popular imaginary device for exploring subjectivity and questioning ethical norms around what it is to be a self.

By inviting the evil genius to place all of our knowledge under doubt, Descartes exposes the one thing that cannot be doubted—that I am doubting and thus that I am thinking and that this means that I must exist. My existence provides me with the certainty I need to proceed to acquire more knowledge on reliable ground. Henceforth, I don't actually need God all of the time to guarantee my thought processes, but rather I am able to do this for myself, using my own analytical thinking skills modelled primarily on the laws of mathematics and geometry, not the observational principles of empiricism or natural logic. The outcome of this is to relegate God to the realm of religious experience, no longer the arbiter of modern knowledge, which now exists in the form of modern science. The subject is, I am, on the model of the *cogito*, existing, but as what? As yet I am an empty entity, without a body and on my own. I am a modern subject, on the precipice of becoming, but as yet in a state of abjection, a stage of being relating primarily to the experiences of fear, horror and anxiety interrogated by Kristeva (in Chapter 5).

If we were to accede to or repeat the *cogito* experiment, how would we return to the body, to each other, to the natural world? The *cogito* is a cold and empty, not to say lonely, place; if (as the Gnostics posited) the body is the prison of the soul, the *cogito* is solitary confinement. Whereas the spirit/mind connotes light, the body generates heat, and the emotions of aggressive and sexual urges we attribute to this state and the loss of reason. As represented in films like *The Matrix* (1991), as a sort of 'construct' (as Morpheus refers to it) it represents a proto-virtual reality and in many ways something that eerily resembles what we now call the digital world (an analogous derivation of Descartes' model of space on extension and geometry), and one that proliferates and mutates just as much as those we are familiar with now. The glass metaphor is here richly symbolic. Glass is a membrane that separates and connects, a window on to and between separate, parallel and sometimes competing realities. As mentioned previously, it is no accident that so many of the geniuses of the early modern period were polymaths who also took a keen interest in optics and lens-grinding. This was the age of the invention of the telescope and other such technologies that made our world smaller and more isolated from the spiritual cosmos, and also brought other worlds in the physical universe closer to us in a way they never were before. In more recent times, we connect worlds, many of us, by the act of stroking a small glass panel—the latest instantiation of the smartphone or tablet—our newest and most widely available and powerful ICT devices that shape our world, our relationships and to a large extent even who we are. While such technologies continue to generate huge optimism and promote a spectacular image of science and the celebrity of scientist/philosophers, at the same time, as the glass delusion suggests, it still instigates deep-seated anxieties and fears about how far this will go, and what it would mean to individuals in terms of self-image, identity, their private and interpersonal, social, and bodily, existence—even the nature of reality and being itself (thereby resurrecting the problem of ontology from the ashes of epistemology). As Saint Paul famously wrote, we view reality 'through a glass, darkly' (1 Corinthians 13). While he was talking about love (evil and love being the subject of Chapter 6), the same applies here to knowledge, including self-knowledge and the transparency or otherwise of who we really are. Will our technologies inaugurate a scientific step into the unknown or frontier of reality too far and enable or even create more and worse evil? Would the knowledge we gain and the expansion of the self thus generated automatically shatter us and destroy our world, with respect to what our real, corporeal, social bodies and/or the environment can actually take? Will we be destroyed by our mirror images or the doppelgängers we create using these technologies, as for example expressed in current anxieties and crimes around virtual stalking, social networking, digital death or (even worse) digital immortality? 'identity theft'? Will the systematic manufacture, development, marketing and obsolescence of such devices threaten the very social and environmental survival of the planet? Will the 'refraction' of what is 'real' as a result of our burgeoning information and technological age, via deceptive or imperfect prisms of knowledge, make it impossible for us to tell what is real and what is false, thereby resurrecting the scepticism Descartes originally sought to dispel in even more evil and persistent chimeric forms?

These kinds of questions and fears are still very much the stuff of science fact and science fiction, and the source of suspicion about human knowledge and power set loose from the bounds of any ethical/ religious/sensual restraint, drawing on our deep fears and experiences of evil. As Speak (1990) astutely notes, the early modern preoccupation with the mind/body split was a product of what were then radical efforts to rethink the nature of reality and the power of human cognition, but one that also manifest itself in the obsessive desire to define and reassert the boundaries between orthodoxy and heresy—or what in criminological language would be civility, regulation, deviance and the refining of mechanisms of social control. And, indeed, difficult and deep-seated questions about the nature of power, freedom and the need to regulate and control in global modernity are more, not less, urgent and persistent, as exemplified in current debates over surveillance, security and human/civil rights (see for example). In theological terms, scholasticism was able to resolve the weak, venal and corporeal shortcomings of the body in an eternal eschatology of the divine will against the temporal background of the afterlife. In modern times, in this life, these same problems pertain and are further complicated by the imperfect 'vessel' of the body being not just fragile but now transparent and febrile, open for any and all to see our deepest, darkest secrets and prone to disintegration and manipulation by the very technologies we develop for self-expansion and expression. What is more, for those of us living in late modernity, the expansion of the subject and the proliferation of evil in virtual realities make the task of being human(e), maintaining an identity and knowledge of good and evil even more anxious and vertiginous. Negotiating this is a price we pay for modern science, one that may be worthwhile and liberating, but nonetheless still high.

What does this have to do with criminology? For starters, there is a substantial and growing criminological research literature on cybercrime, cyberstalking and the exploitation and victimization of vulnerable individuals and children online by predatory individuals and organized criminal gangs. For many people, these are becoming increasing and often tragic and distressing areas of concern with respect to clearence, issues pertaining to identity and body image are dominant.

The evil genius and the Foucault–Derrida debate

These lines about the evil genius in Descartes' First Meditation provided the occasion for an extraordinary and heated exchange between two major thinkers in recent times: Michel Foucault and Jacques Derrida, an interesting and revealing development from which I draw heavily from Hassan Melehy's book *Writing Cogito* (1997). This debate tells us something about the nature of metaphysical evil—that pure, impersonal, disinterested, transcendent evil for its own sake—and the effect of the Cartesian incantation of the evil genius for the modern age.

Derrida kicked it all off by implying in his early paper 'Cogito and the History of Madness' originally presented in 1967 that Foucault, his former teacher and mentor (though only four years his senior), and holder of the most prestigious Chair in French philosophy in the world named after Descartes, had fundamentally misunderstood a basic premise of French philosophy contained in a passage from Descartes' seminal *Meditations on First Philosophy*. In his magisterial *History of Madness* (2006), Foucault referred almost in passing to some of these lines from Descartes' *Meditations* on the nature of the cogito; this formed part of Foucault's thesis about the history of madness in modernity, that it was basically constructed on the exclusion of insanity from all forms of rational knowledge. Derrida commented:

> In his 673-page book, Michel Foucault devotes three pages—and moreover in a kind of prologue to his second chapter—to a certain passage from the first of Descartes's *Meditations*. In this passage madness, folly, dementia, insanity seem, I emphasize *seem*, dismissed, excluded, and ostracized from the circle of philosophical dignity, denied entry to the philosopher's city, denied the right to philosophical consideration, ordered away from the bench as soon as summoned to it by Descartes—this last tribunal of a Cogito that, by its essence, could not possibly be mad.
>
> Derrida (2002: 37 (emphasis in original))

And, indeed, there does appear to be in Foucault's work a tendency toward the study of exclusionary practices in modernity as the basis for exploiting power, specifically the creation of the 'Other' in modern discourse, whether in the form of self/other, reason/madness, good/evil or discipline/punishment. Most students of criminology should be very familiar with this notion in the highly influential work by Foucault on discipline and punishment.

But, Derrida argues, what Foucault doesn't adequately appreciate is the *insanity* that is at the heart of the *experience* of the *cogito*. It is this experience that renders the supposed division between reason and madness less distinct than it might on the face of it appear to be:

> ...what is in question here is an experience which, at its furthest reaches, is perhaps no less adventurous, perilous, nocturnal, and

pathetic than the experience of madness, and is, I believe, much less adverse to and accusatory of madness, that is, accusative and objectifying of it, than Foucault seems to think.

Derrida (2002: 39)

What Derrida is doing here is challenging his teacher the great professor of French philosophy Michel Foucault on his knowledge of one of the most fundamental and canonical texts in French philosophy. This represents a real transgression on a number of levels—Derrida not only violates the filial principle underwriting civilized philosophy (and reportedly makes Foucault apoplectic with rage), but he also opens up the possibility that modern philosophy in general and rationalism, in particular, are underwritten by madness by virtue of the Cartesian reliance on the fabular principle of transcendent evil. Derrida opens up the possibility that the *cogito* has achieved a rather different outcome in modern thought. Rather than inaugurating the project of modernity by excluding madness and banishing error through the establishment of rational knowledge on solid ground, instead what the *cogito* opens up is the possibilities of many diverse and competing *cogitos* that proliferate and branch out in all directions, opening up many alterative avenues of thought as opposed to establishing two distinct poles, as demonstrated in Foucault's interpretation (Melehy, 1997: 40). In other words, as Melehy (1997) explains, the rationality at the heart of the *cogito* is madder than madness itself because it disguises itself as the opposite of madness, completely distinct from it when in reality it is completely deluded, even intoxicated, on its own self-declared self-confidence. Gasche (1986) puts it another way, pointing out that the philosophy of reflection built on the foundation of a self-posited 'thinking thing' that is the *cogito* is somewhat less substantial or critically viable than it might at first appear; modern metaphysics is thus built upon a thin veneer that is the dull and opaque 'tain' of the mirror, the tain being the tinfoil that gives the mirror its lustre and reflective qualities. A transcendental philosophy of reflection that is unable to account for anything beyond the bounds of rational cognition itself (e.g. ontology, theology, etc.) is thin, fragile limited and opaque indeed.

By severing the close ties to a benevolent and omniscient God who guarantees our knowledge in theodicy, Descartes creates the modern subject—a new and disjointed thing that breaks all previous links with established philosophizing. And that's in the end what the encounter with the demonic evil genius does—it enables Descartes to release us from previous limits to thinking, but at a price. Descartes' contemporary

Pascal knew this, and now we do too. Encountering pure evil without God would seem to be a risky business; going spoiling for a fight that is by definition impossible to win.

What Derrida claims in his debate with Foucault is that Descartes' dismissal of the evil genius can never be complete—the evil genius can always return, and haunts modern philosophy like a demonic spectre, occasionally breaking out in the form of evil excess within the context of a fully rationalized modern machine. We have (and will again) see this in the directing of the fruits of scientific technology not at making life better for more people, but rather on making it much worse for many more, for example in extreme manifestations of historical suffering such as the Holocaust, but arguably also in more quotidian and everyday technologies like modern food production, market economies and practices of work.

What Descartes creates in the *Meditations* by way of a totally self-assured and self-evidencing subject is what Montaigne called a 'monstrous child' (Melehy, 1998: 42): an entity that is utterly convinced of its own maturity and certainty by willingly if unwittingly deforming itself the process. Through this damaging act of self-immolation, the modern subject denies its multiplicity, neglecting its true creative and transgressive nature, which is in its rational manifestation is quite insane, and often quite purely evil. This is the real influence of the evil genius, and its powerful ability as Descartes rightly noted to deceive—and to keep on deceiving—human beings.

By his invention of the simulacral image of the Evil Genius, Descartes' attempt to domesticate and harness evil for the purposes of establishing an 'absolute referential ground for truth and certainty' (Merrin, 2001: 93) backfires quite spectacularly. As Deleuze declares, Descartes' introduction of such a dualistic image as foundational to Western philosophy 'can only banish but never destroy its simulacral power' (Deleuze in Merrin, 2001: 93). The real truth is that the ground of the modern subject is ungrounded, or at best founded on a very thin veneer of reflection, and hence the subject (that empty, bloodless and bodiless lone entity) is continually delivered back to the infinite abyss of the demonic images from whence it emerged. And so it would seem to be that our world as virtual/digital reality brings with it many new anxieties and burdens concerning the negotiation of our own shifting identities and relationships in a cyberspace stalked, if not by a single evil genius, but a proliferation of monsters, deviants and trolls.

By turning the tables on his former teacher Foucault, Derrida uses the force of the evil genius to turn the tables on modern philosophy and modern rationalism in particular. Rather than creating a division between truth (good) and error (evil), modern philosophy has instead unleashed an evil more potent, more excessive and more prone to error than ever before: an insanity that masquerades as reason. Giles Deleuze sums it up by describing the history of philosophy as an 'ass-fuck' (Deleuze in Melehy, 1997: 42), and that this filial and sterile way of thinking is responsible for producing the 'monstrous child' that is modern philosophy. It has separated us from God and also from ourselves, each other and nature.

In this regard, we can deduce that Derrida projects onto the history of modern philosophy an understanding of the narrative of evil as excessive and ultimately without consolation. This is in line with the Jewish tradition derived from exegesis of Job of 'making sense' of evil that, even when it is construed from a metaphysical or transcendental perspective, tells us something very real about the manifest nature of human suffering in modernity terms of its proliferating and excessive character and visitation upon the 'innocent' in the wake of modern technologies and science.

Summary and conclusion

In this chapter, we have examined the topic of metaphysical evil, specifically as constructed in the Cartesian fable of the evil genius. What we have encountered is an alternative, flawed and deceiving demon or God, a figure who—if he had been our creator—would be accountable for the limited nature of human cognition and our propensity to error. The story of the evil genius in Cartesian philosophy may have served its purpose of reconstructing modern philosophy on relatively sound epistemological grounds focusing on the clarity and distinction of ideas, establishing human rationality as the standard of certain truth, thereby dispelling the ancient and medieval traditions of ontological metaphysics. However, the domestication if not defeat of the evil genius has been, in contemporary philosophy, anything but complete. Under the auspices of objective, scientific, reliable rationality, we have seen some of the worst and most evil atrocities in modern times, apparently becoming progressively more excessive and 'rationalized' as modern history unfolds.

This modelling of philosophy upon the reflexive subject and activity of self-reflection may be empowering in some ways, but is also a risky business, emotionally as well as socially. The birth of the subject and modern philosophy through the fabular encounter with the evil genius offers a number of insights into the advances and short-comings of centuries of modern thought. Reflecting obliquely upon the wisdom tradition and the story of Job and his encounter with a god and an evil demon, we gain another and potentially rich vision of evil in its metaphysical form. These stories and their interpretations over centuries have highlighted the competing strategies of certainty, self-confidence and the powers of modern science as remedies of evil on the one hand, and the need to take recourse to more ancient virtues of sincerity, authenticity and compassion on the other.

The eponymous figure of the evil genius remains as much a villain-ous bad boy and as much a subject of popular fascination as ever he was. While in the tradition of modern philosophy, engagement with this character is frightening and exhilarating, from the wisdom tradi-tion, it reminds us that evil is not just a challenge to human ingenuity or a chance to maximize our potential, resist, fight fire with fire and perhaps eventually get what we want. It is also about remembering that this world is one of images and deceptions, and that the real challenge of evil is to recognize this as a deeply profound truth and view this encounter with unjustified, disinterested and extreme evil as an invitation to responsibility, compassion, forgiveness and commu-nion with God (Mittleman, 2009). On the other hand, there is the possibility that the invention of virtual reality and/or cyberspace has opened up new vistas and portals for encounters with and predations of newer forms of transcendent, metaphysical, even diabolical evil in contemporary versions of the evil genius who are more pathological and less prone to remorse, forgiveness and reform than ever before. These themes pertaining to human and diabolical evil will be explored further in the next chapter in the philosophical contribution to the study of evil by Immanuel Kant. Kant's engagement with evil and the failures of theodicy will bring to a conclusion the first main section of this book and our encounter with theological, philosophical and metaphysical evil.

3
Radical Freedom, Radical Evil? Kant's Theory of Evil and the Failure of Theodicy

So far in this book, we have examined the problem of evil modelled on the theodicy and as imagined in the fable of metaphysical evil in the rationalist philosophy of Descartes. Here, we began to trace the differences and similarities of the theological and philosophical languages, concepts and theories about evil and what it is and (just as importantly) what it is not, where it comes from, what it means and what we can and should do about it, if anything. What we encountered in those accounts was the origins of a particular and distinctively rational way of construing evil and how, for example, this has been enshrined in legal-judicial discourse (hence of significance to a discipline like criminology). We also saw, in both approaches, how distanced God becomes from what are nascent humanist discourses that focus on the powers of human reason and cogitation alone, and how brutal and paradoxical these can sometimes be in their consequences and outcomes. In many respects, these secular discourses stand in stark contrast to some of the mythical, narrative or wisdom traditions; these stories reveal a benevolent and loving God living among His creation, in which evil is the result of wilful deviation from the moral law by recalcitrant but still beloved human creatures and is dealt with in the here and now, mainly in a compassionate and communitarian way—the roots of another and what we usually identify with a quite contemporary notion of evil in the form of crime, e.g. community or restorative justice. What we also saw were signs from the very beginning of the modern period that the confidence in the 'new science' and modern subject were somewhat less robust than might appear in hindsight, and that despite all the promises of Enlightenment, evil would seem to be as inscrutable, intractable and random—and its effects as extreme and extensive—as ever, if not more so. And that it would be the persistence and challenges of evil as, for instance, encapsulated in the theodicy that would expose these anxieties, limitations and (ultimately) failures of rationality and science.

In this chapter, we will concentrate on Immanuel Kant's take on evil, specifically in terms of what he termed 'radical evil' and 'diabolical evil' and his critique of theodicy. In this respect, we will find ourselves (briefly) in the domain of contemporary moral philosophy, which is where, until very recently, the study of evil has more or less remained since the end of the nineteenth century. Here, we witness the encounter between evil as a distinctively *human* phenomenon and rationality conditioned by social and political norms (as opposed to theology or geometry) as a way of dealing with it for us moderns—as represented in Immanuel Kant's resolution of the philosophical fight with evil (vis-à-vis the evil genius) as originally picked by Descartes. The main question to be addressed in this chapter, before moving on from theological-philosophical theories of evil to more cultural studies and narrative versions, is how is this encounter negotiated, and what does it produce in terms of our perceptions of and responses to evil, then and now? Hence, the aims of this chapter are to trace the development of the understanding of evil in modernity from its roots in religious/theological discourse to modern philosophy, and its ultimate emergence as a problem for ethics/moral philosophy and most latterly human rights. And to do this, readers will be introduced to the concepts of:

- Radical evil
- Diabolical evil

I will then conclude with some summary remarks on philosophical and theological approaches to evil before then moving on to narrative.

The story so far . . .

So far, we have been presented with the problem of theodicy and the (onto/theological) problem that absolves God from responsibility for evil despite the fact that it exists and He created the world, and us. In Chapter 1, we reviewed some of the more (in)famous theodicies that tend to focus on the functional qualities of evil as in some way necessary for the accomplishment of the divine purpose for this world. In Leibniz's phrase, notwithstanding the undeniable fact of evil, ours remains 'the best of all possible worlds'. Or alternatively, for those such as Bayle, Malthus and in the current advertising campaign for a promi-nent brand of oven-ready potato snacks, 'it's all good'. This approach pins its hopes on the outcomes and the fact that evil has a purpose, albeit one we humans are pushed or possibly unable to (fully) under-stand. Whichever position you take, the payoffs in terms of acquiring a better understanding of evil and being better equipped to come to grips with it, especially when it happens to you or someone you love, are of dubious worth.

We have similarly been presented with a view of evil that has emptied it of its content by denying its ontological substance in the form of 'reality', i.e. the Neo-Platonic Augustinian view of evil as non-being or privation; something that is increasingly marginalized and pushed to the side (Rogozinski, 1993). While evil does exist in the respect that real people really suffer it and do it, it is not so much a matter of fault (a positive offence) as default (a shortcoming or mistake) (Rogozinski, 1993: 31), sins of omission rather than commission, if you like.

We have also encountered the evil of the devil or 'seducer' and the evil genius, tracing the trajectory of a type of metaphysical or transcendent evil whose radical otherness and 'fictional' and disinterested, god-like power does little to disguise the fact that he is as elusive and ineffable to human understanding as evil itself. Or, maybe he is all too under-standable, being less a god and more like us; who's to know? What all of these theodicies have in common is that they are quite abstract in their conceptualization of evil. They portray evil variously as radically other in its binary opposition to the good, a non-entity, or as something that, when you think about it and try to make rational sense of it, breaks down the boundaries separating what we normally think of as good ver-sus evil completely—so things like the good of sensual pleasure become evil and the evils of suffering and famine become good. Or they use human phenomena such as time, history, justice or political ideology to extend and expand reason beyond the point of acceptable speculation about things like divine will. This is not very satisfactory. As some con-temporary philosophers argue, the residual presence of evil in modern secular thought in terms of the many unanswered questions about its nature and the what we can possibly know or do about it remain. Not only that, but in the wake of a science and epistemology built on the Cartesian model, the forms and scale of evil we have to deal with seem to be proliferating, not receding, even as we seem to use our knowledge and technologies to firefight its pernicious effects. More than ever, when it comes to evil in our midst, we may well ask, what the hell is going on?

Despite these attempts at rational philosophical explanations, we may feel that evil remains as unknown and rampant as ever, possibly more so. We still find ourselves insisting that evil exists, in the face of the perfection of God or the limitations of humanity and the world. Its impact and duration would appear to be much more than just a residual effect of human faultiness or the entertainment of transcendental demons. For some reason, people still do evil, and there are perceptively evil people, as is well evidenced by the testimony of many innocent victims and the exposure of truly shocking crimes. Our experience of evil resists reduction to these abstract onto-theological and metaphysical explanations with consummate ease, and they do little to help us understand it or eradicate it, except possibly to accept it as a fact of life. Rational explanations that argue for its logical consistency or ontological status, absolute alterity and transcendence, or socio-economic necessity appear to leave us feeling a bit flat when it comes to the crunch, especially when evil is upon *us*. We still ask the questions:

Why? And, more to the point, why *me*?
Where do we go from here?

Such questions motivated the eighteenth-century German philosopher Immanuel Kant (1724–1804), leading him to address himself to the problem of evil, with it has to be said somewhat limited success, before eventually dropping it never to return to the vexed topic. In his works on moral philosophy such as *Groundwork for the Metaphysics of Morals* (1785) and the essays 'Religion Within the Limits of Reason Alone' (1793) and 'On the Miscarriage of All Philosophical Trials in Theodicy' (1791), Kant set out his thoughts on theodicy, and what he would in the end consider its ultimate failure. Notwithstanding his limited success, Kant's efforts would lay the foundation for how evil has been treated in modern thinking, at least until recently. What is different about Kant's approach to the study of evil is his rejection of the onto-theological problem of theodicy and the finitude of the world, of how to make sense of the existence of a good God and the reality of evil in the world. Instead, he concentrated on how human *actions* and *agency* pertaining to evil can be explained along the lines of freedom and responsibility in relation to the civil moral law.

Kant focused his attention on what he called *moral evil*: that is, human evil for a real, material, human world. This represents what will become entrenched as a specifically modern conception of evil that refers to evils that human beings are responsible for, as opposed to the catastrophes of nature as transcendently ordained punishments or the suffering emanating from the faults, limitations or imperfections of us or the planet (despite the contribution of philosophers such as Rousseau and again until quite recently when nature and the natural world have resumed their significance in the study of evil). In her book *Radical Evil* (1996), Joan Copjec observes that in 'Religion with the Limits of Reason Alone', Kant enacted a conceptual revolution by which evil 'ceases to be a religious or metaphysical problem and becomes, for the first time, a political, moral and pedagogical problem' (Copjec, 1996: xi). By situating evil as epiphenomenal to human *freedom* rather than as a derivative of mortal *finitude*, Kant opened the way to what María Pía Lara (2001) calls a 'postmetaphysical' understanding of evil (Schott, 2003: 2). In other words, we are leaving our friends (or enemies) in the cosmic or other transcendent realms behind, and to their own devices, from now on—at least from the mid- to late-modern philosophical point of view. Evil geniuses now become fodder for popular culture and entertainment industry, not serious thought.

Henceforth, Kant's focus on moral evil means that he is only interested in how human beings are responsible for the evil actions that take place in this, the 'real', world, and the social and political and, indeed, ethical problems that arise out of this. In this sense, evil is about human action and moral agency: what people *do* (or sometimes don't do). To reiterate, this is not metaphysically oriented, abstract or linked to transcendent beings or reality in any meaningful way, hence the designation of 'post-metaphysical evil'. From Kant's perspective, if something is transcendent or metaphysical in its origins, then there's no way we can know about it, so it's not worth worrying about. Kant was quite pragmatic when it came to evil. Whatever we say about such phenomena will be speculative by its nature, as we have no direct access to the mind of God, Satan, evil geniuses, etc. The same applies to deep philosophical questions about the 'true' nature of reality; there is a limit as to so much we can actually really know. So, to the encounter between Morpheus and Neo in *The Matrix*, compelling as the options put to Neo are in the scene about the red or blue pill, Kant would have probably chortled, or just looked a bit bored or more likely bemused. Red pill, blue pill: what difference does it make? Take one, take neither or blend them both in a smoothie, the reality or realities we find ourselves in we can still never absolutely know whether or not they are actually 'real'. Kant was a philosophical genius but also a practical person. His view was to just get on with it, whatever reality you live in or are presented with:

WYSIWYG, in other words, or a prototypical variant thereof. Whatever world we live in is and must be taken as real for us. Whether or not it is the 'best' or most 'good', it is in effect all we can do.

For Kant, this practicality and pragmatism are at the heart of one thing that is the problem with theodicy. It is based on a fundamental confusion because theodicies are by their nature speculative and refer to things that are impossible for us to know. This is a main reason why all theodicy arguments ultimately fail. This approach makes Kant the first philosopher to deal with the problem of evil in a way that does not refer to the cognitive or ontological properties of a supreme being (Bernstein, 2001: 57). What is more, neither are acts or states of being intrinsically good or evil in themselves vis-à-vis sins or virtues—so happiness is not a good in itself (e.g. the happy hitman is still evil), nor is courage (e.g. the soldier who storms an outpost to kill children). Rather moral worth is conditioned upon the context in which decisions are made and actions take place that determine goodness or evil. The only really good thing is goodwill, which is conditioned in its relation to duty and the moral law.

In fact, Kant argues that morality does not, strictly speaking, need religion at all, though it cannot be completely divorced from a concept of God (Hanson, 2012), but can operate according to the principles of reason alone. While this construal of the problem of evil frees us from the necessities of speculating about the mind/purposes/motives of metaphysical or transcendent beings, at the same time, we are still nevertheless situated as moral actors between two different 'worlds', evocative of the Gnostic and Cartesian mind/body split, relating to our rational and sensual/animal natures. 'Man, according to Kant, belongs at once to two worlds. One is the world of sense, the other the intelligible world. As a member of the former, he is subject to natural inclinations; as a member of the latter, he is subject to a universal moral law' (Fackenheim, 1992: 260). This, among other aspects of being human, will cause trouble for Kant, but we will return to this again presently.

What matters for the moment, in Kant's initial engagement with the task of understanding evil in 'Religion Within the Limits of Reason Alone' is three things:

1. Freedom/choice—at the heart of Kant's treatment of evil as a category of human agency is his allied concentration on the issue of *choice*, that is, our *freedom* to choose to do good or not
2. Duty—the ethical code by which members of different societies are socially and morally contracted to abide by

3. Moral law—Kant is similarly concerned with how this freedom to choose and to act is taken in relation to the maxims of the moral *law*, the code of principles, which duty (and also true freedom of the will) impels us to obedience in our actions and choices

Hence, evil becomes something that is understood as being intrinsically socially and politically oriented and shaped according to things like human freedom, choice, agency, duty and the law, and very much a problem to be dealt in the here and now, preferable via the organs of moral philosophy. So, strictly speaking, to understand evil, we don't need the speculation of theodicy, metaphysics or religion at all, according to Kant. These are, at best, distractions, at worst, excuses for moral turpitude and passivity, that we were 'seduced' by some transcendent wicked being. As Kant states:

> ...for its own sake morality does not need religion at all. So far as morality is based upon the conception of man as a free agent who, just because he is free, binds himself through his reason to unconditioned laws, it stands in need neither of the idea of another being over him, for him to apprehend his duty, nor of an incentive other than the law itself, for him to do his duty. At least it is man's own fault if he is subject to such a need; and if he is, this need can be relieved through nothing outside himself: for whatever does not originate in himself and his own freedom in no way compensates for the deficiency of his morality. Hence for its own sake morality does not need religion at all (whether objectively, as regards willing, or subjectively, as regards ability [to act]; by virtue of pure practical reason it is self-sufficient.
>
> Kant in Bernstein (2002: 12)

This investment in self-sufficiency and agency is the basis of Kant's deontological or duty ethics (from the root of the Greek *dei*, or 'one must' and *deon* meaning 'duty'). In his later writings, Kant will return to the seminal importance of the existence of God and what are the implicitly transcendental aspects of *a priori* moral maxims such as the categorical imperatives, but for now, we will concentrate on his initial argument.

Human agents are free to choose their actions—but according to the exercise of their reason and duty. With this freedom comes responsibility. Consequently, actors are also fully responsible for their choices and subsequent acts. This is the other side of the freedom coin in modern liberal societies. This combination of free will and the constraints of reason and the moral law lead to a number of problems for Kant, and continue to provide fodder for ongoing debates in moral philosophy (as you can see from the commentaries cited here, and indeed many more).

Let's look at some examples of moral acts to try to flesh out what Kant means. Consider the four famous cases of the shopkeeper he discusses in the *Groundwork for the Metaphysics of Morals*:

1. Acting against one's duty. A shopkeeper might cheat her inexperienced or naïve customers (e.g. children, cognitively impaired people or just the inattentive) by, for instance, regularly short-changing them as a matter of course. Such acts would be dishonest and clearly a derogation of her moral duty, a violation of the moral law and thus evil.
2. Acting in accordance with duty, but not from duty. The shopkeeper might not cheat her customers because to do so would be to act against her own self-interest. Customers might choose to shop elsewhere and her business would then suffer. This is not morally worthy because the act is not done from duty but rather motivated by self-interest or 'self-love'.
3. Acting in accordance with duty but from natural inclination. The shopkeeper is honest with customers because she is a nice person and really likes her customers and so acts out of a sense of altruism, and expression of her love for her fellow humans. Not morally worthy because dependent in the first instance on personal disposition, not the moral law.
4. Acting in accordance with duty against one's own inclinations. The shopkeeper behaves honestly with her customers because it is the right thing to do, despite hating them and feeling that her goods are underpriced, for example. Kant also gives the example of the depressed suicidal person who does not kill himself because it is the wrong thing to do. These actions have moral worth, because they prioritize the moral law over individual inclination.

What we can infer from this example of the shopkeeper that the *outcome* of acting in a morally correct way, in this case being honest, does not satisfy Kant's conditions for acts of moral worth even if, or arguably because, they coincide with long-term self-interests and/or personal dispositions. While they may be prudent or fortuitous, they are not done out of a sense of duty and obedience to the moral law, but are instead to some extent conditioned by things like consequences and outcomes (which introduces the element of self-interest, self-love or selfishness) or inclination/disposition (which we don't control, isn't a matter of moral choice and, indeed, is serendipitous, we cannot take credit for being nice, nor can we be held morally culpable for having a mean disposition). What is key to Kant here is the matter of *principle*, not the calculation of consequences or reliance on chance or things that are beyond our control as determinants of true moral worth.

While what is observable in the works of thinkers like Descartes and Kant are the roots of secular ethics, it is important to note that neither Descartes nor Kant were what we might now recognize as secular fundamentalists; they were not forerunners of the forms of virulent atheism on offer in some quarters today. On the contrary, there is ample evidence that both were devout Christians: Descartes a committed Catholic and Kant an observant Protestant. And, indeed, we can see the influence of Kant's Protestantism here in the example of the shopkeeper, that implicit reference to the gospels and the focus on individual morality. So, for example, the shopkeeper who is a nice and decent person by disposition: how can she take credit for this? We can hear the echo of Jesus' admonishment to those who love their friends as a sign of their moral goodness—of course, we love our friends; where's the virtue in that? Why should we be rewarded for how God created us? It's in loving your *enemies* that you show true moral strength and character. And you can detect the influence of that ethos here. Kant adopts a similar attitude consistent with Protestant morality, that simply obeying the rules and that's it is not enough. Because in more serious situations of moral decision-making, the influences of things like self-interest and personal inclination might lead us astray. What if the morally worthy thing is to act in a way that violates longer term self-interest, as for example sacrificing your own happiness or even life for a greater good? What if it means acting against your own inclinations, as for instance when you feel like killing yourself but refrain because it is against the moral law? If Cartesian hyperbolic doubt was heavy artillery, this is morality on steroids. Kant may be taking away the excuses and buttresses of demonic temptation, but in putting morality in our hands, the demands he places on humans as 'free' moral agents are high.

In Kant's view, moral worth or culpability pertains, in particular, to the actor's choices and actions in terms of observing and obedience to the *moral law*, which he argues can be defined according to rationality on its own. So, you can't say that the devil or God or anyone else made you do something and is thereby responsible for the consequences of your actions. This implies that to deviate from the law is in itself irrational and also that such deviation from the moral law is also not really free, which is problematic for Kant. This is part of what makes Kant's resolution of the problem of evil unsatisfactory, because 'freedom' in his usage of the term doesn't really seem to equate to what most people (especially in our times) usually mean by the word. Kant and some of his commentators (notably Bernstein) engage in some fairly elaborate philosophical acrobatics to solve this dilemma, based on the meaning of the 'will' in free will, with debatable success, but we are not concerned with the philosophical calisthenics here. The outcome most people agree with is a feeling that Kant never really sufficiently solved this problem, and there is also evidence that Kant was aware of this himself, as he abandoned and never returned to the problem of evil. Notwithstanding this, he does offer some concepts to help move things forward, such as his notion of radical evil.

So, while our free will makes us autonomous agents to choose to do good or evil, our nature as rational beings and the moral freedom derivative of our social human condition keys us into the advantage of constraining our absolute and selfish autonomy according to the moral maxims of the law (something like what political philosophers such as Hobbes, Rousseau and Locke describe in notional terms under the aegis of the social contract). We may be capable of doing evil, but it seems there are other types of constraints (both external and internal) that tend to prevent us from making bad choices.

Against this background, we can start to flesh out precisely what Kant means by looking at the two types of evil he discusses in his essay: radical evil and diabolical evil.

Radical evil

What is radical evil?

First of all, what Kant means by radical evil is not the same as what a thinker like Hannah Arendt in her early work, e.g. *The Origins of Totalitarianism* (1948) (whom we will encounter later in this book) meant by the phrase, i.e. that it is extreme by its very nature, exceeds measurement or comprehension, beyond the pale, in some sense qualitatively different from anything else in normal human experience (Louden, 2000: 135). In the Kantian sense, we wouldn't restrict the term 'radical evil' to someone like Hitler or Stalin. Radical evil applies to everyone.

Instead, Kant's use of the word 'radical' has its derivative etymological meaning from the Latin *radic-* or 'root', 'source' or 'origin' (Kluge in

Huang, undated: online). Hence, radical evil is the evil that is at the heart of the human condition; it is 'rooted' in human nature and in the individual human being. Kant states '[the human] way of thinking (what concerns the moral disposition) is corrupt in its root' (Kant in Louden, 2000: 135). This means that not just the monsters of history are radically evil, but rather that all human beings are evil as part of their being. This is, for Kant, where the true 'radicality' of evil lies; that it resides in everyone, not just a few villains, however malicious.

To be human is to have a propensity toward evil. Even the best of us have this latent proclivity; it is universal and an elemental part of being human. Radical evil is, however, not the same as original sin (in the Augustinian sense), it is not traceable to a 'first' man or woman or their deeds. At the same time, there is an intrinsically *historical* element to Kant's theory, with reference to human time as opposed to divine eschatology. Duncan (2012) describes Kant's view of evil as 'resolutely anthropocentric (or more accurately, rational-being-centric)' (975). While we may not have access to or be able to conceive the mind of God, by no means does that leave us bereft or without substantial resources to draw upon in our understanding of and fight against evil. For Kant, our (practical) rationality can tell us a lot about the history and future trajectory of evil, and for Kant, this constitutes a 'journey' in the modern sense, albeit a painful one, but one that contains great hope. This type of rationality and its limited, pragmatic and realistic scope contrasts with the hyperbolic optimism and abstraction of the rationalism of Descartes. Think about it, from a Kantian perspective. Perhaps the real significance of the story of Adam and Eve is not the designation of original sin or taint; rather, it is that, were we in their situation, knowing what they did and being human, we would have acted in the same way; and why? Because we know that Adam and Eve didn't have the advantages of historical and cultural knowledge and development that we do; hence, we are able to use this knowledge, these values and experiences to make better and more informed *choices* about our actions now and henceforth. Duncan (2012) argues that this is at the crux of Kant's thinking about evil, that it is fundamentally about the notion of progress and the process of harmonizing our desires as a species and as individuals with the moral law, and that this is by its nature a work in progress in human time. For Kant, this is not inconsistent with the goodness (or coincidentally the existence) of an all-powerful God, but rather a shifting of focus on the *historical* aspects of human moral development; our propensity to make mistakes is for Kant balanced by our capacity to learn from our mistakes and become better people and more consistent and reliable as moral decision makers. But this is an essentially human endeavour founded upon a conscientious deployment of moral will power buttressed by a duty to follow the moral law, as opposed, for example, to a consequence of our nature as created beings or the intervention of divine grace. Unlike Adam and Eve, whose 'conjectural beginning' (in Duncan, 2012: 979) exposed their lack of self-awareness, agency and other resources, we are in contrast in a position to improve ourselves and make better and more ethical choices in the future, founded upon human reason; this is in itself indicative of God's plan for humanity. In the context of biblical narrative, this is an alternative if slightly oblique view of what Ricoeur called the wisdom tradition.

Control is key (and will ultimately be the downfall of Kant's position). Kant is not saying here that we are somehow *innately* evil (or good for that matter) in the sense that these moral states are, strictly speaking, essential to our being and hence beyond our control (Bernstein, 2001). Rather, what he is stressing is the *propensity* we have for being good or evil. It is a predisposition for action, and so something that all human agents as actors are susceptible to and ultimately responsible for in terms of the consequences of their own deeds. And this is why free will and choice are so important; we are morally responsible for the choices we make as individuals and the deeds we consequently do. And in the real, cultural-historical world that is shaped by experience and maturity, even with our faults, appetites and limitations, we can and sometimes do learn and thereafter do better, choosing not to repeat the same old mistakes.

As commonsensical and persuasive as this approach is, it still does not solve Kant's problems in relation to the failure of the theodicy argument. Clearly, there is a tension here between the human susceptibility to evil that is intrinsic to the human condition, and the responsibility for evil actions that are a consequence of a person's free will or choice. How can we be morally culpable if we are disposed to evil (however weakly or contingently) by, for example, having a (potentially) depraved nature, and thus (at least to some extent) have no choice in the matter? Some argue that Kant never sufficiently resolves this paradox, and there is quite a lot of scholarship devoted to it. What he does seem to propose as a way of dealing with this is to insert a layer between our evil natures and the exercise of our free will—i.e. *disposition (Gesinnung)* or *character*.

Thus, the propensity toward evil can be negated or attenuated (depending on your point of view) through the exercise of good moral character as a kind of filter separating out the evil before it becomes manifest in our actions. So, something like self-awareness is important. We can be disposed toward evil by nature, or indeed, as we saw in the shopkeeper example, naturally disposed toward the good. It is not these 'natural' inclinations or default dispositions Kant is drawing attention to here, but those we choose, those that require effort and the exercise of agency and will, which by their elective quality imply moral decision-making. Hence, through our exercise of moral character, we have the potential to prevent evil actions being chosen in the first instance, thereby pre-empting evil and suffering. This is primarily accomplished through our self-consciously positive relationship with the principle of duty and the moral law, and further conditioned by the more stable, university rules or 'maxims' that Kant called the categorical imperative. The categorical imperative equates to basic moral principles such as not treating other human beings as means to an end but as ends in themselves, and also acting in a manner that we would wish everyone else in our situation to do the same (a variant of the Christian 'golden rule' of 'do unto others as you would have them do unto you').

For Kant, the very fact that we struggle so much in our moral decision-making is indicative of the power of the drive toward evil and the strength of the moral law (Sullivan, 1989: 124). 'So what then is radical evil? Simply put, it refers to our propensity knowingly to choose maxims contrary to the moral law' (Louden, 2000: 138). Radical evil is the (occasional) deviation from the moral law, even though we know what it is and what we should do. According to Kant, this happens because of three factors:

1. frailty (or weak will);
2. impurity (lack of integrity of our actions, deviation from the categorical imperative); and finally
3. wickedness or perversity (this being the most serious because it implies not just weakness but forethought).

But at the end of the day these three have one common root: selfishness or self-love, and ultimately it is this that accounts for our inability to put the moral law, our duty and the universal good first over our own self-interests.

Kant's notion of radical evil departs significantly from previous Enlightenment thinking on the human being as inherently good, or even perfectible, but by no means does that mean that we are beyond hope. While Kant pointed out the intrinsic predisposition of human nature to both good and evil, it is important to remember that by saying this he was not consigning human beings and human society to the moral dustbin or a bad fate. On the contrary, while people are susceptible to radical evil, they also have the means to pull themselves out of it, by recourse to good character, duty or simply by following the moral law. But this requires a degree of determination, self-awareness, maturity and effort on our part as responsible moral agents.

Meaning that while human beings might be radically evil, we are not *irrevocably* evil (Sullivan, 1989: 125). In a way, we are equally susceptible to the good because we have such a drive toward the law and toward good moral character (Sullivan, 1989). Otherwise, we would not be so torn and conflicted over our actions. This, Kant would suggest, is basis of the battleground of morals where humans live, situated between good on the one hand and evil on the other: not between two worlds or two gods, but between two paths of action. Or, if we are situated between two worlds, these are the very human realms of sensual appetites (what we want, desire and corporeal creatures) in competition with rational intellect (what we aspire to as thinking and reasonable beings) (Huang, undated). We are innately disposed to desire both good and evil (from both our animalistic and rational natures), and this is manifest in our actions and in our feelings about morality and ourselves. It is that side of our human nature that is rational, practical and ethical that offers the potential for hope.

However, the fact is that this is how we were made, and we are limited creatures, not always in control of our appetites and continually and forever subject to factors that are strictly speaking outside of our control despite how much or how hard we try. This is the 'passivity' at the heart of theodicy as recognized by Ricoeur (1984), meaning that because of our limited and corrupt natures, we cannot be held fully responsible for our evil actions because we are not fully in control of ourselves nor other external circumstances that further contribute to and exacerbate our inherent limitations. The difficulty for Kant is that, again, this means that in essence we are not really 'free', and hence a central plank of his position relating to human freedom is decisively undermined (Duncan, 2012). Moreover, there is the issue of rationality itself and how this is construed; a central problem for Kant is that he considers only the morally viable or worthy options to be rational, so that when we choose to do evil (as all of us will sometimes do) this in itself equates to an 'irrational' act. This perspective contains echoes of Descartes' view that doing evil is like being in error, or making a mistake, as opposed to intentionally—or wilfully, even gleefully—going astray. Like Adam and Eve, or those who lived during the era of slavery or through the Holocaust, how can I be blamed for living during a time when there was insufficient cultural mores to enable me as an individual agent and member of society to behave in a more morally worthy manner? Are such pernicious historical evils really my fault, or the fault of all those living at those times in those situations? Am I, or were those people, partially or fully to blame for the external conditioning factors I cannot control? Also, consider the fact is that God could have made humans without the desires to do evil but He didn't; that is not our fault (Duncan, 2012). These are the problems that haunt theodicy, and Kant never sufficiently resolves these difficulties. On the other hand, without going too much into the technical detail, it has been argued that the point Kant was trying to make in his theory of radical evil wasn't about the notion or problem of an absolute freedom (that we do not have), but instead about the freedom of human *will*, the freedom of human beings to *choose* what they do (Alford, 1997), which while imperfect and limited, is still a real choice.

Diabolical evil

For Kant, while radical evil is ultimately about being motivated by self-interest, diabolical evil is distinguished by the lack any self-interest or self-orientation. Both forms of evil divert from the course of duty, but a diabolically evil person would do so just for the hell of it, as it were, not in order to advance any self interest or selfish motivation as a means to an end.

Diabolical evil is an extreme or 'pure' form of evil that is like something identifiable with the evil genius in Cartesian philosophy or Satan in Job—it is impersonal and unmotivated by self-interest or personal gain. An act is thus ' ... diabolical evil when he surrenders any personal judgment and responsibility for his own deeds to the extent of being self-effacing, of morally collapsing in the abyss of "doing it for its own sake" ' (Rangelov, 2003: 761).

Is this effacement of the self in diabolical evil is what renders human beings the inhuman 'monsters' that we are familiar with from history, such as Hitler, Pol Pot or Stalin? Rangelov (2003) claims that this is where Kant's theory is in practice subverted, because people who are guilty of diabolical evil are those who satisfy the condition of the categorical imperative, which constitutes a fundamental or *a priori* principle of Kantian ethics that some argue means that he is either practising

or reaching toward metaphysics. However, what the categorical imperative generally states is that we should act in a way in which we would
will that action to become a universal principle, i.e. that everyone
should behave in that way in the circumstances. But what about these
monsters such as Stalin and Hitler, they really *do* view their actions as
'rational' and justified, and would want to them to apply universally?.
What is more, they really do believe that their duty is to the 'master'
cause, in the form of the state, the party, the group, whatever. And
finally, they really do consent to the effacing of their own self and subsequently their self-interests in this regard in the depraved degradation of
others, replacing this with the interests of the 'party' etc., and absolving
themselves of any moral responsibility for their actions as a result Many
(e.g. Card (2002)) have argued this problem is resolved by the undermining of the principle of the categorical imperative. However this is still a
real problem for Kant. While he recognizes that there is the possibility
(some would say, in the wake of the multiple atrocities of the twentieth
century, an inevitability) that socially, politically and culturally determined things like moral laws, duty, character etc. can be perverted with
consummate ease. And the reality is that indeed they are, and this is a
serious fault in his ethical theory that seeks to humanize evil in rational
and socially and politically oriented contexts that are exempted from
the absolute realms of theology and metaphysics.

In the wake of an atrocity-ridden 'long' twentieth century, philosophers such as the Claudia Card (2002) have sought to recover and
reconsider the notion of diabolical evil as meaningful for our times. Card
defines it as 'knowingly and culpably seeks others' moral corruption by
putting them in situations where in order to survive they must, by their
own choices, risk their own moral deterioration or moral death' (2002:
357–358). In her book *The Atrocity Paradigm* (2002), she focuses not on
the obscurity of moral absolutes but rather on the all too common and
familiar 'gray zones' of ethical culpability that result from the enacting
of the kinds of diabolical acts that result in the deeply pernicious suffering that envelops both perpetrator and victim in atrocious situations.
For example, she refers to the concentration camp victims that inflict
evil on their fellow inmates in exchange for the lessening of their own
punishment, or the active participation in the sexual exploitation of
children by others who have been 'trafficked' in order to release them
from the burden of doing such sex work. Card wants to resurrect and
re-invigorate the concept of diabolical evil to describe and designate
these very serious and pernicious types of evil acts, by virtue of their
scale, depravity and dehumanizing impact.

We may ask, however, is this what Kant really meant by 'diabolical evil', or is this something else? Isn't this sort of act, however pernicious, in the end acting out of self-interest? Card criticizes Kant by pointing out that according to his theory and typology, it is impossible to distinguish in scale between mere wrongdoing (e.g. short-changing a customer) and extreme evil (e.g. genocide). We find ourselves again in the kind of contradictory territory of the traditional theodicy, whereby acts against the moral/religious law of the time (e.g. fornication) are considered be evil whereas 'rational' acts such as deploying nuclear weapons or withholding foreign aid or international assistance that lead to large-scale suffering are to be regarded as excusable, inevitable or otherwise, in the end, okay, possibly even good.

To be fair to Kant, it is unlikely that he or anyone else could have seriously envisioned the depth and extent of evil and depravity that would characterize some of the seminal events of the twentieth and twenty-first centuries. Writing from his hometown of Köningsberg (which he famously never left) in the nineteenth century, Kant refused to accept that human beings could be really diabolically evil because he thought it was impossible for them to be sufficiently unself-interested in their motivations or perverse enough in their understanding of and relationship to the moral law to satisfy the conditions for this type of evil. He also thought it was impossible for the human subject to lose the degree of common sense, compassion, empathy and humanity in general for such a conversion to take place and still be a human subject. Such a diabolical stance was for Kant irreconcilable with his understanding of human nature. But as Alford astutely observes, distinguishing different categories or typologies of evil was not Kant's aim; rather, in actively collapsing these categories in the single human category of radical evil, he is making a point about the generic qualities of evil that are ultimately attributable to our propensity to be selfish and to pervert the moral law, which is inherently human. 'Kant defines radical evil not in terms of the enormity of the deed but of the human inclination to corrupt morality so that it becomes a servant of self-love' (Alford, 1997: 69). These conditioning factors not only allow evil to be enacted and suffered, they enable us to feel 'good' about it while this it is happening, whether through the grandiosity of envy or enraged self-righteousness (Alford, 1997). The ongoing legacy of Kant's theory of radical evil will be returned to in Chapter 8.

In any case, Kant considered this a problem for modern moral philosophers, not for theologians or religious leaders. Was he right? Has history since born this out?

Summary, conclusion and a little heavy metal to finish

Theodicy is an attempt to use rationality to resolve the problem of evil emergent in a world created by an absolutely good God but still subject to evil. Kant seeks to extract the problem of evil from onto-theological and religious frameworks and reconstitute it as a problem for moral philosophy. Through what is a resolutely anthropocentric stance, Kant focuses on the importance of action, responsibility and free will in the moral decision-making process, introducing new conceptualization of human nature in relation to the propensity to do evil (and good) and emphasizing the role of reason in moral action in his concepts of radical and diabolical evil. However, for many commentators, these concepts fail to capture some of the more 'shady' and pernicious aspects of evil; for example, in terms of the scale of depravity, corruption and suffering entailed. Not all evils are the same, and for some, the problem with radical evil is that it is not radical enough (Alford, 1997). The limitations inherent in the rationalization of theodicy-type arguments means that we can never be completely free or to blame for the evil that we do or encounter. What is more, the post-metaphysical construction of evil that takes a more socio-historical perspective on morality raises significant questions for the role of stabilizing *a priori* moral 'maxims' such as the principles of human rights within a Kantian system of deontological ethics.

In the wake of the Holocaust and other atrocities, the question of diabolical evil has been reinvigorated. How else might we think about or engage with diabolical evil? What do you make of the cultural studies analysis of evil, for instance in relation to the body or in heavy metal music? Does this enhance your understanding of (radical or diabolical) evil? How do or should we interpret and assess such data from popular culture in terms of the analysis of such deep philosophical-moral issues such as identity, culture and human rights? Let us now briefly consider an example: Deena Weinstein's (2000) analysis of the Van Halen classic 'Runnin' With the Devil'. What follows could and should be expanded and refined, and perhaps some of my readers or students will be minded to do so. But really this is an opportunity to incorporate other lesser-known and developed methodologies into social science research, not least on the topic of evil, here specifically music and the body.

Heavy metal music (hereafter HM) in many ways can be perceived as an antidote, maybe even a by-product, of theodicy and meta-physical thinking on evil. First of all, it exceeds and actively, willingly and unapologetically transgresses any sort of rationalization of evil—whether radical (human) or diabolical (meta- or super-human). So it is residual and/or resistant to theodicy and Cartesian metaphysics, wilfully going places that traditional/classic philosophy and theology do not reach. And what are these places? After Kant, they really have to do with the emotional, hedonistic and moving body as a way to reconnect or otherwise 'know about' what he claims we cannot know: the diabolical (or alternatively the divine). And in contemporary culture, knowledge of evil is often sought through the sensing, moving, dancing, costumed, corporeal, venal, private, erotic and social bodies. The thumping bass beat that is a staple of HM (and other popular dance forms) gets into our lungs, hearts and souls, pervades us and makes us want to move, maybe even headbang. And headbanging or swaying is a great way to use the body as its own physical resource to confound reason—who can think 'straight' while doing that?

Somewhat paradoxically, this extends the excess and hyperbole of Cartesian doubt and Kantian moral worth by taking physicality (in this instance, in the head department) to its extreme. This is the case in the trance-dancing tradition of Middle Eastern belly dance such as in ancient temple dancing or the Khaleegi dance of the Arabian Gulf peninsula, where mythically dancers repetitively circle or throw their heads around to achieve a state of mental if not spiritual transcendence. Like headbangers, belly dancers do this in isolation as well as in choreographed synchronicity with each other. The effect is to draw upon and emphasize the darker alterity of, in the case of belly dance, female sexuality, and its transgression of phallocentric logic and rationality. Such moves highlight the sensual and carnal aspects of femininity, as well as highlighting the cyclical and repetitive elements of nature intrinsic to (human) corporality, whereby so many of the moves of belly dance are circular and pelvic oriented to highlight the mythic earthiness and cyclical nature of animality as well as sensual desire (Buonaventura, 2010). Philosophically speaking, this constitutes a resurgence of the sensual knowledge and the experience of nature in Aristotelian thought that were suppressed by Enlightenment philosophies centred on rationality such as those of Descartes and Kant.

From a cultural studies point of view, drawing on Eagleton's analysis of the witches in *Macbeth* (2010), what is also of significance is the departure from linear, historical or civil time, in favour of a much more amorphous, disoriented and cyclical present. Difference from the standpoint of identity, individuality and morality are erased, and chaos—whether in the form of indiscriminate suffering or pleasure (or both)—not only ensues, but is actively pursued, for no particularly discernible purpose apart from the sheer hell of it. Experience of such cyclical-performative time contrasts starkly to both the eschatological ends of divine eternity and the utilitarian ends of rational-linear temporality of social history and capitalism. The witches in *Macbeth* dance in a circle and in circles; they 'bend' time, perverting it from its linear direction toward aspiration and achievement to the 'endlessly stretching' delirium of desire, the winding path to a sort of prophetic knowledge of the future that is blatantly spiritual and shamelessly irrational (Eagleton, 2010: 83). This cyclical-present bears a much closer resemblance to the time of nature, with scant concern for difference, consequences, productiveness or tomorrow; on the contrary, the 'vaulting ambition' of such negativity in the present stretched into the future is to annul '...eagerness for the next achievement' (Eagleton, 2010: 83). The purpose is that there is no purpose; no practically measurable one anyway. The pointlessness of such deception and delirium is the point, as in art, and particularly performance arts like dance. 'Here then we arrive at an insight which seems central to the idea of evil. It has, or appears to have, no practical purpose. Evil is supremely pointless' (Eagleton, 2010: 84). Evil is also, as Eagleton notes and we will see in subsequent chapters, repetitive, relentless, insubstantial and boring, always the same, as represented in the Sartrean version of hell or possibly the Sadean heaven (Chapter 6). But what both heaven and hell contain are sovereign deities who run the place and do what they like for whatever reason they like, at the end of the day, much like the amoral gods and goddesses of ancient Greek mythology. Embracing the cult(ure) of HM, belly dance, drama, dance and other performance arts enables mere mortal humans to partake of and pretend to such elusive pleasures and powers, or at least their effects, if only by opting out of the demands of human daily life they claim to repudiate. And it feels good. It certainly beats working, and for many, this is what the proverbial working for the weekend is all about.

The presence of belly dance can also be perceived in some classic HM music videos, such as Van Halen's 'Runnin With the Devil'. Here, singer David Lee Roth exhibits his impressive dance moves with particular effect, not just as a display of his physical dexterity (much as Descartes is said to have incorporated an original ontological proof for the existence of God in his *Meditations* even though strictly speaking he was arguing there that he didn't need God to guarantee his system but included such a classic proof anyway as a display of his genius; thus, showing that it wasn't because he couldn't accomplish such a philosophical/theological feat of intellect, but that he could and chose not to, or simply didn't need to). Unlike the later and much more pop-oriented 'Jump' (1984),

'Runnin With the Devil' displays many of what have become the conventions of classic HM music—from the isolation, alienation, solipsism and introspection of each band member during the performance, to the driving beat, repetitive and not terribly deep or even coherent lyrics, to the androgynous/fetishist costuming, the darkly demonic staging and repetitive, circular moves. In the accompanying 1978 video to the song, there is little sociality between band members, even though they are in the very act of performing together. There is darkness and smoke, and no discernible audience, the scene is fairly bleak and unadorned, very simply staged as a 'live' performance. Roth's costume and hairstyle are distinctly feminine, even what we would call girly, from the long blond tresses he tosses around with seductive and sensual abandon to his pink pearlescent jacket, silver-cuff bracelet, silver lamé belt, tight trousers, at least one visible earring and necklace. Though he does indulge in a quite aggressive masculine punch of the air, many of his moves are classic to belly dance, one of the most erotic, sensual and feminine forms of dance: the hip bumps, pelvic circles and back-bending. The screams are evocative of a visceral animality, defying conventions of making the words discernible or understandable; they are like an animal in pain or even shrieks of orgasmic ecstasy.

As Weinstein (2000) reiterates, HM is meant to be listened to *loud* and these excesses of audible and transgressions of gender norms and social civility encapsulate its distinctive qualities. Norms of masculinity (individuality, power, aggression) are exaggerated; norms of femininity (dress, movement, sensuality, animality) are switched and also exaggerated. The effect is to defy reason and rationality apropos of theodicy thinking about evil. The outcome is to provide alternate routes to perceive and connect with the other realm of the 'diabolical', though individual and collective means located in the body (as opposed to spirit/mind/*Geist*). Essentially, this equates to a rejection of reason as a human trait and the embracing of sensual and venal corporality as emanating from another transcendent reality, where even the devil himself might live and reign. For many fans of HM and other popular dance 'crazes' such as belly dance or salsa (e.g. Rendell, 2011), the music and movement of these popular forms provide potent sites for escape from the demands of social civility and everyday society and open channels to 'other' imagined, desired, fantasized or fetishized realities where the diabolical sovereignty of unfettered or more loosely fettered sexuality and deviance reign. Gods and goddesses are born and there is murder on the dance floor. Corny, maybe, but I defy even the mighty Kant to have resisted the temptations of a thumping beat. On a more serious note, the atrocity of the Holocaust and its aftermath took and continue to take place to music, both as a soundtrack to Nazi politics and the spiritual healing of concentration camp victims and their descendants (Beker, 2007; Bergen, 1996). It is these sorts of cultural and artistic forms of expression that in so many ways and so easily supersede the limits of rationality and the moral law, and to which we now turn our attention in our exploration of theories and concepts of evil.

Part II
Evil and Narrative

4

Telling Evil Stories: Understanding Cultural Narratives and Symbols of Evil in the Phenomenological Hermeneutics of Paul Ricoeur

This chapter begins the second section of this book devoted to evil and narrative, exploring how narrative (or narratology, the study of narrative) can be used to explain and explore evil, as both a philosophical schematic and a methodological tool. We will concentrate in this chapter once again on the seminal work of the distinguished philosopher Paul Ricoeur. As Franzosi (1998) puts it, and I have to agree, Ricoeur is not for the faint-hearted, but do not despair. Though challenging to read, Ricoeur's work is immensely rewarding of effort. *The Symbolism of Evil* (1967) represents one of the most significant and sophisticated works on the subject of evil to date. While it would be erroneous to claim that Ricoeur's recourse to narrative solves the 'problem of evil' on a theodicy-type model (nor does he claim to), by embracing and acknowledging the power of narrative in its fullest dialogical dimensions it would not be an exaggeration to claim that in some sense the narrative approach deals in a more sophisticated way with the passivity-agency problem that beleaguers theodicy. This chapter is intended to show how this is done by introducing Ricoeur's phenomenological hermeneutic approach to narrative generally and to outline his theory of evil in terms of its symbolism and narrative forms—that is to say, the words we use to talk about evil and the stories that we tell to each other and listen to. For those interested in evil, and/or crime and deviance, I hope that this chapter is just the start, and that some of the examples provided here and subsequent chapters drawing on narrative and storytelling will inspire you to delve further into the work of this fascinating and important twentieth-century philosopher and the phenomenological/hermeneutic approach.

It is worth reiterating here that a primary objective of this section of the book is to further develop skills in interdisciplinary research for criminology and the social sciences, that is, utilizing theoretical concepts and frameworks commonly used in other disciplines (e.g. literary criticism, cultural studies, psychoanalysis) in a social scientific and specifically criminological context. Such conceptual and theoretical knowledge and critical skills are becoming increasingly necessary for those working in the field of criminology today, as a way of enhancing what have become well-worn concepts, frameworks and techniques. Being able to knowledgeably discuss the cultural aspects of evil in relation to crime and to be creative, imaginative, flexible, resourceful, innovative and enterprising, envisaging possible new ways of dealing with old and persistent problems in a fast-paced, increasingly diverse and ever-changing world is necessary to continue the development and reinvigoration of criminology as a vibrant academic discipline.

And as we know, but are not particularly forthright at acknowledging, criminology is a discipline dominated by storytelling; the production of stories from a number of usually contested angles often happens as a result of some form of wrongdoing or the suffering of evil. We can see this, for example, in the competing narratives put forward and tested in an adversarial manner by legal representatives in the criminal justice process, or indeed as prolegomena for those who commit a criminal act (as in rational choice theory). It is for formal actors such as police, juries and/or judges and informal interpreters such as journalists, co-workers and friends in what is a highly mediated society to make up their minds about the credibility of these stories, and where crime is concerned, that is a major preoccupation. The fact of the matter is, we do this all the time, share these stories and they shape to a considerable degree our individual and collective, private and public understanding of good and evil.

The outline of this chapter covers:

- Narratology
- Narrative and evil—Paul Ricoeur
- Ricoeur's method—phenomenological hermeneutics
- *The Symbolism of Evil*

We will briefly consider aspects of Ricoeur's thesis in *The Symbolism of Evil* (1967), focusing on the potency of the symbols of evil as a driving force behind storytelling in virtually every society since the earliest times up until today, and beyond. We will also discuss Ricoeur's typology of the symbols of evil, and how his phenomenological hermeneutics helps us to recover the rich experiences of evil that enhance the more modern, abstract, philosophical approaches we looked at in previous chapters, and indeed those to come (and more). I will conclude by considering some examples of the application of Ricoeur's theory to the evil of racism as set out in Ronald Jacobs' analysis of the Rodney King beating.

Narratology

What is narrative? For most people, what immediately comes to mind when they hear the word 'narrative' is the activity of storytelling—an act which comprises both telling and listening, i.e. an event with more than one person present. So, immediately we get the strong impression of narrative as an interactive and indeed a deeply social and temporal event, comprising more than one person (or maybe only one person but at different times, as with the private practices of storytelling in journals and diaries), as well as something which takes place all the time, inclusive of virtually all people, as part of ordinary everyday life. Second, what often comes to mind when thinking about narrative is the telling of certain kinds of stories, such as folktales, sagas, myths and so forth. It is through these kinds of narratives that consensual values, collective concerns and the cultural transmission of all kinds of knowledge between individuals and across the generations takes place, connecting us in the present to a receding past and anticipated future. Hence, we may say that every culture has developed ways of identifying narrative forms so that they can be easily recognized and told apart. This idea was developed in a systematic way by the Russian folklorist Vladimir Propp (1895–1970), whose name is closely identified with the development of *narratology*, the branch of literary theory devoted to the study of narrative.

Third, to develop the second point, what often comes to mind when thinking of narratives—especially in a modern context—is their use as art forms. Here, the notion of imagination, creativity and even performance, usually associated with an individual (and named) author is of key importance. Hence, in modern 'Western' societies, we tend to link narratives with established cultural forms such as the novel, play or short story, rather than the myth or epic poem, although the saga in the form of the soap opera or serial drama is still very popular. And this is instructive, as in modern societies, narratives are not limited to such high cultural forms, nor are genres rigid or immune to change. Rather, they develop and morph as people use and transform them to tell their stories, and often relate to more ordinary or pedestrian forms of storytelling and entertainment such as movies, magazines and television programmes. In their intimate link to the individual, popular narratives in modern cultures often have to do with individual and/or private lives, as reflected in popular forms like auto/biography and memoir.

We all use storytelling and narrative forms as ways of making sense of what is the 'raw' experience of daily life. Commentators on narrative identify this as a universal human trait. While all of these forms have their recognizable narrative tropes (i.e. figure of speech such as metaphor, simile, metonymy etc.)—such as triumph over adversity, love lost and found, rags to riches, life as a journey etc.—what is universal is the concern with individual creativity, using these forms as the springboard for telling one's one particular—and changing—unique story. In this way, we are culturally predisposed to recognize and be able to choose *genres* which are especially meaningful for us or which we particularly enjoy, while also hearing something new and having these genres changed and transformed into previously unknown forms.

So, narrative is about the transmission of historical and cultural values on a collective scale as it is about making sense of the everyday experiences of ordinary life for individuals and their social collectives. In addition, though we rely on narratives which are familiar to our society in the form of genres as a quick way to identify or enter into stories, at the same time we value these as much for their potential to tell us something new and possibly unique, and also as modes of changing these same genres as an essential part of our cultural life. It is the ubiquity and universality of narrative which makes it such a rich and attractive resource for interpreting and analysing sociocultural life. This makes narrative analysis a powerful tool for social scientists, one that is already utilized and embedded far more than is commonly acknowledged, even within the most positivistic number-crunching methodologies:

> The narrative analysis of the text helps to bring out not only the properly linguistic characteristics of the story...but also a great deal of sociology hidden behind a handful of lines. It is precisely because (a) narrative texts are packed with sociological information and (b) much of our empirical evidence is in narrative form that sociologists should be concerned with narrative. [Just think: Even the quantitative sociological method par excellence, the sample survey, often hides powerful narratives behind its numbers (Mishler, 1986: 72).]
>
> Franzosi (1998: 519)

A comprehensive summary of narrative or Ricoeur's methodology is beyond the scope of this chapter, but the points below give a flavour of some of the main principles of phenomenological hermeneutics as set out by John Lye (1996). To briefly summarize, these are that we live in the material world in our own space and time, not any other worlds, but the one we know and share; it is from this that we derive meaning. This meaning is arrived at through our raw experiences and the tools we have to hand to make sense of these, primarily language and narrative (e.g. storytelling and myth). Especially in relation to experiences of evil, we are symbol-using creatures and utilize and share these symbols to make sense of the inscrutable, insufferable and disturbing happenings and realties around us. While these help us to make sense of—and to some extent at the same time also 'make' the world as we know it—there is always something that escapes symbolization, that exceeds language, what it cannot capture and what remains unsaid, but nonetheless still needs saying.

At the end of *The Symbolism of Evil* (1967), Ricoeur presents his reflections on method. He writes:

[M]odern hermeneutics entertains the project of a revivification of philosophy through contact with the fundamental symbols of con-sciousness. Does that mean that we could go back to a primitive naivete? Not at all. In every way, something has been lost, irreme-diably lost: immediacy of belief. But if we can no longer live the great symbolisms of the sacred in accordance with the original belief in them, we can, we modern men, aim at a second naivete in and through criticism. In short, it is by *interpreting* that we can *hear* again. Thus it is in hermeneutics that the symbol's gift of meaning and the endeavor to understand by deciphering are knotted together.

Ricoeur (1967: 350–351 [emphasis in original])

So, what phenomenological hermeneutics offers us is the opportunity to try to recreate a sort of dialogue with the past through a revived appre-ciation of *language* and the *act* of interpretation as an activity that is something like untying knots. While it is clear that we can't go back and reclaim a sort of naïve or recovered first encounter with sacred texts that is like that the people who lived by them in the past had (or indeed cur-rent believers do), what we can do is to try to find this 'second naivete' through the active and interpretive activity of criticism. By 'criticism' Ricoeur doesn't mean finding fault with these texts; if anything, just the opposite. He means that we use our analytical skills for listening to and attempting to understand and engage with and interpret these texts within our own realm of meaning and signification. This means striving to 'hear' from the past as well as trying to speak for ourselves in the present and the future. This is how we create a kind of dialogue with the past, and indeed dialogic is important in narrative and in Ricoeur's understanding of it.

Hermeneutics is a phenomenological method that reflects on meanings which are not constituted primarily by the subjectivity of the interpreter even though this interpretation must be guided by the interpreter's understanding. Subjectivity is involved, but the meanings are not founded on it entirely. Interpretation also involves consideration of the subject matter within its historical (i.e. previously understood) framework.

There is no doubt about it: the style of *The Symbolism of Evil* is difficult; it is very technical philosophically and compressed. In it, Ricoeur builds upon Kant's concept of the symbol as it appears in his third critique (*The Critique of Judgment*, Kant's treatise on aesthetics and ethics, encapsulated in what he considered the fundamentally practical assessment of 'the good'). Here, Kant states that 'symbols give rise to thought', and this is really where Ricoeur wants to start; for him this is really where the action is in terms of the melding of human experience with philosophical reflection. As Kant indicated, this happens largely through the use of *language*, as both experience and thinking rely on language substantially for their form and content. But language/speech/narrative doesn't just appear from nowhere, and neither does reflection. Human beings are born into a world which is already underway, and we use symbols as a way of relating our own experience to our pre-existing culture, to each other, to history and to the future as a way of recovering meaning and making sense—to ourselves and to each other. It is in this act of recovery and striving to understand genres and other narratives we receive from the past in our present world that we overcome the false dichotomy of passivity–activity in evil as represented in theodicy. In narrative, both are required: passive reception of stories about what has gone before or happened to others and active articulation and interpretation of what is happening to or for me now; this is a living, historical, and future-oriented project. It is in this sense that Ricoeur considers narrative and symbols of evil as constituting our 'gift' from history, the 'givenness' of language, the world, our experience, each other, these genres and we keep them alive and pass them on through our use of them, especially in articulating and narrating experiences of evil. In this way, narrative overcomes the limitations and frustrations of theodicy, philosophy and metaphysics that as we have seen in the previous chapters that become stuck in the unresolvable dichotomy of agency (action) and passivity (what social scientists would call 'structure', but what more generally is known as external reality, i.e. real life, the stuff we can't do much about or can't control), whereby the suffering of evil remains ultimately inscrutable. Ricoeur acknowledges this dichotomy but does not attempt to reduce or eliminate it through any rational or logical exercise—such a venture would be fruitless. Instead, he acknowledges this tension for what it actually is—a limitation, a sign of our finitude, but also a freedom, a launch pad; more than that, a *demand* for creativity, for us to contribute by telling our own stories as a result of our experiences of good and evil. This tension is irreducible; but what Ricoeur's theory can contribute that philosophy and metaphysics can't is an awareness of narrative and inclusivity of (religious) myth. This enables him to acknowledge the primordial realities and pain of evil and the limitations of human being while being able to reiterate the primacy of the good as a prior and fundamental condition (Wall, 2005).

In *The Symbolism of Evil*, Ricoeur develops his argument about the primacy of symbols and myths of evil above all other subjects for human beings. It is worth repeating, he describes these symbols as like 'gifts' that make possible but also *demand* philosophical reflection. What he means by this is that there is a special urgency about these types of experience and there are a cluster of symbols that have been used throughout the ages by different cultures to 'bring to language' people's own experiences of evil and suffering in the world. Every person in every age must do this for themselves, but the symbols are there, pre-existent and pre-philosophical, our inheritance from history, to help in this duty to 'make sense' (an active and essentially mandatory task) of the world.

So the symbol comes first, before the narrative and reflective, philosophical understanding.

Symbols are incredibly rich in meaning, but also indeterminate, open to and demanding interpretation. Symbols give rise to thought, and not only make storytelling possible, they make it necessary for cultures to develop and survive. Ricoeur describes symbols as connecting us to the experiences of the past while also opening up the possibility for our own speculation on it and on our own experiences. Symbols are charged with memory and hope.

As indicated already, among all the symbols, Ricoeur argues that the symbols and myths about evil are especially important. This is because of the enormity and urgency of the experience of evil and human suffering and the need to get some kind of handle on it, make sense of why it happens, how it can be dealt with when it happens, and how it can be anticipated and ideally avoided in the future. The alternative of simply surrendering to evil as a raw, brute, 'un-storied', non-narratable reality is just unthinkable, too daunting, too chaotic and frightening to contemplate. Without such stories, it is impossible to mingle the suffering of evil with the balm of hope, to make evil mean something through the possibility of sharing, healing and reconciliation. So, in all cultures at all times, we see some expression of the mythical stories about the origins and end of evil generated from the symbols of evil. This is, Ricoeur argues, universal, and a deeply pervasive need. To the question of evil, these symbols provide, if not an answer, at least the possibility of one, or a partial one; one that could last us for our time on earth during which we need it.

The book *The Symbolism of Evil* (hereafter *SoE*) is presented in two parts. Part 1 is the most theoretically oriented and philosophical, and most difficult, setting out his typology for the primary symbols of evil. They are:

- Defilement—analogue of stain
- Sin—analogue of deviation
- Guilt—analogue of accusation (*SoE*, p. 18)

'Analogue' here means foundational symbol. Ricoeur gives the example of 'water', which as a symbol of threat or destruction in the biblical tradition is expressed in the myth of the flood, or as a symbol of renewal and rebirth is expressed in the story of baptism. Let us now look at each symbol in turn.

Defilement

'With defilement we enter into the reign of terror' (*SoE*, 25). It evokes fear and magicality, it is about conflation of the moral order with the cosmic and physical/biological orders in the explication of evil, something Ricoeur thought we as moderns were culturally beyond, to some degree. It is about the imputation of evil with punishment, that those who suffer misfortunes such as death, failure and loss are somehow impure and in need of purification.

Symbols of defilement are about impurity, corruption and contamination, usually through interaction or proximity with sources of impurity, focusing on the contagion of evil. These sources can be actions (e.g.

sexual intercourse, purified through the ritual act of marriage), thoughts, words, places, even people. Such interaction with these results in the 'staining' or defilement and thus rendering evil of something that was previously 'pure' and good. This is a very ancient symbol of evil, and is often remedied through some sort of *ritual action*, to restore purity via the means of symbols. This symbolism relates to the distinction between the sacred and the profane. These are the sorts of concepts that the criminologist Jack Katz (1988) utilizes in his analysis of 'cold-blooded' killing (which we will consider in more detail in Chapter 7).

There are many purification rites that serve this function, e.g. the rites of baptism, confession, exorcism and so forth that are traceable to early religious traditions that still continue today. In our contemporary world, there are also notions of 'purification' that are much more postmodern (e.g. re-birthing) and violent in nature, exerted on the bodies of the 'impure' as the source of evil, either our own or probably more commonly on the bodies of others. This is expressed most graphically in the phrase 'ethnic cleansing', which is symbolically identified with the primordial evil of defilement. So, for example, in the Balkans conflict in the late twentieth century, the idea was to 'purify' the racial identity of the local community through the annihilation of the 'other' whose 'sins' or 'faults' were imputed to mythical origins from time immemorial. In this way, ethnic purity could be restored through the mass murder of an entire population. An example of true evil symbolized in defilement that is as applicable today as it was millennia ago, and a potent causal factor to the very modern phenomenon of genocide we will revisit in Chapter 8.

Sin

Ricoeur discusses the transition from the symbols of defilement to those of sin; a process which adds to (rather than replaces) the meanings of contagion, contamination and impurity which are primarily external in nature, emanating from a source outside the self. To the meanings of defilement are added the additional dimensions of transgression and iniquity which are much more internal sources of evil, coming from within the self. Though both might be the result of possession (e.g. by a demon) the need now is for the sufferer to recognize his imputed fault and confess or repent as a condition of being delivered from evil by God.

Ricoeur identifies the symbolism of sin in the first instance with the Babylonians and the ancient Hebrew religious traditions. While they do retain the connection of evil as defilement and impurity (e.g. in Leviticus), they add to it the historical and legal dimensions of life with God under the Covenant. So the evil of sin is experienced as a violation of this covenanted relationship, evoking the difference of life before and after the establishment of the covenant with God. This is an *ethical* realm, more devolved from the close identification of evil with a chaotic cosmic order that is the realm of amoral gods or a biological sphere of indiscriminate bacteria or viruses in which humans have little power or control than defilement. Humans are not just pawns or hosts here, although the influence of transcendent or physiological factors may still sometimes be in force. Sin refers instead primarily to the relationship between human beings with God and the law, under which humans have agency and choice or freedom to act, but also bear moral responsibility for their actions as individuals.

What emerges as particularly significant in this symbolic encounter with evil is the experience of evil in relation to God via the *Word* (logos). God's holy will is encapsulated in the law, which then becomes the focal point of ethical concern. These considerations of evil in sin become more juridical and philosophical in nature, and the key relationship is between the alignment between the Holy Spirit and the word as God's law or even the personification of the godhead as in the figure of Jesus for Christians; this is often represented in terms of the *personal* relationship with God. The symbolic language relating to good and evil in this model are often to do with the symbolism of 'darkness' and 'light', about the apportioning of 'righteousness' and 'justice' as opposed to the crude separation of the sacred and profane. Sin is determined by God according to His law and the dread of human beings of being in violation of it.

Guilt

As with sin, guilt retains the previously described dimensions of the other symbols of defilement and sin. What is different about the symbols of guilt is that they add to the imputation of sin the element of *subjective* fault. So, evil is not just an ontological reality as it was with sin in terms of the violation of the law and the relationship with God, it also brings into this the *consciousness* of being at fault and of deserving punishment. This is symbolized in the language of evil and suffering as 'burden' or 'weight', whereby the sin weighs on the conscience of the guilty, and victims who suffer evil should divulge in speech their experiences as a necessary step in unburdening themselves of trauma in order to facilitate subsequent healing. It is a burden of evil that the individual must bear subjectively, and it is deeply personal in addition to being ontological and communal.

Guilt is about assuming the personal responsibility for evil as actors, as producers of evil; *real* agents. It links the juridical notions of punishment and responsibility with the pain of suffering an accused and condemned conscience. Guilt is experienced as a weighted conscience, chastisement and dread. This experience of evil is the most distanced from that of defilement in that it is not so much then about the reality of evil as a violation of interdictions and the vengeance that follows such violations, but rather about the 'evil use of liberty' (*SoE*, 102) as the consummate need for the individual to make amends. We could relate this to something like Kant's focus on human freedom as opposed to finitude, and the individual moral responsibility and imputation to conscience, character and integrity that became part of his main concern, in addition to his appeal to the law. From a victim's perspective, such language is evocative of what is the clinical discourse of therapeutic healing. Both encapsulate the twin demands of understanding and justice in the face of evil as a necessary resolution, primarily accomplished through the testimonial and legalistic organs of witness, adjudication, punishment and healing.

Ricoeur identifies the symbolism of guilt as constituting a 'revolution' in the symbolic representation of evil; instead of guilt being engendered from the indiscriminate suffering of vengeance, guilt is now about finding liberation through punishment in healing, of being delivered from a guilty conscience and seeing those who have caused suffering brought to account. This healing becomes a solitary and fully individual experience, but one that culminates in that most communal experience of justice. Eventually, the symbolism of guilt is transformed, for example, in the language of the 'tribunal', whereby it is no longer the violation of a covenantal relationship with God that is the primary concern, but rather the violation of humanly ordained moral law as carried out objectively in formal institutions. This is more administrative and rationally oriented, as is the imputation of the degree of guilt and the subsequently decided form of punishment not as vengeance but as corrective—rational and proportional.

Part 2 of SoE: The four 'great narrative cycles' of evil

The second part of *SoE* traces the four main narrative myths of evil in their different sacred traditions in terms of the story of the origins and resolutions of the problem of evil. Ricoeur identifies four main 'great narrative' cycles of the myths of the beginning and the end of evil (Ricoeur, 1967: 171–174):

- The myth of primal chaos
- The myth of the wicked god
- The myth of the soul exiled in the evil body
- The myth of the historical fault of the individual ancestor/prototype 'man'

The myth of primal chaos refers to the drama of creation in which the origin of evil coincides with the origin of things, and foregrounds the chaos with which the god struggles in the act of creation. It is fundamentally linked to the cult re-enactment of the combats that took place at the origin of the world as the basis of religious ritual. Evil is identified in these types of myth with chaos. Examples include the Babylonian-type creation epic, also found in Hesiod's *Theogony* which regards evil as the original condition. In this myth, Apsu and Tiamat make and produce the Gods, who are wicked. Evil is thus personified in gods and goddesses who are amoral, meaning that deities can also be evil. Good is a later emergence, but comes not from moral evolution but physical revolution, a violent struggle between latter better gods and older wicked gods. In this myth, Marduk is the highest of the better gods. Creation is not the making of the universe out of nothing as in the Judeo-Christian mythology; rather, it is the attack on the old, chaotic order in a violent way, whereby as creator-god Marduk kills the sea monster from the primordial waters, Tiamat, and creates the world out of her carcass. Creation is construed here as the negation of original state of being replaced by a new victorious being, in which existence as 'chaos' is replaced by being as 'cosmos', marking creation as a 'new birth' (Eliade, 1958: 401). But some of the original evil remains— the revolution is not a complete success. In the Babylonian creation myth, humans are fashioned from the carcass of the executed evil god Kingu, hence human beings retain some of this residual evil, rendering us different from the new 'good' gods. There is a way to resolve evil, through ritual enactment; each New Year's Eve and Day Marduk's victory over evil is re-enacted (see Eliade, 1958). This ritual re-enactment represents a way for humans to gain redemption through the celebration of this important festival that marks the sovereign heroism and magic of Marduk. The central figure in this festival is the king—a more primordial role than political. He is Marduk's representative on earth and in real human time, retaining his sovereignty in historical time and something of the magic. As in the symbolism of defilement, this way of construing and facing evil is cyclical and founded in a realm of magic and nature; it is heavily reliant on ritual as a necessary and repetitive response.

The view that evil is the primordial, original condition and gods are evil is objectionable to later thinkers like Plato who argued that the future guardians of society (children) should not be exposed to Hesiod's myths, so they were censored. Henceforth, goodness and godhead become synonymous. The prophets of the Hebrew Bible also objected to the notion in the Babylonian myths of a wicked god. Despite some of the destructive acts attributed to Yahweh, biblical creation myths are contrary to the Babylonian-style creation myth in this regard, though again this residual possibility (e.g. in the story of Noah and the flood) is not completely eradicated.

The myth of the wicked god—Ricoeur identifies this as the Greek tragic type, the god who tempts, blinds, leads astray etc. as in the narratives of Aeschylus and Sophocles, Nietzsche's *Birth of Tragedy* and Aristotle's *Poetics*. The origin of evil here is located in the suffering of the hero, not so much the hero's fault but the malevolent side of God (in the example from ancient Greek myth, Zeus), who is also the highest form of goodness. How is evil then resolved?

The real resolution of evil in this narrative is in the aesthetic trans-figuration of suffering in the figure of the hero. Although the sufferings are evil, the spectacle is somehow experienced as deliverance (*SoE*: 173). There is a salvation in the revelation of the tragedy of evil which con-veys a sort of deliverance in the tragic spectacle itself. The narrative and receptive focus is on the phenomenal cycle of spectacle, pity and catharsis. Human freedom coincides with understanding this necessity to do with evil. Thus, beauty has the power to transfigure evil via the spectacle, but that is all. Acceptance of the tragic through the catharsis of the storytelling (*poesis*) is the best that can be achieved, as opposed to transformation through a call for action (*phronesis*) (see Wall, 2005). In this respect, the repetitive qualities of ritual contained in the myth of primal evil are retained, but with the emphasis now on performance as opposed to religious observance. The affective and collective experi-ences of human emotion in the catharsis of tragedy replace the priestly role of sacrament and the re-alignment of the sacred and profane in a theological or metaphysical sense.

The myth of the soul exiled in the evil body—This is an Orphic myth. Orphism was a Greek religion which influenced the Greek tradition of philosophy. Good and evil are not so much defined by good and bad gods; they are a distinction within every human being. The good is represented by the soul or later the mind; the bad is represented by the body. Resolution of this dichotomy comes from the destiny of the soul, the soul's escape from the body, later through death but in the here-and-now via knowledge (*gnosis*). The cosmogonic and theogonic aspects of myth play a much less prominent role here, if at all. Platonism comes out of this, influencing early Christian thinkers like Saint Augustine, which in turn influenced modern thinkers like Descartes. The wickedness of the body is ultimately rejected in Plato, but this tradition is still highly dualistic.

The myth of the historical fault of the individual ancestor/prototype 'man'— This is the story of the 'fall', as represented in the Hebrew Bible/Adamic myth. Ricoeur states this is the most complex in how it relies upon and is related to the others. It also is closest to the Greek-tragic type. In this type of narrative, the origin of evil is not with or before creation, but after creation. The significance of the creation drama gradually becomes eliminated here; salvation becomes much more important, with the drive toward eschatological myth and the end of time rather than concern with evil as an original or conditioning reality at the beginning in creation. This type of myth is historical rather than cosmological. The concentration is on human time, even with its (occasional) emphasis on the eternal life of the soul.

Evil according to these myths is the fault of humans, as the fall took place after and in the context of a perfect creation. God is good and what He created is good; that is the original and eschatological condition, not evil or wickedness in God. Genesis 3 explains the wrong choice that Adam and Eve made. Ricoeur observes a tendency in these myths to excessive moralism. That tendency is so radical that both writers of Genesis 1 and 3 introduce inconsistency in the narratives they relate. In Gen 1, God broods over waters; in Gen 3, we encounter the snake. Both are already there, either preceding God's creation (in the former) or containing the malevolence or evil of temptation (in the latter). How can this be? It can't, and be consistent with the notion of creation *ex nihilo*, from nothing, or with the notion of God as omnipotent, omniscient, all benevolent and the creator of everything that exists. As with the theodicy, this inconsistency interrupts the tendency to put all the blame on human agents for evil. The story of Job's suffering also does this—he was innocent of his suffering. Then again, the serpent as the creature personifying evil speaks to Eve in her own language, something she can understand, persuading her as she later persuades Adam; this, as Wall (2005) notes, is suggestive more of the human qualities of the serpent as opposed to its divine or demonic attributes, thus saying more by implication about the human condition than God in the narrative of this creation myth. What is the resolution and how are such inconsistencies to be resolved? Should they be, and what advantage would this proffer?

This type of myth comes closer here to Babylonian style, according to Ricoeur, in the respect that there is a saviour king in the figure of Jesus Christ. It is thus not coincidental that in the Judeo-Christian Bible, the earliest psalms are about kingship. The king is a representative of Yahweh on earth. But, after the split of Israel and 2 Kings, the king in the Judeo (and to some extent Christian) tradition is transmuted into the king who will come in the future, the messiah.

Summary and illustration

So far in this chapter, we have explored narratology, the study of narrative, as initiated in the work of Propp, and what narrative is and does. This is mainly been done through a consideration of Ricoeur's methodology of phenomenological hermeneutics and the special place of evil in the symbolism of evil (defilement, sin and guilt) and the four 'great narrative cycles' of evil (primal chaos, wicked god, body/soul dualism, original 'man') as set out in *SoE*.

For the remainder of the chapter, and by way of applied summary if you will, I would like to cite an example from the recent research literature to show how Ricoeur's method can be used to explore what is by any measure a persistent and pervasive evil of our times: racism, and police brutality. The purposes of this section are to enable readers to:

- use Ricoeur's typology for the symbolism of evil to conduct a narratological analysis of media stories about evil (in this case the racist incident of the Rodney King beating);
- begin the process of learning interdisciplinary theories and methods for social-scientific/criminological analysis;
- evaluate the strengths and weaknesses of this type of approach in socialscientific research; and
- be able to determine the appropriateness of applying such narratological analysis of evil in criminological research.

In his article 'Civil Society and Crisis: Discourse, and the Rodney King Beating' (1996), Jacobs applies Ricoeur's theory to two media representations of the infamous incident involving the violence carried out by police upon the motorist Rodney King. One of Jacobs' central concerns is trying to figure out how the beating of Rodney King by these police officers came to be seen as itself *symbolic* of the race problem in Los Angeles and beyond. How did these series of events become perceived and understood by the different communities in this way? How did they then proceed to try to confront or resolve these narratives? What impact has the narrating and symbolism of the Rodney King incident had on the broader understanding of race relations in the US subsequently? And how do the continually unfolding stories around these people and events reflect back upon the utility of narrative methods for social science and criminology?

Jacobs takes for his sample data set what he calls the 'entire universe' of the newspaper reports on these events from two Los Angeles newspapers, the *Los Angeles Times* (a daily newspaper with a huge circulation) and the *Los Angeles Sentinel* (a much smaller weekly newspaper read mostly by the local black community) and compares them in narratological terms. This is very much like the narrative method of phenomenological hermeneutics developed by Ricoeur, and indeed Jacobs refers to Ricoeur and *SoE* a couple of times. In this section, we will seek to build upon Jacobs' analysis in terms of concentrating on *SoE* as an analytic reference.

Narrative is a central concept for exploring and making sense of the dynamics of 'civil society' according to Jacobs. It helps us also to understand the construction of social crises and the significance of social events:

> ... [N]arrative analysis has become an increasingly important tool for social scientists interested in explaining social process and social change. There are two main reasons for this. The first has to do with the role narrative plays in constructing identities and enabling social action. Narrative helps individuals, groups and communities to 'understand their progress through time in terms of stories, plots which have beginnings, middles and ends, heroes and antiheros, epiphanies and denouements, dramatic, comic and tragic forms.' (Alexander and Smith, 1993: 156)
>
> Jacobs (1996: 1240)

Jacobs argues that the discourse of 'civil society' is organized around a bifurcation of citizen and enemy (1242). So, in a fundamental sense, talk about citizenship and civility is about identifying those who are socially 'worthy' and those who are 'unworthy', defining deviance and the lines of demarcation. Hence Jacobs' analysis concentrates on the different ways the events of and surrounding the Rodney King beating are narrated and also 'read into' continuing historical/possible future narratives of civil strife and racism. He focuses on *character* (heroes and anti-heroes) and *plot* (tragedy, comedy, romance etc). He tries to see how public narratives are used to 'purify' one set of actors and their allies while at the same time 'polluting' their enemies.

The 'polluting/purification' metaphor could be readily assigned to Ricoeur's *SoE*, which Jacobs doesn't really do. And there are many examples in the newspaper reports he cites relating to Ricoeur's symbols of evil. I have set some of these out in the following table according to the symbolism of defilement, sin and guilt (Table 4.1):

Table 4.1   Ricoeurian analysis of symbols of evil in Jacobs

Symbolism	Defilement	Sin	Guilt
Language	Corruption, pollution of police; contagion of guilt by association of Commissioner Gates with corrupt officers	Deviation dereliction of duty by police; irrational and excitable officers; deception; 'darkness' of surroundings in film and its significance as a record of police brutality in 'black and white'; moral light represented by black community	Subjective fault; individual officers using their powers in illegitimate ways; police officers as 'bad apples' and questions about 'goodness' of the 'barrel'; violation of openness, fairness and transparency; frustration/miscarriage of justice
Response	Requires ritual purification—e.g. through violence of rioting? Exorcism of racist police officers from LA force?	Implies need for repentance, confession	Implies personal subjective fault, need for punishment, institutional reform and healing

Table 4.1   (Continued)

Symbolism	Defilement	Sin	Guilt
Realm	Evokes primordial, cosmic experiences evil; 'non-rational' (Jacobs)	Ethical realm; evokes social covenant of the law, juridical– philosophical in nature than cosmic	Not cosmic, theological or ethical; subjective and individual, focusing more on individual moral culpability
Outcome	Chaos; innocent victims situated between malevolent and impersonal forces; cyclical, repeat pattern of behaviour that people have to come to terms with as a pre-eminent and pre-existing reality that is very difficult if not impossible for them to change (e.g. through mechanisms like consciousness-raising or legal reform); contagion through the generations of racism	Dread of humans to violate law; denial of blameworthiness, legal, moral responsibility on part of officers; crisis of the video evidence and moral justification on part of police in the eyes of the world, there is a case to answer; questioning of institutional power and responsibility (e.g. Commissioner Gates); victims seeking righteousness and justice	Victims reject the authenticity of the officers' confession and repentance and seek redress through exculpation in the law; when the law fails to deliver this, many victims revert to the chaos and violence of defilement. Failure to achieve justice through lack of lament and remorse and apportioning of blame and punishment prohibits healing and means the evil is unresolved

Probably the most prominent symbols Jacobs cites in both newspapers' reports are those of defilement, e.g. the corruption, pollution and the need to 'purify' the LA police. But in addition to this, there is also the symbolism of sin with reference to the language of deviation; irrational and excitable officers; deception. Also guilt—officers using their power in illegitimate ways; violation of openness, fairness and justice; lying; guilty by association with the officers of the Police Commissioner Gates.

Layered on top of the symbolism of evil, we can detect in the stories recounted by Jacobs the presence of Ricoeur's four narrative forms into which these symbols are formulated and shaped at the level of storytelling, as represented in Table 4.2.

Ricoeur's great mythic cycles of evil:

Table 4.2 Ricoeurian analysis of great narrative cycles in Jacobs

Great mythic cycles	Myth of primal chaos	Myth of the wicked god	Myth of soul in exiled body	Myth of historical fault/prototype 'man'
Action/ plot	Violently, wildly, pounding, pummelling, uncontrolled actions of the police	Faultlessness and moral purity of black community on who undeserved suffering is visited upon by corrupt and evil authority figures	Dualistic distinction of goodness of black community versus evil of the police/racist American society	Representation in *LA Sentinel* of the malevolence of racism, which is an ongoing occurrence in a long history of evil suffered by poor black communities in the US
Ontology/ reality of evil	Evil as primal cosmic condition; cyclical, chaotic nature of suffering of innocents; ritual identification with the suffering good secondary god (e.g. Christ)	Catharsis; transfiguration of RK's suffering as a spectacle and symbol of racism in the US through police brutality overseen by the state	Gnosis; strength of black community in their more nuanced historical understanding of racism and racist crime and endemic	'Original man'; not something that's just emerged as discrete event or can be solved by the sacking of one corrupt police commissioner (*LA Times* solution)

How does the above analysis based on Ricoeur differ from the genre theory adopted by Jacobs? Comparatively speaking, genre theory (such as Norbert Frye's) tends to be quite structural in character, meaning that overarching narrative structures are deemed noteworthy over more detailed use of language and related experiences of emotion, power, morals and embodiment. In his article (and later book), Jacobs focuses on genre constructions of the various narrative versions of events in terms of their romantic, tragic, comic or ironic representations. Ricoeur's framework arguably incorporates more in terms of 'grand' narrative structures and perhaps more importantly the minutiae of symbolic language pertaining specifically to evil (e.g. in the use plot and metaphor). It also seems to encapsulate the experience of evil as it unfolds as a public event in a way that captures the deep-seated emotions involved.

What does this more phenomenological hermeneutic narrative analysis tell us about evil, in this case the social understanding of the evil of racist violence, in contemporary society? For one thing, the primacy of certain sets of metaphors (e.g. polluting influence of racism as institutional and social defilement as opposed to the need to excise a 'few bad apples') utilized by the producers and recipients of the different narratives about who the 'enemies/deviants' are and what 'really' happened in the beating of Rodney King exposes a number of underlying assumptions underpinning this seminal and richly symbolic event. The presence of what is a deeply primordial and emotive language of evil as experienced by many in the black community in Los Angeles suggests the long-standing experience of racism, whereby new episodes are read into previous narratives of tragedy, in which victims exist within this 'cosmic' force and have little if any control over the course of events or their eventual resolution. It is no coincidence that the symbolism of defilement is the most prominent in the narratives represented in the *LA Sentinel* and the symbolism of sin in the *LA Times*. This says something about the nature and experience of racism in American society, that it is experienced and understood as a basic, primordial form of evil that is visited upon the innocent repeatedly and has not yet sufficiently moved on to being subject to healing and reform (in the former case) and the need only to locate and excise a few 'bad apples' (in the latter).

What is more, the eventual outcome of excessive and transgressive violence in the riots is anything but unpredictable or 'mindless'; on this narrative arc, the violence of rioting is entirely predictable, and makes sense in terms of its ritualistic nature in response to what is perceived to be (with good reason) a cyclical experience that will in all likelihood happen again. Here, we can see the power and utility of an interdisciplinary theory in what are conventional and vitally important areas of criminology—racism and police brutality. I suggest that it is valuable and commendable to consider other such disciplinary and theoretical approaches to address what have proven to be entrenched and pernicious problems relating not just to these issues, but similarly to analogous and equally topical issues such as youth and gang crime and riots (here construed as ritual violence). Paying attention to the *language* and how symbols and narratives are utilized and developed could help individuals and communities to better understand, interpret and communicate their experiences and responses to evil in a new and potentially less divisive way.

On the other hand, alternative community interpretations of these same events as relating simply to a few rogue officers whose actions are not regarded as representative of a malady at the heart of the police force as represented in a narrative of evil as sin/guilt or the fault of an Adamic man character indicates a very different perspective on the ontological reality and remedies that are applicable in this situation. That a legal trial of a few officers should take place and be regarded as sufficient to 'close the case' even where guilt is not apportioned simply does not recognize the experiences of evil represented by the master narratives of racism as experienced by the black community. What is evident is that the two communities and versions of events are using the same 'raw' experiences of evil to 'speak from' and 'speak to' very different histories and realities; the upshot is that in relating these narratives of evil without a reflexive awareness of the symbolism and narratives of evil, they are not really able to speak to or hear each other in a particularly meaningful way. This entails that mutual understanding will not be achieved, neither will justice, and the cycle of misunderstanding, hurt and mutual suspicion will continue, making the repetitive and tragic outcomes of such a case more likely to happen again in the future. When people living in the same community cannot appreciate and live through the story as told by the proximate 'other', what hope or scope is there for mutual understanding and possible healing, justice and resolution?

Then there is the issue of Rodney King himself, literally and figuratively the 'king' of religious myth, the 'first man', the one, who comes to defeat the originally wicked and amoral 'gods', the better, or less evil, god. Before, during and after the incidents directly surrounding the filming of his beating by LA police officers, King's own personal narratives of identity as shaped by the external forces of racism and indeed fame if not infamy have been multiple and dynamic, showcasing the plasticity of narrative and its scope as a mode of creativity even for those caught in the maelstrom of celebrity/notoriety. King's continuing efforts to articulate and come to terms with the trauma of experiences emanating from things like his addiction to alcohol, family problems, criminality, victimization and the trauma of the events of 3 March 1991 led him to engage in a number of public spectacles in which one or more of these experiences of evil were formulated in line with normative legal or media narratives of what such experiences mean, and how they should be dealt with. But, as Wall (2005) notes in his assessment of Ricoeur's narrative theory, as a mode of 'moral creativity', such highly mediated and deterministic narratives often fail, as they are insufficient to encapsulate or express the complexity, subtlety, originality and authenticity of the primary experiences of suffering and harm that initiated the need to tell one's own side of the story in the first place. Other, more exploratory and less repetitive and stereotyped engagements with language and narrative are required here, and indeed, that is where we will be going in the next chapter on psychoanalysis.

While there are many tragic aspects of the Rodney King story, there are also stories of hope, love and change too. And in the final analysis, we are yet to reach the end of this story in terms of its meaning for the people of Los Angeles, the 'city of angels', or beyond. How this story will be told and re-told will be part of the legacy and potential 'gift' of this extremely tragic and painful story of the evils of racism and state violence, leavened as it is with the possibilities of hope. As Wall (2005: 99) states, ' ... all of us find ourselves, like Sisyphus, having constantly to begin creating our lives over again. The capability for creating a narrative unity of life involves not only the realization of creative freedom in the world but also the renewal of this broken world itself.' An essential part of this endeavour is the exposure and receiving of these multiple and necessary 'truths'.

Becoming aware of the nature of these discursive aspects of evil could help to make such underlying premises and experiences clearer, adopting a more phenomenological hermeneutic perspective on the divergent 'realities' and stories. Awareness of such cultural and philosophical aspects of social evils such as racism and/or policing could help to advance such communication and reconciliation in a way that does not entail that one community is compelled to accept the 'factual' discourse or the hegemony of the other, or that the other is enabled to disregard or derogate the narratives of the other as a result of the unequal distribution of power and influence in society at large.

This analysis tells us that there is much beyond the 'factual' or rational in media representations of deeply affecting public incidents. It also reveals additional dimensions of moral action as at the root of evil as emphasized by Kant. While human action in the phenomenon of evil is undeniably of vital importance, it is the arrangement and meanings of such actions within stories by different actors and listeners that is crucial, including elements such as chronology, characterization and plot (Franzosi, 1998). As noted as far back as Aristotle, though there may be a real distinction between *poesis* (literally 'to make' in ancient Greek, 'production' or 'art') and *phronesis* ('practical wisdom', including ethics), nevertheless in the real life and ongoing historical construction of morality and 'the good', the two are very intimately linked (Wall, 2005). While this means we may never solve all of our problems or eliminate evil, the continual need to narrate and tell stories about such evils, and listen to those who suffer, offers us the opportunity to change for the better and to become more compassionate and understanding. This in itself is a sign of hope and, as Ricoeur states, makes such discursive language and methods truly a gift from history. How we use these gifts now, in our society, is the question for social scientists and criminologists. In the next chapter, we will continue our exploration of evil and narrative, this time from the perspective of psychoanalysis, another sort of hermeneutic and cultural theory relating to and highlighting other forms of evil and their sources in human psychic development.

5

'Something to be scared of'—Evil, the Feminine and Psychoanalytic Theory

This is the second of three chapters comprising the second main section of the book in which we continue our explorations of theories, concepts and perspectives on evil from a cultural studies or narrative point of view. In this chapter, we will venture briefly into the fascinating territory of evil and psychoanalysis, with a specific emphasis on the work of the French philosopher and psychoanalyst Julia Kristeva, and the political scientist and commentator on psychoanalysis and evil C. Fred Alford. Psychoanalysis and the approach to evil will be considered specifically in relation to Kristeva's *The Powers of Horror* (1982) and the very familiar and popular figure of the vampire as the contemporary epitome of evil. Using the vampire as an example, we will explore some of the approaches and ideas of psychoanalysis in relation to evil and ask, are vampires scary, pitiful or 'baby stuff'? What is the 'power' of this very popular and lucrative form of 'horror'?

So far, in the context of just this book, we can observe the magnificent variety and scale involved in the study of evil, from the vast outer limits of the eternal, metaphysical cosmos to the very innermost, darkest, secret and private desires of the single soul in the process of becoming a subject or self. And that is a massive scope in scale on any measure. The challenge presented by psychoanalysis is that it covers all (or much) of this, and none. Meaning that it takes into account the collective and timeless cultural experiences of symbolism and myth from the past as well as stories of the most personal individual trauma in the present, while at the same time rarely using the term 'evil'. But as Stein (2002) argues in her analysis of the letter written by the 9/11 Al Qaeda leader Mohammed Atta to his other cell members, it is time this wariness toward evil changed and psychoanalysis took such an important and seminal phenomenon in modern culture and interpersonal relationships much more seriously. There is a need to engage more directly with the proliferating evils that result in the epidemic forms of violence, aggression, depression, addiction and associated multitude of neuroses in contemporary society. Where 'evil' or the 'dark side' of the human psyche are concerned, this mainly has to do with things like close encounters with the unknown or inscrutable, often in relation to primal urges of a sexual or aggressive nature. Such urges and drives are directly relevant to a social science discipline like criminology, when it comes to making sense of the psychological factors that motivate people to commit crime.

What has also tended to feature in previous encounters with evil, such as in theodicy, metaphysics and moral philosophy is a concentration on the 'rule of the father', what is known as *phallocentrism*, and indeed 'the father' is elemental to psychoanalytic theory. This can be roughly defined as rationality, civility, a concentration on the public sphere and the rule of law and order all converging around the sociocultural power and predominance of masculinity of a narrowly construed kind. In Kristeva's work, in particular, we see a major departure from this phallocentric approach, and the return of the repressed in psychic experience, specifically with respect to the recursion to the feminine, the maternal and the private/subjective/personal. In this context, the activity of storytelling retains its qualities of moral agency and subject-construction as described in previous chapters by Paul Ricoeur, but here the attribution of power and the embodied and subjective experience of agency are somewhat messier and less 'in (or subject to) control'. What is more, while symbolism and myth are still very much in evidence as potent tools for analysis and sense-making in psychoanalysis, the value of genre is perhaps less prominent than in other narrative theories. This is especially notable in relation to the type and level of language through which the pain and trauma of evils that are not fully understood or controllable by the person in question whose need to articulate and decipher them is urgent and specific, in many ways intensely private and unique. It is also to some degree attributable to the psychoanalytic scepticism toward the utility of norms (such as genre) as sufficiently stable anchor-points for critical analysis; as far as psychoanalysis is concerned, such norms and archetypes are as much objects of scrutiny are individual subjects.

What is psychoanalysis?

- The 'talking cure'
- A 'theory of culture' (Ricoeur, 1970)

Psychoanalysis is a twentieth-century theory relating to society and the self, though a different kind of self to the one we have encountered before, not as consciously self-assured, self-certain or 'pre-formed, pre-linguistic' (Grosz, 1989) as the Cartesian subject. The self here marks a revolution of a Freudian notion of the divided and collective as well as a 'languaged' self, i.e. a subject that is formulated in and through the use of language. In this respect, as Paul Ricoeur (1970) astutely notes in his commentary on Freudian psychoanalysis, there are two distinct areas of psychoanalysis: there are the multiple discourses of psychoanalysis itself with its unique and diverse concepts and theories that form the basis of therapeutic praxis and an interpretive framework for analysing society and/or culture as a whole. This binocular perspective on the individual and sociocultural contributes to the complexity but also the richness and diversity of psychoanalytic theory. In both aspects, language is elemental, but it isn't everything, at least not as we normally think about it. What language is *not* is a reified, reductive, ideal 'representation' of material 'reality', i.e. factual, objective empirically verifiable discourse about what 'is' and what is 'out there'. Language in the arena of psychoanalysis is much more than that, covering not only the 'real' (whether as it is or as it appears to be) but also the imaginary, e.g. our dreams, fantasies and imaginations, it is fictional and factual, descriptive and artistic. It is from these diverse and sometimes contradictory sources that we recover meaning through storytelling and make sense of ourselves and our lives (Ian, 1993).

> If, as these writers [e.g. Julia Kristeva] suggest, language is not simply a set of practices much like any other, but is the condition for the meaningful existence of all other practices, then analyzing the structure of language may help make clear its crucial role in the functioning of power itself.
>
> Grosz (1989: 39)

Language is as much about what is, as what is not—tracing as it does what we fear and what we want. Harking back to Descartes in Chapter 1, as Ian (1993) notes, the language of the psyche is rich and recalcitrantly self-contradictory; it can have us believe p and *not* p at the same time, reversing, or simply ignoring, the law of non-contradiction or the excluded middle that is fundamental to (phallocentric) logic. Other, contradictory, or possibly no logics or rationalities pertain here, not as Descartes and many others would have recognized them.

There are a number of distinctive approaches within psychoanalysis which for reasons of space will not be delved into in any great detail here detail here, but basically what they have in common is the notion that we all are made up of an individual conscious self (itself a complex construction) and also a common or collective conscious which we share and which extends back throughout our sociocultural history which comprises a vital part of our inheritance as social and above all language and symbol using and storytelling beings. This collective conscious is a deep and rich communal reservoir from which we derive and interact with our cultural histories and subsequently transform them and ourselves, often through the experience of our own everyday private and social lives, codified in and interpretable through mythologies. In relation to evil, this process is often animated by personal experiences of suffering and trauma and interpreted through the myths and symbols derived from our ancient collective past.

In this sense, psychoanalysis is not exceedingly different from Ricoeur's hermeneutic theory, and indeed he considers psychoanalysis to be a kind of hermeneutics. But there are significant differences between the two, impinging on the foundational ontologies of phenomenology and its concentration on consciousness and language, compared with what would appear to be more substantive claims about the ontological realities of the id or collective conscience, for example, which we won't go into in any detail as they are not directly relevant to our task, and there are ample external resources for those who are interested in delving into this more deeply. Suffice to say that we are still very much in the territory of relating our own individual 'raw' experiences of evil to the symbols and narratives of our cultural histories and myths; hence, the generation of language and activities of interpretation and storytelling based on the symbol and myth are vital here as is the process of knowledge creation in the act of communication and subject formation. It is through articulating our experiences that we can gain a greater understanding of our world, each other and ourselves, and thereby at least harbour the hope of achieving a better (or at least bearable) acceptance of the human condition as we experience it. Often, in practice, this need for articulation is driven by the emergence of neuroses and psychoses as the result of a deep psychic disruption between our conscious understanding and our unresolved unconscious drives, activating the collective, linguistic notion of the speaking self. This is what the French psychoanalyst Jacques Lacan called the 'de-centred self'. Dealing with this de-centred self and the thoughts and actions that emanate from it is often what motivates people to seek counselling or other types of help. This basically sums up the experience of evil from a psychoanalytic point of view, the fear of the unknown that is unwittingly propelling our as worrisome yet inscrutable behaviour, and the urgency of deep-seated sexual and aggressive drives and unresolved trauma.

In the opening chapters of this book, our explorations of evil focused on things such as God, demons of various kinds, rationality and the moral law—all normatively and (from the perspective of many feminist commentators) very masculine figurations of power and/or masculine constructions of power relations in terms of assigning deviance, guilt and punishment. Throughout her work, Kristeva offers a very different route for engaging with the problem of evil by in the first instance concentrating on the *feminine*, or perhaps more specifically the maternal, rather than the masculine/phallic/paternal as the source of our first formative psychic experience. She is especially interested in the overlap between psychoanalysis, literary theory and the liberating—potentially revolutionary—text, with a focus on the speaking subject. In *The Powers of Horror*, what she terms 'abjection' is at the core of our primal experiences of evil, as for instance manifested in the emotions of fear, horror and dread. In delving into these primal experiences, her aim is to critique, challenge and also subvert the attendant ideologies of phallocentrism, or masculine dominated social order, that emanates from the predominantly patriarchal or Oedipal discourses of law and norms which tend to repress, subvert or deny the feminine.

> Hate is not the opposite of love. The real opposite of love is individuality.
>
> (D.H. Lawrence cited in Ian, 1993: 1)

We could put the above sentiment another way: the opposite of love is being alone, being isolated, abject.

Just as Ricoeur identifies the symbolism of evil as having primacy above all other symbolic systems of meaning, so in *The Powers of Horror*, Kristeva identifies being abject and the experience of abjection as among the 'primers of my culture' (1982: 2). This primary experience relates to the individual subject occupying the role of the abject, that is, the crushing experience of being alone, separate and isolated from others (particularly significant others such as the mother and father, but also the community with which one shares a common language and culture, and even oneself). Abjection is manifest in primal experiences such as in the revulsion, repulsiveness and nausea of being in the presence of filthy, decrepit, polluted and unclean objects like rotting food, sewage and other waste products—again, not unlike Ricoeur's symbolism of defilement—things that we have instinctual drives to expel, avoid (like the plague!) or render wholly 'other' in ritual or symbolic ways. Similar 'othering' processes apply to people we deem to be corrupt or 'evil'. At the same time, such repulsive and disgusting objects also have their compulsive qualities, such as when we cannot help but to look at the car accident or roadkill as we pass by. While glass and mirrors were the eponymous objects of the Enlightenment, the mascerated, visceral or dead body is its counterpart in psychoanalysis, with its guts spilling out and fluids escaping, such disgusting objects make what is normally hidden 'inside' undeniably visible 'outside', a compelling analogy for knowledge acquisition. Similarly, we want to know all the most intimate details about the eponymous serial killer or child killer (at the time of writing, Mick Philpott, the British man convicted of the manslaughter of his six children in an arson plot is the current recipient of the 'PURE EVIL' designation by the British tabloid press; previous recipients have been Vanessa George Ian Huntley, all offenders against children, consistent with Kristeva's focus on this relationship and its violation). The ultimate defiled or 'dirty' object is the human corpse, that feared and dreaded 'abomination' that is the dead, decaying body devoid of a soul—i.e. resolutely abject—represents the source of the monstrous and staple of horror in modern film (e.g. in the form of zombies, vampires and the like) (Creed, 1993).

It is no coincidence that every culture has its rituals through which to purify and dispose of the (human) corpse, again consistent with Ricoeur's theory of evil symbolized as defilement. Ironically, it is their biological connection with the effluents of birth, sex and menstruation that culturally link women/females with the corporeal defilement of death and monstrousness. But even when their reproductive function comes to an end, women's cultural links to the monstrous are by no means exhausted, as demonstrated by the (post)menopausal attitudes of disgust, ridicule and revulsion directed at older women in Western societies in particular (e.g. as crone, hag, witch, bitch, old bag, demonic mother, evil queen etc.), especially when they dare to exhibit signs of sexual agency or desire (e.g. whore, slag, slut, cougar, man-eater, mutton dressed as lamb etc.). By their very existence after the expiration of their biological reproductivity, older women symbolically represent the unwelcome, disruptive and/or repulsive presence of deterioration, atrophy, mortality and death; even in their physical bodies, the stretchmarks of childbirth, flaccid flesh and desiccated features evoke the disgust of 'living decay' that is tolerated petulantly by their alignment with vestigial monstrosity and abjection (Ussher, 2006: 128). Older women in contemporary Western societies are expected to be, and sometimes even consider themselves to be better off, 'invisible', otherwise they are exposed to a repertoire of punitive censure based on their deviation from and violation of norms of femininity and power (see, for example, Lessing, 2002 and Greer, 1991). Even when older women strive to (and indeed are expected to) conceal signs of age through recourse to an array of technological 'remedies' such as creams, hormone-replacement therapy, cosmetic surgery and/or a wide and increasing variety of non- or semi-surgical medical procedures, their efforts nevertheless usually attract scorn and derision. Advancing age in women constitutes a violation of a cultural norm of femininity in modern Western societies. When they get it 'right' and preserve their 'youthful appearance' and hence attraction as sexual objects to (younger) men, as in the popular cultural figure of the MILF ('mom I would like to fuck'), or lists of best-dressed women over 40 or 50 in women's magazines and other popular media, these only serve to highlight their atypical, analogous and deeply ambivalent qualities. The attraction of the MILF incorporates the taboo of sex with an older woman, the lure of the risky and forbidden act with a woman who could, or possibly even did, once fulfil the maternal role. The notion of MILF sex opens up a new space for the exploration of the forbidden/unknown and the acquisition of power played out on the body of the mother, whether over one's contemporaries via the sexual conquest of the maternal figure, or as a sign of the woman in question's sexual potency beyond motherhood:

> The 'milf' term describes an extremely attractive older woman in her 30s, 40s or even 50s who is the mother of a friend, girlfriend, or other acquaintance. The milf is so sexy that a young male would risk his relationship with a friend or girlfriend to have sex with the mother.

> The 'milf' fantasy combines the sexual knowledge of the experienced older woman with the danger of doing something forbidden. For some males, the turn-on involves the idea of sex with someone who's acted like a mother to them ('this woman used to make me peanut butter and jelly sandwiches.') Others desire to penetrate the 'place' that the friend came from. And for some, the fantasy serves as a power play as it enacts the age-old insult, 'I did your mother.'

Initially made popular by the raunchy 1999 teen comedy film *American Pie*, the milf concept became more widespread thanks to pop cultural references such as the 2003 song 'Stacey's Mom' by the band Fountains of Wayne.

The rise of the milf roughly parallels the rise of the cougar, another older and sexually voracious female figure who pursues younger males.

While some women dislike the milf term, others regard the label as proof of their sexual attractiveness to those young enough to be their children.

For many women closing in on menopause, being seen as a milf suggests a certain physical power over men; this perception confers a sense of prolonged youth, as aging women who lost their fertility have traditionally been regarded as crones, wise perhaps but with no sexual worth. A whole category of pornography has evolved around the milf concept, with many older women evidently enjoying the exposure.

Lowen (undated: online)

For older women who make the 'best-dressed' lists, it is their anomalous qualities of 'youthful' beauty by which they are distinguished; it is no accident that many of these women are either celebrities or models, i.e. women who have the cultural and material capital to devote to their appearance (Ussher, 2006). To put it another way, the sexual attraction of these older women is intimately linked to their possession of time and money, and the fact that they are not afraid to spend both on hedonistically oriented consumer goods, something that is not inconsequential to many young men who may have plenty of time on their hands but little money in an age of austerity. But let 'ordinary' women not in possession of such extraordinary capital openly display a sense of sexual agency or attractiveness and they are particularly exposed to types of criticism and scorn that reinforce restrictive norms of femininity and the intrinsic deviance of older women as sexual beings or as objects of erotic desire. Sex involving other/maternal women is still very much in the category of defilement, with its lures and repulsions, and intricate social mechanisms for policing the older female body, such as in fashion magazines, television shows and other media aggressively marketing products and information on 'How Not to Get Old' (Channel 4, 2013), then pillorying women (and increasingly also men) for buying them.

Defilement is what Ricoeur called primordial and Alford 'precategorical' evil, preceding the abstraction of philosophy or theodicy; it is about what is dirty 'coming out', oozing, leaking or spurting into the open, about '... the loss of boundaries, the way in which inside and outside are no longer distinct, and the dread this loss incurs' (Alford, 1997: 60). The potency of these unstable, vacillating poles of compulsion and revulsion and breaching of (social) boundaries in the living, secreting body establishes their power in policing the symbolic manifestations of evil in the course of everyday life and management of subjective identities, even sanity:

> The abject is a condition of symbolic subjectivity; and is also its unpredictable, sporadic accompaniment. It is the underside of a stable subjective identity, an abyss at the borders of the subject's existence, a hole into which the subject may fall when its identity is put into question, for example, in psychosis. The subject needs a certain level of mastery over the abject to keep it in check, at a distance, to distinguish itself from its repressed or unspeakable condition.
>
> Grosz (1989: 72)

Kristeva points to the experience of crime as a species of abjection, a violation of order that exposes the fragility of society and the law, in particular, in the face of these dreadful experiences and dark drives. So, we see immediately how Kristeva's different types and ways of treating abjection relate to the self and its inner drives and the body, as well as to higher levels of psychic and social experiences to do with feeling disconnected from culture and society and the proximity of the dirty, corrupt, dreadful, deviant, monstrous, feared 'other'. Note that Kristeva diagnoses the *fragility* of the law and by extension the patriarchal function of 'the father' in contemporary culture, not its collapse or total renunciation; this is no Nietzschean declaration of the 'death of God', but to call into question the fraught psychic coexistence of the father, mother and child and the crisis of the 'maternal vocation' of love in modernity (Kristeva, 2008: online). In this context, 'love' is transformed into erotomania: the desperate, hysterical need to love and be loved. Hence, in the form of online dating, we 'shop' for partners much as we do for other consumer goods, and judge potential mates in much the same manner, while marketing and packaging ourselves as objects of desire in the same objectifying, impatient and superficial way.

Such efforts in the realm of looking for love do not relate just to the ideal partner or one's idealized erotic self as necessarily 'good'. The libidinal attraction to abjection means that the roles and experiences that make us desire such deviant or prohibited phenomena themselves become more attractive. Paradoxically, this compulsion puts at risk the very constitution of the formative subject, whereby psychic crisis is deferred in the temptation to surrender personal agency in a kind of sadomasochistic fantasy. In her article 'Every Woman Adores a Fascist' (2000), Laura Frost explores such themes in as encapsulated in the erotic thrall and compulsive allure of the male tyrant and modern independent women's desire to be dominated as represented in women's literature (in this instance, in the works of Woolf, Plath and Jong). We will return to the topic of erotic literature in the next chapter.

What emerges here is the importance not just of language, society and symbolism, but also the immense importance of gender, sexuality and the *body* as important and neglected primary sources of experience and knowledge about something as important as good and evil. Kristeva insists that it is these embodied experiences that converge in cultural roles and discourses of caring and the symbiosis of birth and infancy that are the primary sources of psychic development and knowledge of evil. This represents a shift in focus from the competition with the father or the entrance into the legal-linguistic-symbolic realm, as posited by Freudian psychoanalysis. The body also features prominently in other psychoanalytic analyses of 'evils' such as pain, terror and agency in sadomasochism explored in Darren Langdridge's essay 'Speaking the Unspeakable: S/M and the Eroticisation of Pain' (2007). Langdridge draws upon Elaine Scarry's work on the body in pain, specifically torture, to explore how pain represents an evil the unfathomability of which is encapsulated in its inexpressibility in language and how undeniable it is in human experience. What could be more consummate of abjection than the tortured body, this side of death? We cannot ignore our pain; we cannot feel someone else's pain. Like the *cogito* (Chapter 1), this is emblematic of the hyperbolic binary of *certainty* (our pain) and *doubt* (the pain of the other) in modern culture and thought—central Cartesian themes, as we recall. In the Cartesian schema, evil here pertains to the human propensity to error, i.e. to be wrong or mistaken, possibly deceived, such as by a demonic influence or sensual experience (including emotions). The arena of law and human rights, an Oedipal or patriarchal realm, reasserts the evil of torture as 'error', regardless of any utilitarian or cathartic expiation. In other words, however good it feels to do, or however effective it might seem, torture is wrong, period.

Pain marks the boundaries between self and other in a stark way that nothing else can or does. Nothing makes us more alone or isolated, helpless and bereft as being in pain; in the material, living world, it is abjection. The pain of torture, the intentional infliction of pain against our will is the ultimate experience of this, denying the agency and personhood of the victim. Scarry (1985) states that torture 'unmakes the world' (subtitle); it annihilates, pure and simple. It denies agency and silences language. It ruptures knowledge and reality and scars histories and truths, both personal and collective. It is reductive, and returns the victim to something like a state of infancy, if not in the imbalance of power it 'creates' (though it is morally repugnant to think that torture could ever be generative), then in the semblance of the balance of power it destroys. '...Physical pain is not simply inherently difficult to articulate: it is also something which actively destroys language through a resultant recourse to a state anterior to language, the verbalizations of the baby before it has acquired language' (Langdridge, 2007: 87–88). If Cartesian hyperbolic doubt and Kantian morality are agency on steroids (as argued in chapters 3 and 4), this is the vulnerability on steroids as a response to evil. In his analysis of bondage, dominance and sadomasochism (BDSM), Langdridge goes further, identifying the very language of (moral) agency with the language of weaponry, of possessing power and having power over others. And, indeed, much cultural and political language about social evils converging around suffering, victimization and harm relate to the war metaphor, e.g. the war on terror, war on crime, war on drugs, war on want etc., which is a construction of evil we will return to in Chapter 9. Of course, this is much more than a linguistic phenomenon; this nexus of evil and agency in the human psyche is a pressing issue, especially when it comes to asking questions about how someone can actually and intentionally do the evil they commit on others and still retain their humanity.

While this is true of actual physical pain, in many ways the same can be said of psychic or psychological pain, and indeed we see such analogous usage of language in popular discourses about the pain of abjection in erotic love, particularly in relation to the feminine; for example, when Erica Jong writes about her heroine's longing to be 'annihilated by love' in her iconic novel of female sexuality *Fear of Flying* (1973). These are 'real' in the sense of primary and primal, if not always material experiences, and they are as Jong's among others' works suggest, highly ambiguous as the source of both intense sexual pleasure and deep libidinal pain, and also their links to subject formation, especially for (today's) women. In much of contemporary erotic literature written for or by women, such 'torture' and abjection are themselves the purported objects and destinations of desire, and this is held up as emblematic of a post-feminist ideal of independence, that most exemplary modern icon of agency after two feminist 'waves'. While these are themes that are worth visiting here, they will be examined in more detail in the next chapter.

Kristeva invites her reader to consider the primary experience of breastfeeding and the types of language and rules pertaining to the encounter with the bodily fluids associated with birth and childbearing, especially milk. This relates to what she defines as *semiotic* as opposed to *symbolic* language; pre-Oedipal language that precedes the symbolic language of the law/father and the rationality of logos. Breastfeeding marks the infant's entrance into language, as a subject as yet undifferentiated and unformed, demarcating a space or locus of the 'subject to be' according to embodied formations of erotogenic zones. In the infant/child, these are not yet confined to distinct corporeal or genital areas, but are experienced over the entire body as the source of the satisfaction of sexual pleasure drives (Grosz, 1989). In contrast to symbolic language, such semiotic articulations are unformed and chaotic. They precede stable subject or identity. Kristeva's demarcation of semiotic language designates the contribution of sexual drives to signification (making of signs, symbols and the subject) (Grosz, 1989). The semiotic is feminine-, subject-formation-, mother–child-oriented, whereas the symbolic is male, phallic, ordered, regulated and more social in the civil sense.

In *The Powers of Horror*, Kristeva notes the kind of gagging reflex or nausea that many people typically feel in response to 'dirty' objects like shit, vomit, blood etc. and the skin that develops on the surface of milk. Consider also the practices in Jewish culture pertaining to the consumption of milk and the early prohibition in Leviticus against cooking a young goat in its mother's milk and its significance as a sign of rejecting what was a prevalent religious practice of the dominant 'other'. The presence of such dirty, disgusting objects as manifestations of evil (material and symbolic) threatens the very stability of civil society and exposes the fragility of civility by breaking down boundaries, violating codes regarding what should remain 'separate', private and hidden. The devouring of the mother's body by the infant and the abjection experienced after birth by separation from the breast underpin our pre-Oedipal experience and influence our subsequent language of *fear*. This experience of fear introduces a '*drive* dimension' (Kristeva, 1982: 42, original emphasis) that makes even very young babies want to understand or 'index' what that 'other' thing is so that they too can categorize and control it, that unknown and perhaps unknowable 'other' that is causing the infant so much anxiety and pain by his/her absence.

Importantly, this 'other' (the mother) is experienced first as a kind of 'nothing', literally a no-thing, a source of deprivation, frustration and want. This evokes the two stages central to the establishment of a stable identity/subject: the narcissistic mirror stage and the Oedipal/castration stage. Both are semiotically articulated and symbolically undone in the construction of the image of what she terms the *maternal phallus*, where the stability of such categories of good/clean and evil/dirty collapse. With corruption comes the erasure of difference and the inauguration of psychological and emotional chaos of confusion, fear and despair. Here, we note echoes of the Augustinian notion of evil as deprivation (as discussed in Chapter 1), as nothing, and the glass delusion that disrupts the confident optimism of Enlightenment (Chapter 2), but is this what Kristeva has in mind?

The maternal phallus/phallic mother

It would seem that Kristeva is not applying this idea of evil as 'nothing' in the Augustinian sense of being an ontological non-entity, nor is she positing a rational 'thinking thing' (*cogito*) Cartesian subject, although deprivation and anxiety definitely feature as complicating factors to the durability of either or both. According to Kristeva, the question of what this 'other', this unknown and seemingly terrifyingly unknowable thing *is* is the question that the analyst must help the analysand (the one who is going through psychoanalysis) to understand, and this is what the process of the psychoanalytic 'talking cure' essentially is. How this is done is not by recognition of the emptiness or non-being of the 'other', but rather with the conscious encounter with it in the unconscious, in all of its terrifying impossibility as something which is and also something that is not. What would this other thing be if it didn't exist, if I didn't exist? Which I might not, as I cannot transmute, articulate or transmit my own pain? What if I actually am alone? What if I am not at all? While we may hear echoes of the hyperbolically doubting Cartesian subject here, significantly, this is not the empowered, confrontational, heroic figure of Descartes in his battle with Aristotle via the Evil Genius; this fight is much more difficult, less intellectual, much more intimate, emotional, dangerous and fraught.

Kristeva describes this as that thing which is not, yet is still something to be really scared of, the exemplar of which is the *maternal phallus* (1982: 42), symbolic of the entrance into the phallocentric realm of law and renunciation of the mother. The encounter with such an impossible and non-existent psychic object serves the purpose of bringing fear to the surface for the analysand, thereby introducing the transformation of this 'no thing' into the lost object of desire, and henceforth the thing to strive to articulate through the creative and diverse language of the imagination, often through (sexual) fantasy. This is the moment, Kristeva argues, where genuine reflection and creativity, especially in the form of *writing*, become a possibility. Such signifying practices in the adult open up the return of the infantile inscription in more mature form, vis-à-vis the return of the repressed (in Freudian terminology). This moment of creativity provides an opportunity to reconsider, revisit or even remake the hierarchical and erotic domain of the subject, even if it is as a result of pain; to recreate the maternal other as 'no thing', the as yet unknown and unregulated erotic economy of the self as in infancy. Here resides the primacy of the *oral* impulse as opposed to genital or phallic. Laughter features here, as do other forms of levity, ridicule and hysteria. Here also resides the demonic, this time in relation to the quasi-hermeneutic process of language and interpretation: '...the process of writing itself [is revealed] to be a demonic process, held in check only by a rehumanising process of reading' (Hodge, 2000: 24). Contrary to the stereotypical cultural discourse of secularism, the disruptive power of the demonic is even stronger and less inhibited in modernity than in previous eras. This is because the power of this 'demonic force' affecting subject formation via self-reflection is exacerbated by the 'erasure' of metaphysics post-Descartes and its replacement by technology (Hodge, 2000: 24). However, even in a post-metaphysical/religious age, not all is lost, as the 'rehumanising' dimension is preserved in the relationship with the 'other' as reader and receiver remains possible. But before this relationship is realized through articulation in language and storytelling, the demonic presides, taunting, beguiling and terrifying the abject, in the psychic struggle.

This is where literature, art and the creativity of culture come into their own as remedies for the fear and horror of abjection in the rich and carnivalesque realm of imagination fuelled by the potency of sexual fantasy and desire. This possibility offered by writing connects the symbolic-linguistic realm of the (infantile) subject with (Oedipal) culture in a particularly generative way. The products of this encounter are often seen in great literature (or possibly in the low culture of porn, as considered in the next chapter) or in the creation of new possibilities for the modern subject in terms of exceeding the restrictions of conventional practices of the self (specifically in relation to transforming the role of gender and sexuality). This is where pain is contrived and endured in a consensual way (with all the problematics that come with this use of consent); it can be both transgressive and formative, and even extremely pleasurable.

A possible way we can make sense of this is by looking again at the psychoanalytic study of BDSM by Langdridge (ibid.). One of the key features of pain (erotic or otherwise) is that, as previously stated, like evil, it elides language. This is because it disrupts the normative relationship between language and a referent. This is a dangerous and fearful rupture, not unlike the disruption in theodicy between guilt and suffering. It destroys the normal intersubjectivity of communication because there is nothing external, no referent out there 'in the world' to point to, to communicate to another person the nature and experience of *my* pain. Phenomenologically, it has no correlation with the external world and, therefore, in a deep philosophical sense threatens the integrity and even existence of the phenomenal world at its core—again, not unlike the *cogito* in some respects, or Kant's concept of the noumenal 'thing in itself', or possibly Husserl's concept of *noema* with its concentration on the urgency and need of the expressive power of such articulations of direct, first-hand experience (Smith, 2011). But when we are in pain, when we suffer, where is the (m)other? This question speaks to the dilemma of hermeneutics and phenomenology in terms of their commitment to the dialogical elements of language and the other in an acutely challenging way.

> Pain, however, is not of or for anything, having no referential quality. It almost uniquely speaks to the heart of phenomenology, challenging the very core of this philosophy, trapping us in an egocentric predicament. That is, since pain is not intersubjective—being uniquely private—it is not shared—not turned out on the world—and therefore not readily accessible to others.
>
> Langdridge (2007: 88)

It is at these boundaries that Kristeva lingers in her reflections on the evils of abjection and horror.

This kind of deep existential pain is revolutionary in its potential; it can destroy the world, or alternatively in some circumstances possibly open it up, expanding the frontiers of language again to new horizons with new partners through the experience of erotic pleasure, taking the subject back to a pre-linguistic place were pain can be the starting point for re-inscribing novel experience and renewed subjectivity, investing language with new meaning(s). In erotic s/m play, as Landridge and others argue, this can be extremely pleasurable and liberating, creative and even healing. Entering into what can be painful experiences of power imbalance consensually can be positively transgressive (in an erotic sense), as opposed to crudely and negatively destructive (as with torture). Because here the boundaries that conventionally separate individual bodies through binary norms of public and private, self and other, internal and external, decency and obscenity, concealment/privacy and self-exposure, good and evil, break down by being wilfully transgressed. The resulting experience can be extremely gratifying and creative, 'fusing horizons' to borrow Ricoeur's phrase, between what are regarded and usually experienced as quite separate realms. This transgression can be excessive (as explored in the works of Bataille, addressed in the next chapter); devastating, reactionary or intensely liberating, and creative. Think of the value of such unique experiences, breaking conventions of language and identity, and the significance of re-inscribing them with speech/writing in a new way other people can understand or recognize— the basis of creative writing. This can be scary and unpredictable, but also thrilling, generative and cathartic.

Landridge's basic argument goes something like this: that the loss of language/agency at the hands of the Dominant in BDSM and eventual regaining of speech by the submissive can result in the re-inscription of narratives of previous sexual trauma, and the opening up of new directions and re-establishment of agency on one's own terms. This is perhaps why the instructional discourse of BDSM for Doms is so much about care and the compassionate use of power and control. Whether or not this ideal is manifest in reality is another matter. But what we encounter here is the fusion of horizons at (and across, and against) the boundaries of language, the world, the self, social norms, discursive conventions and the other. This is a dangerous, risky and exhilarating place. There is nowhere more alive, no place more deadly; nowhere so abject, but also a place where the serenity of a kind of solitude occasioned by erotic pain claimed in BDSM sex play can be found. A place notably encoded by restrictive roles but also, paradoxically, for some, where the erotic encounter with the other can fuse the divide between self and other through the experience of flesh with flesh. In pain, in what makes us the most unique and isolated, and its insertion in the context of BDSM, we find that even as we are most helplessly isolated and abject, we are like everyone else. This is a shared and embodied revelation about the human condition. Some practitioners describe this as a sort of quasi-therapeutic liminal space, in which previously experienced sexual trauma can be replayed in a way that enables a cathartic working-through of the original experience via the recovery of a renewed sense of power, control and agency, as in the following reflection on an episode of BDSM role play: 'So my special day with Daddy had turned out to have a special gift in it—a visit to my own past, and a reawakening of a buried memory, a chance to re-experience feelings of injustice and frustration—and to see where, perhaps, similar feelings today might have their origins' (Easton and Hardy, 2004: 165).

And now our focus shifts from daddy back to mummy. The general structure of Langdridge's thesis is in some ways remarkably different and yet also similar to that put forward by Kelly Oliver (2008–2010) in her analysis of Kristeva's reflections on the 'maternal passions', whereby the sexual-erotic-political ambiguities of motherhood are to be considered as not only primary but emblematic of all human passion and desire. ' ... [M]aternal passion is quintessential to human passion because it can be a form of working through conflicting emotions of attraction and aversion, which are the result of animal drives, by turning them into the human passions of love and hate' (Oliver, 2008–2010: 5). In motherhood, the psychic and political dramas of semiotic and symbolic language, love and hate, reason and hysteria, and more, eventually become resolved in the 'serenity' of dispassion that is the 'good enough' mother who loves, gives and eventually lets go. This is another version or perspective on the maternal phallus as 'lost object' of desire. This sacrifice born of love and indifference allows the child to separate from the mother and occupy a place of suitable detachment as an independent subject in his or her own right, and thereby to be in a position to 'sublimate' desire for her using language to achieve a sense of serenity through the preservation of laughter and love (Oliver, ibid.). Oliver cites Kristeva's comparison of the mother to a 'good fairy' who tirelessly performs small acts of care for her 'little ones', not noticing her own pain and fatigue. The reification of the feminine in biological maternity in this scenario is precluded by the emphasis on rebirth as opposed simply to birth; the 'good enough' mother loves, and eventually leaves, in time becoming 'dispassionate' toward her offspring. This cycle of creativity and destruction that characterizes the dynamics of maternal passion differs intrinsically from that of the masculine-Oedipal Evil Genius (as, for example, in the contemporary exemplar in the popular cultural form of 'the banker' on the television game show *Deal or No Deal* (see Dearey, 2012)). In this scenario, the masculine Evil Genius keeps a careful tally on the infractions and weaknesses of the player/child and the inflections of their use of language, especially in highly emotional circumstances; in the course of the happenstance of 'live play' of the game, the player's random choices are weighed up as advantages or mistakes and continually calculated according to a crude monetary value in a gamble to win or 'spank' the father/banker. This type of confrontational, legal-judicial and punitive calculus does not characterize the maternal passion, which elides such commodification (or has the potential to do so).

As a post-structuralist, Kristeva's concentration is on discourse, and in this sense the discursive language of gender is not reduced to the essentialist biological categories of the body, meaning that a mother doesn't necessarily have to be a woman (nor the father a man). By this she means that even though masculine and feminine might have meaning in a symbolic or mythic sense and certainly are important in our current social order, these don't equate to biological realities whereby 'woman/feminine' is related only to biological females and 'man/masculine' only to biological males. But this is not to say that biology doesn't matter, rather it is dialogically related to meaning: 'More radically than any other human science, psychoanalysis, playing close attention to the unconscious, allows us to think about transcendence as an alterity immanent to the human being, anchored in sexuality at the frontier of biology and meaning' (Kristeva, 2008: online). When it comes to phenomena like breastfeeding, this point may be a bit fraught, but she is not overly concerned about such matters. Her focal point is the challenge to the phallic order, the discourse of civilization which is 'erected' on the maternal and on the basis of the repression of the feminine (Grosz, 1989). By recognizing the power dimensions inherent in these gender roles and the social advantages given to the masculine in access to symbolic language, both women *and* men can recover access to such language and experiences of sex, mothering and/or care. Deconstructing and subverting this power relationship represents a truly revolutionary act and one that not only disrupts language and meaning, it creates new and joyful discourses (*jouissance*—enjoyment or pleasure, particularly that associated with sexual orgasm). This process enables oppressed subjects (many but not all of whom are women) to gain access to symbolic language.

Though Kristeva has been criticized for the lack of a political edge to her work because of the singular concentration of language and discourse typical of post-structuralist deconstruction which tends not to recognize the historical and material realities of power and oppression (see Weedon, 1987). There are also many political and ideological tensions with feminisms. Nonetheless, she argues strongly for the revolutionary potential of this type of discourse emerging from experiences of abjection. In her work, she concentrates on the revolutionary powers of the avant garde and art that

> ...induces crises of representation, expressing and liberating the otherwise inarticulated jouissance of the semiotic. It captures and expresses libidinal, rhythmical impulses which threaten the symbolic with what it must repress, making explicit the social stakes vested in the repression and suppression of the semiotic by its own focus on semiotic elements.
>
> Grosz (1989: 55)

Art gives symbolic expression to the semiotic; helps it 'break through'. But these forces unleashed by art are extremely volatile; they can inspire political revolution in poetic language as well as instigate totalitarian rhetorics of fascism and oppression through the return of the repressed in the form of violence and aggression. These extremes are observable in fetishism (in the case of the feminine) or psychosis (masculine), both of which Kristeva associates with gender.

Kristeva insists that art has huge potential in terms of threatening the existing social order by disrupting discourses (particularly around conventions of gender and sexuality) that are hugely important to propping up the existing phallocentric/capitalist power structures. This is why such ostensibly 'deviant' and disruptive discourses are so vigorously and stridently policed by those with vested interests, with potentially serious social (if not criminal) consequences for those who trespass these normative boundaries. One way of divesting the semiotic of its revolutionary potential is through the process of commodification of gender and sexuality. Once again, we have encountered this type of phenomenon before, e.g. in the policing of the sexual other and the body as in Malthus's theodicy, in Chapter 1. What is important to note is that such encounters with and articulations of evil not only hark back to previous centuries, they raise issues and experiences that pertain now, and are still pervasive in popular cultural discourses of evil. Consider, for instance, what have been the 'crazes' historically of the witch hunt (see among others Lemert, 1997) and currently surrounding the popular erotic novel *Fifty Shades of Grey* (2012) by E.L. James. It is interesting and instructive that such a book has been categorized generically as 'mummy porn', given its concentration on the character of the young female ingénue (similar to the popular *Twilight* franchise) and the reflections on the maternal and the erotic as discussed above. We will turn more specifically to the topic of literary pornography and erotic literature and evil in the next chapter. For the moment, suffice to say that what the phenomenon of *Fifty Shades* evidences is a deep-seated and previously untapped general interest in such issues of female sexuality, violent/'deviant' sexual fantasy and motherhood. Let us first turn to the work of C. Fred Alford and that stalwart symbol of sexual transgression and excess in popular culture, the vampire: the figure that would inspire the *Fifty Shades* phenomenon.

The vampire: Sexual revolutionary or baby stuff?

It is probably not coincidental that *Fifty Shades* famously originated from the contributions first made on a fan site associated with another hugely popular and lucrative publishing and film franchise, the *Twilight* series of vampire stories. Both relate to the sexual awakening and initiation of a young, female ingénue by a slightly older and dangerously attractive but also conventionally attractive young man. How are we to interpret such stories about evil and sex?

In his book *What Evil Means to Us* (1997), psychoanalyst and political scientist C. Fred Alford undertook what for our purposes here proved to be an interesting—though admittedly unscientific—study of evil, comprising a comparative study of two sample groups. For the first sample group, he put an ad in a local newspaper seeking volunteers to take part in a qualitative study of evil:

TALK ABOUT EVIL

Have you experienced evil? What is it? Can you forgive? Talk with a professor doing research on the topic. Students, faculty, staff and all others invited. Pays $10.00 for 1–2 hours on-campus interview. Call xxx–xxxx.

He received a large response, comprising more than 100 people, 60 of whom he later interviewed. This group he categorized as the 'free informants'.

The second sample group consisted of 18 inmates recruited from a local maximum security prison in the US, housing inmates doing long sentences for serious crimes, including theft, (multiple) murder, child murder, infanticide, patricide, matricide and fratricide. These prisoners belonged to a group organized by Alford entitled 'Popular Concepts of

Evil' that met for two hours a week for more than a year to discuss the topic of evil. Alford also used some other ethnographic material (e.g. video tapes of psychiatric interviews with inmates) and data from Internet discussion boards, but for the most part he concentrates on these two sample groups.

Alford's primary interest was not to collect the different definitions of evil, but rather to try to understand how evil is interpreted by people today as an 'active' cultural phenomenon. Alford uses psychoanalytic theory (derived from the work of Melanie Klein, Thomas Ogden and D.W. Winnicott) to do this. In this section, I want to begin with some remarks on Alford's analysis of the vampire in the study, and how this relates to Kristeva's work and some other commentaries on this iconic cultural figure of evil.

One of Alford's findings in his comparison of the inmate and the 'free' groups was the divergence in terms of the types of cultural references and emblematic representations of evil they identified. This difference was also evident within the free group in terms of age, with a distinction between older and younger (under 26 years) participants. This difference was the influence of popular culture in the media forms of film, television, computer games, Internet sites etc. and the figure of the vampire as represented in contemporary popular culture as the icon of evil. What was striking to Alford was how unlike the older participants, the younger informants focused on this figure as a symbol of evil and also a source of fascination, even envy:

> 'Oh man, that's what I want to be. I'd give anything to be a vampire. I could go anywhere, do anything. No one could stop me,' said Ralph C.
>
> (a younger free participant)

Tom A. concurs:

> They're so sexy, I didn't even think about it until an English professor said so. But they are. It's all about sex.
>
> (Alford, ibid.: 88)

Seeing how Tom A. brings it up, let's look at the various cases, beginning with an English professor who considers vampires as the modern epitome of sex.

Nursel Icoz (2006) is a Professor of English who published an article on the vampire figure in *Dracula* and 'La morte amoureuse'; her reading would be typical of the case for the highly suggestive sexual nature of the vampire myth as recalled by Tom A. Icoz's argument is based on the premise of the extreme sexual repression of the Victorians in the nineteenth century, and how the vampire story evoked horror and dread but also intense sexual desire among its readership as a result of the fear and anxiety over female sexuality, homoeroticism, the instability of gender roles and heterosexual desire, adultery, paedophilia, sex with multiple partners, oral sex, necrophilia, loss of innocence, sexual depravity and so forth. Icoz contends that it was the severity of sexual repression and the social consequences for those who deviated from the prevailing moral code governing sexual behaviour that presented the possibility for such suggestive tales implicating the forbidden yet compelling qualities of all of these 'other' unspoken and generally unknown sexual drives. She even suggests that the vicarious evocation and transgression represented in the Gothic fiction of the time actually reinforces the ideological normativity of heterosexuality, monogamy, racial, gender and class purity and sex in marriage, by making it possible for readers to at least temporarily satisfy their urges through fantasy alone, thus leaving untouched dominant middle-class bourgeois values. Once the book about the sexy vampire was closed, she argued, it was back to reality and business as usual.

Icoz and others argue that the vampire myth as a narrative of evil is deeply conservative of the existing capitalist social order, whereby the proletariat has its 'life blood sucked from it' symbolically and literally speaking by the parasitic 'undead' of the capitalist entrepreneur. On the other hand, it is possible to argue that the vampire has his (or her) transgressive and potentially treasonous side too. By existing outside the normative (Oedipal/phallocentric/rational) laws of space and time, and with the contagiousness of their condition, vampires represent an alternative to the political and cultural hegemony of industrial capitalism and the normative natural selection of biological evolution. They thereby open up the possibility for the disruption and even displacement of British colonialism through the Empire-building ambitions of popular characters like Dracula and the elimination or sublimation of the human species at the hands of this 'master race'. What is more, this other master race has the potential to turn the tables on the colonizing power that is Britain to make the British the slaves of their interests as a result of their insatiable lust and desire.

Yet, these disruptive and potentially revolutionary elements of the vampire story are somewhat undermined by the narrative resolution that demands the restoration of existing power structures and normative gender roles and heterosexuality expressed through marriage and the restoration of the British colonial Empire in the ways they are consumed. Dracula, for instance, is the cunning and evil foreigner who can and must be slain forever *par excellence*. Bram Stoker's ending of the story leaves the possibility of Dracula's return open, thus preserving the frisson of future erotic encounters while more significantly implying the need to remain ever vigilant against the foreign 'other' as a civic and moral duty.

This invocation of the vampire as epitome of evil Alford compares to the older participants in his study who didn't tend to mention the vampire when discussing evil, and inmates who laughed off this image of evil as juvenile when he asked them about it. 'Only kids and weirdos believe that stuff. It's for babies' (Alford, 1997: 88) said one inmate. These groups were either uninterested or unmoved by the image and myth of the vampire, or else found it risible and childish.

In his psychoanalytic interpretation of the vampire as symbolic of evil, Alford is himself quite dismissive of the potency and maturity of this revolutionary threat to the social and moral order:

> The vampire is the perfect baby, perfect, in the sense of being so dependent it knows nothing of the limits of its power, the way its unlife depends on others' real lives. It is the way life ought to be— but only for babies. Psychoanalysts use the term 'primary narcissism' to describe this state, a state of dependence so unconscious and complete that the other's power is an extension of one's own.
>
> (Alford, ibid.: 88–89)

Alford states that this primary narcissism also harbours within it the potential for real terror (89), because of the vulnerability to exposure this state of power dependence incorporates. The infant's total desire for fusion with the mother is matched by the total abjection and terror it would experience without her. This makes the fictional representation of the vampire in contemporary culture (as opposed to the folkloric vampire) one of social isolation, abjection in Kristeva's terms, not cultural regeneration (whether on an alternative (r)evolutionary model or not).

Alford's interpretation of the vampire is emblematic of a pre-genital infant sexuality which is untouched by a real conception of the 'other' and the reality outside its own desire for immediate gratification and its image of itself as all-powerful, lacking ego boundaries. However, as with any real figures (e.g. criminals) who subscribe to such a 'badass' mentality (anticipating Katz in Chapter 7), this psychic vision is all too soon and all too easily dispelled by the very real presence of the other, who is in many cases just as insistently needy and suffering such egocentric delusions of grandeur.

It is a truism that vampires don't indulge in sexual intercourse (although some current and virtually pornographic popular media interpretations ignore this); they suck their victims dry, an image that could be more readily applied to a baby eagerly breastfeeding than to the symbolism of phallic penetration or sexual intercourse. Here, we can make an analogy to the pre-Oedipal, pre-phallic interpretation of Julia Kristeva—rather than the blood the vampire seeks to drink symbolically representing semen (as Icoz argues) it might alternatively be interpreted symbolically to represent the mother's milk. And perhaps it is arguable that the 'life force' internalized by the vampire in drinking the blood/semen/milk is more akin to the phenomenon of breastfeeding than to the oral ingestion of semen in the act of fellatio (which is somewhat subverted in terms of its specific generative qualities when ingested by mouth). Such an interpretation of the vampire myth has potential to reveal alternative and perhaps more fundamental cultural dynamics relating not so explicitly to a phallocentric political dichotomy of imperialism, but rather to the semiotic language of love, the self, the other and the disarray of erotic desire and bonding.

Following Kristeva, what we may derive from the constancy and ubiquity of the vampire narrative in industrial and late capitalist modernity is something about the latent and chaotic urgency of desire, and its restless shifting from compulsion to repulsion in the erotic body and imagination in ecstasy as well as fear and pain. This neediness, not unlike that of the pre-Oedipal infant, is not so much observable in relation to the law-oriented symbolic order dominated by the phallic father as it is mired in its struggle with the pre-linguistic emergence of the desiring and abject subject of the maternal and semiotic language, with its recursion to the dynamic and unscripted language of desire, horror and love. While this can be original and liberating, it can also be crude and vituperative, reasserting the dominance of capitalist hegemony through the mere production, as opposed to a more creative generation, of speech. What Kristeva has in mind when she discusses the revolutionary is not glossolalia, talk for the sake of it, neither does she advocate a version of postmodernism in which subjects and cultures are the products of a deconstructive and auto-referential vortex of meaningless chatter. Consider, for example, the confessional 'airing of dirty laundry' that makes up the oral content of the more trashy television chat show can demean and objectify the people whose very trauma is its daily diet (see Grindstaff, 2002: 19); whereas the testimonials of those who have endured and survived some of the worst atrocities or most horrible abuse taking place every day all around us are among the most inspiring and heartbreaking stories, the meanings of which exceed language and transform subjects and ethics. 'Poetics is associated with a "deconstructive" tendency in postmodernity toward "self-generating and self-justifying inventiveness to produce for each moment something better—or, nihilistically, just to *produce*." Mere production itself would—and today in large part does—reduce ethical life to the utilitarianism of the marketplace' (Wall, 2005: 65 [original emphasis]).

As Kristeva argues, it is this poetic and evocative language that exposes and has the potential to transform the static and sterile language of Oedipal discourses, as evidenced for example in what she identifies as the epidemic levels of depression in contemporary Western societies, thus revealing the need to return to these excessive and transgressive articulations. Dismissing such discursive narratives as merely 'babyish' is to ignore their revolutionary potential to initiate widespread and vitally necessary cultural change, and to divest them of their true meaning in a dominantly phallocentric social order that continues to repress, exploit and deny the feminine.

> On the whole, postmodern cultures, despite their fascination with ghouls and vampires, have had little to say of evil. Perhaps this is because the postmodern man or woman—cool, provisional, laidback, and decentred—lacks the depth that true destructiveness requires. For postmodernism, there is nothing really to be redeemed. For high modernists like Franz Kafka, Samuel Beckett, or the early T.S. Eliot, there is indeed something to be redeemed, but it is impossible to say what. The desolate, devastated landscapes of Beckett have the look of a world crying out for salvation.
>
> (Eagleton, 2010: 15)

The answer of salvation to the question of evil involves what are the unruly, uncontrollable and sensational powers of love, the sacred and sacrifice. These will be explored further in the next chapter, which will conclude this mid-section of the book on evil and narrative (Table 5.1).

Two deconstructions of vampire myth:

Table 5.1 Vampire myth

Alford, Icoz	Kristeva
Phallically sexual vampire; penetration; civil/public; symbolic	Pre-genital vampire, latent sexuality; sucking, oral (speech); nocturnal/private; semiotic
Stresses Oedipal sexuality, conflict	Emphasis on maternal pre-Oedipal relation between mother & child, bonding
Child's struggle with father to possess mother—reinforces symbolism of patriarchal power, law, civilization	Story of psychic development, eruption of semiotic into public discourse; subject formation; fragility of law & order
Phallus source of fear or envy; evil as lack or privation; loss (castration); psychosis	Maternal phallus—drive to index the 'Other' & work through language of fear; jouissance; art; evil as generative, creative; neurosis
Conservative of existing sociopolitical order, bourgeois values, oppression	Revolutionary, transformation and excess; can descend into anarchy, terror, fascism
Repression, escapism, pornography; torture	Return of repressed; transgression, fantasy; fetishism; S/M

Perhaps what distinguishes the 'English professor's' deconstruction of the latent sexuality of the vampire myth is its concentration on the phallic, Oedipal sexuality to do with the struggle with the father and the drive to contest his possession of the mother. From a Kristevan point of view, this narrative could alternatively be about the maternal pre-Oedipal relationship between the mother and child re-enacted in a more adult (or in the case of *Twilight*, adolescent) realm, a story about the experience of psychic development and the unresolved dread of abjection prior to or during the child's entrance into the realm of symbolism, the law and language through an exploration of female coming of age sexually.

As remarked above, Icoz's thesis regarding the political conservatism of the vampire myth in terms of the contradictory desire for and fear of the foreign 'other' could also be interpreted another way, using the interpretive device of the maternal phallus. In this sense, the language of fear and the need to index and know the 'other' represented in this instance by the vampire fantasy could have a more generative, transgressive, even fetishistic dimension in its avowal and disavowal of the 'lost' and imagined female object:

> 'Fetishism,' as Freud describes it, involves a managed relation to that 'lost' object, the maternal phallus. The peculiarly 'double attitude of fetishists' (218) involves a pragmatic contradiction; the fetishist 'retains this belief' in the existence of the maternal phallus 'at the same time he gives it up' (216). In other words, the 'fact' of female castration is managed by a disavowal—a self-consciously artificial 'belief' in some past when she was not castrated, when her body was whole. That phallus she once had, always already lost, is the part for which the fetish is a substitute. It is a 'penis-substitute,' a fiction of sorts which completes the body of the woman, interpreted as incomplete (214). In short, fetishism revolves around the irreducibly contradictory fiction of the maternal phallus, the thing which, despite the fact that it never really existed as such, made the woman whole in some always distant past, despite the fact that she was never really incomplete as such.
>
> (Becker-Leckrone, 1995: 240–241)

The obvious concentration on not just the oral but also its imbuing with the phallic accoutrement of the fangs is indicative of the maternal phallus in the portrayal of the vampire.

This tendency of the semiotic/feminine in the maternal phallus toward fetishism would sit well with Alford's thesis that evil is about this deep-seated dread, this fear of isolation and separation, something very close to Kristeva's notion of the horror of abjection. Whether or not such an interpretation deserves to be dismissed as merely 'babyish' in a derogatory sense is another question. Does this have the potential to challenge the criticisms of Kristeva that her theory lacks political power? Is Alford's implicit dismissal of the female-maternal-infant interpretation of the vampire story an oblique devaluation of pre-Oedipal and feminine psychic experience in comparison to Oedipal-male-phallic sexuality as one that is 'properly' political?

And of this issue of the politics of sexual desire in these myths of evil: if the vampire is so connected to such a strict Victorian sexual code and the colonialism of industrial capitalism, then what is the source if its fascination as an icon of evil in much more sexually permissive times? And why does the vampire seem to be at once undead but also 'alive and well' as an icon of evil and psychic transgression in the virtual world of the Internet?

Summary (and a bit more vamp)

Psychoanalysis, in its implicit perspective on evil, aims to delve into, recover and articulate psychic experiences of fear, trauma, terror and abjection, and come to some sort of understanding about how these are driving painful, inscrutable, uncontrollable and/or self-destructive behaviours and subject formation. It retains, along with previous theories, binary concepts but intrinsically *dialogical* theory of the binaries of self and of culture. It also retains tensions in existing sociocultural norms relating to evil, particularly gender relationships, sexual identities, power, the body and sexuality. As Ricoeur notes about psychoanalysis, in its devotion to knowledge gained from interpretation as opposed to abstract reason, it has hermeneutic overtones in that it is about the individual but also about culture, and this very much takes into consideration narrative and myths and the receiving 'other'.

Is part of the role of telling stories about evil to help us not so much to come to terms with it intellectually (as in the religious and philosophical narratives) as it is to either reinforce existing power structures out of which the experiences of horror and abjection in modern capitalist societies emanate? Or is it about seeking alternative interpretations of these stories as a way of facilitating radical change to these existing structures? At the end of the day, is narrative just about catharsis, or is it about making real, global change? Or just having a good time?

In seeking answers to such questions, we may pursue a historical line of inquiry, comparing and contrasting the vampire in, for example, a film like *Nosferatu*, or as portrayed by the actors Bela Lugosi or Christopher Lee. These are older men (but still somehow attractive) whose age is exaggerated by make-up and costume to resemble something like animated corpses, the dirtiest thing, as Kristeva notes. These fantastical sexual encounters enable the audience to imagine the pleasures and horrors of illicit sexual encounters (between female sexual ingénues and others?) with the living dead. The horror and dread of mortality and death are elemental aspects of what Bataille called *erotism*. Such highly symbolic and erotically charged attributes such as sucking blood evokes the oral as opposed to being more graphically oriented around penetrative sex. It also reignites fears of the 'other' as 'bloodsucking' parasite, an object of fear and derision whose alluring and exotic presence enervates and weakens its 'host'. Such recursive fears are often directed toward foreigners, women and children, all of whom have featured prominently in twentieth- and twenty-first-century versions of the vampire narrative (e.g. *The Hunger* (1983); *Interview With the Vampire* (1994); *Let the Right One In* (2008)) and even in popular children's culture (e.g. the cartoon *Mona the Vampire* based on a series of popular short stories for children). I cannot help but mention here that the typical seven-year-old (as my youngest daughter is now) with their missing front teeth bear an uncanny resemblance to a very cute vampire!

Contrast this to other and more recent popular interpretations of the vampire story; for example, in the popular television series *True Blood* and the book and film franchise *Twilight*. These are about young, beautiful, perfect and normatively desirable bodies, marketable and attractive. They bring forth none of the dread and fear of sexual initiation, just the opposite! In *Twilight*, Bella is metaphorically if not literally gagging for it, while Edward holds back; this represents a reversal of the power dynamic of the conventional phallocentric order, exposing the latent fear of the sexual female (even if represented by the seemingly innocent ingénue) experienced by men. Regardless of Bella's youth and inexperience, Edward dares not trust himself with respect to his sexual voraciousness for fear of destroying her, and hence a decidedly puritanical stratagem of sexual and other patterns of venal abstinence (e.g. devouring animal as opposed to human blood) are adopted by him and his vampire 'family'. It is this abstinence and social control achieved through developments in technology that is the price for the tolerance of vampires in a newly diversified civil society in which sexual deviance is at least putatively tolerated, as in the television series *True Blood*, while ironically in a sexually permissive society enhancing their deviant power as exotic objects of desire.

True Blood partakes of a more or less blatant pornographic ethos, merely citing the vampire narrative. The *Twilight* spin-off *Fifty Shades* also adopts a more vulgar pornographic discourse, rendering the characterization and narrative of sexuality in rather scripted, predictable and concrete language culled from BDSM; there is little or no room for the semiotic or symbolic here, little scope for imagination; it is difficult for me to read myself into this story, unless I can identify with one of the characters (which given their multiple ideal qualities, few readers would). Such popular erotica will be the explored in the next chapter.

Vampires as evil: Sexy, childish, filthy or funny?

Consider also the representation of evil in the ironic, parodic and comedic representations of evil such as in *Austin Powers* and the Bond/007 films: funny vampires? Does this express a crisis in masculinities and sexual potency, male abjection? Is the vampire now just another 'drag king'? (See Halbersham, 2001; 2005). Do these comedic narratives divest the semiotic of its revolutionary potential by rendering them as deserving of ridicule, or are they revolutionary by virtue of their sending up of a type of masculinity and/or actual humiliation of men? But even in these iconic franchises of classic masculinity, the maternal features more and more; consider, for example, the centrality of the character of Judy Dench's 'M' in the most recent Bond film *Skyfall* (2012), and the latent sexual presence and power of the older/other woman 'Mrs. Robinson' in *Fifty Shades*, a friend of Christian's mother and his first sexual partner and initiator into the practice of BDSM (and a clear reference to Mrs. Robinson in the 1967 film *The Graduate*). What we have here, to borrow from another phrase of classic twentieth-century cinema, is a reinstatement of the powerful, fearsome/fearful, knowing and sexually predatory older woman as figure of ridicule and desire: the evil older woman, whether cougar or MILF.

Anticipating the next chapter, many aspects of the maternal as put forward in the work of Kristeva are observable and illuminated in the work of Georges Bataille (a subject of the next chapter). 'For Bataille, the maternal relation conceals a psychotic element that threatens the very basis of society' (Lukacher, 1994: 14). This focus on the archaic mother emphasises the darker side of the human impulse to creativity, in this instance the link between writing and the demonic, with the devil having the best stories, imagining gruesome things such as witches killing and devouring and children (as in Snow White and Hansel and Gretel). The mother is paramount here, as in Bataille's work, as well as in the character of the cougarish Mrs Robinson in *Fifty Shades*: the evil, sexually knowing, older woman. Let us continue this story in the next chapter.

6
Evil and Literature: Love and Liberation

This chapter is the third of the three chapters devoted to the subject of evil and narrative that comprise the second main section of this book. Before moving on to consider evil and the social sciences in the final section, in this chapter we reflect on the encounter with evil via narrative in 'obscene', pornographic and/or erotic literature. This chapter addresses the meanings of evil as represented in literature, specifically the works of the Marquis de Sade and Georges Bataille, as well as in some more popular contemporary and/or 'instrumental' texts. For it is in the disparate works of these writers and this stroppy tradition that many of the themes relating to evil of previous chapters converge and expand: namely subjectivity, agency, ethics, aesthetics—to name but a few—in the arena of erotic writing, commonly but not exclusively fictional. For the benefit of those who are not familiar with this tradition of writing, I will briefly review the important themes of romanticism, literature and evil and their focus on nature, creativity, the erotic, horror and the macabre. I will then proceed to discuss two major figures described variously as the metaphysician of evil, Georges Bataille, and the libertine, the Marquis de Sade, before concluding with some remarks on the phenomenal popular success of novels such as Erica Jong's *Fear of Flying* (1973) and E.L. James' *Fifty Shades of Grey* (2011), and the implications for the study of evil.

In *The Many Faces of Evil* (2001), Amelie Rorty identifies the approaches discussed in this chapter generically as the 'romanticism of evil'. By this phrase, she means a perspective that is distinguished by being as much about recognizing the repulsion and (more to the point) the sensual and erotic *lure* of evil, as it is against traditional reactions to many previous ways of construing and dealing with it. As a movement, romanticism was about the exploration of more innovative and exploratory cultural forms deemed to be better fitted for express-ing the prevailing anxieties about evil in a morally ambivalent age when the influx of relativism was usurping the moral certainties of the past. While narrative still played, and continues to play, a vital role in this approach, the kinds of stories, characters and plots and the types of human experiences and modes of expression, interpretation and reception that get highlighted and their consequences are some-what different. Some examples will be provided here. First, let's briefly look at what romanticism is before relating these themes to evil and literature.

What is romanticism?

'Romanticism' is a loosely descriptive and sweeping yet nevertheless indispensable term for a profound shift in attitudes toward human creativity and the work of imagination that is usually traced to the first half of the nineteenth century. Romanticism is a complex and diverse movement, so we'll concentrate on the main themes and aspects that relate specifically to the topic of evil, in particular the translation of the experience of evil into art, with an emphasis on literature.

Romanticism can thus be summarized as comprising the following elements:

- Chief emphasis on the freedom of self expression—sincerity, spon-taneity, originality the new paradigms, in reaction to what were considered to be the dry and sterile formalism that focused on a decorous imitation of the past (e.g. neo-classicism)
- Rejection of Enlightenment thinking as dehumanizing, artificial and overly abstract, in favour of a more emphatic embracing of other more neglected human faculties, most especially the emo-tions, the directness of personal and subjective experience, and the boundlessness of human imagination
- Hero worship of the artist (as opposed to the scientist) as a free spirit and expressers of their own undeniable truths; new cult(ure) of celebrity
- Rejection of rationalism, giving way to a more abandoned attitude toward emotional intensity, manifesting itself in rapture, nostalgia

(including the past and childhood), horror, melancholy, sentimentality and (for some Romantics) also the bizarre, exotic and macabre

- Recourse to dreams, folk legends, superstitions and delirium (including drug-induced) as sources of inspiration and knowledge
- Conventional rules of art based on the mechanics of formal (re)production replaced with more 'organic' forms based on free development and natural growth
- New emphasis on nature as the 'mirror' of the soul (transcendentalism)—stressing nature as opposed to knowledge/science/technology as the primary transformative influence on the human subject (as in rationalism)
- Draws on the 'revolutionary spirit' of the diverse political ideologies and revolutions of the time, though the tendency to sentimentalism and nostalgia also contribute to the conservative, reactionary and/or anarchic elements of romanticism
- Unleashed a new wave of gothic horror (e.g. Edgar Allen Poe, Bram Stoker, Nathaniel Hawthorne, Herman Melville) and women writers (e.g. Mary Shelley, George Sand, the Bronte sisters)

(Adapted from Baldick, 2008)

So, though romanticism is by no means synonymous with evil or literature, it was crucial in terms of inaugurating a movement away from what were considered the cold, hard realities of rationality and moral propriety in favour or more unrestrained irrational, ambiguous and recalcitrantly immoral forces. Art, or the aesthetic, and evil, or the amoral/deviant/malevolent, were central to this cultural transition and philosophical revolution. In many ways, this marks a strident reaction to the primacy of science and reason as a force for good that are foundational to Enlightenment thought.

Romanticism represents a strong reaction against the dominance of rationality as the primary and distinguishing human attribute and rationalism (and the moral and civil law) as the fundamental organizing principle underpinning social order. In stark contrast, the Romantics unleashed a full-scale attack on reason, turning instead for their inspiration and source of legitimacy to the power of human imagination, natural drives and individual creativity. Whereas previously pious, religiously ordered societies would view this sort of will to power based on self-creation as virtually synonymous with evil (e.g. in the form of the sins of pride and licentiousness), the Romantics would embrace this reaction against rationalism as the formative principle of a new social and political order (e.g. reflecting the virtues of individuality and expressiveness). Previously, as we have seen, morality and society were built upon conventions of civility that required high levels of (self-) surveillance and self-denial, a sort of watered-down asceticism and stoicism. The Romantics rejected this outright, desiring and demanding indulgence of all sorts.

Many Romantics attacked the idea that the legitimate role of moral and legal codes is to reign in natural human impulses and drives in order promote the common good; instead, they insisted on the legitimacy of the individual and the 'goods' of sensual pleasure, spiritual communion with nature (as opposed to organized religion) and the authenticity of creativity emerging from the domain of the sensual and emotional self. If this crossed the line into the wanton pursuit of evil, then so be it; that only reflects more authentically what human nature is really like and, hence, is more honest and credible than some holy or abstract ideal. The role of the state also came under scrutiny by many of the Romantics in the eighteenth and nineteenth centuries, providing a focal point for emotive nationalism and the revolutionary spirit for change, even to the point of anarchy—whence the evils of 'the terrors' in post-revolutionary France. The Romantics were similarly unbridled and intense in their fascination with (human) nature, to the point of obsession with things like moral depravity and the lure of corruption and decrepitude. And they loved individual mavericks, rebels and risk takers.

Bataille and Sade: The metaphysician of evil and the libertine

The infamous Marquis de Sade (1740–1814) described himself as a *libertine*, that is to say someone who took both his personal and political impulses from the spirit of rebellion, destruction and corruption to extreme limits, by any accounts.

In a letter to his wife Pélagie written in 1781, Sade made the following admission:

> Yes, I admit I'm a libertine: I've conceived everything one can conceive in that genre, but I've surely not done all I've imagined and surely will never do it. I'm a libertine, but I'm not a criminal or a murderer.
>
> (Quoted in du Plessix Gray, 2000: 330)

While it is true he hadn't actually committed murder in real life, he had certainly done so many times and in every possible way he could yet think of in his writings. But this confession, such as it is, gives us an important insight into the thinking of this controversial writer. Clearly, Sade does not suffer from a personal crisis of conscience in terms of the wantonness or extremity of the violent sexual fantasies he describes in his writings; but is this because, as he suggests, he has not acted them all out? Probably not. For what Sade professes, and what he desires, is much more complex than merely expounding fantasy or an increase in licentiousness, though he certainly seems to endorse both, which are not enacted. What he wants and advocates, as argued by commentators such as Bataille, is not non-action but rather a kind of *nothingness*. We may explore this notion through our previous reflections on what we might call the ironic or even paradoxical role of 'nothingness' in various theories of evil discussed earlier in this book—e.g. the Augustinian/Neo-Platonic doctrine of evil as privation or non-being; the empty yet richly potent cypher of the symbols of evil in Ricoeur's phenomenological hermeneutics; the abject impossibility of Kristeva's maternal phallus as a manifestation of non-being—*nothing* can, in the context of evil, mean quite a lot. As the saying goes, with respect to Sade and Bataille, the devil is very much in the detail.

In his collection of essays *Literature and Evil* (2006), the French writer and philosopher Georges Bataille—himself a notorious figure and bad boy, called the 'metaphysician of evil'—describes literature as generally 'guilty', and Sade in particular as a 'monster':

> He was one of the most rebellious and furious men ever to have talked of rebellion and fury; he was, in a word, a monster, obsessed by the idea of an *impossible* liberty.
>
> (Bataille, 2006: 107 [original emphasis])

Bataille is certainly not alone in this judgement. In her biography of Sade, Francine du Plessix Gray (2000) goes to some lengths to present a balanced portrait of the man and his life, yet inevitably gravitates toward the 'monster' depiction. Though enjoying the social status of a family man and minor royal, Sade was someone who took the pursuit of his sexual desires to the extreme, debasing himself and more significantly his victims and the process denying their humanity, agency and suffering in the pursuit of his own basest urges. As is clear from his writings, Sade's immorality knows no bounds; in his pursuit of the evil of sexual violence, there is *nothing*, not even life itself, which is sacred to him. All borders and boundaries that define the moral law or separate the victim from the criminal are not merely breached, as in Kristeva's concepts of the maternal phallus or the abject, they are wantonly and actively obliterated in any and all conceivable evil acts of sexual violence. This evil as an active species of nothingness is not something that is happened upon in the daily rough and tumble of emergent neurotic or depressive symptoms, but is pursued as an end in its own right and one that justifies any means (in a perverse reversal of the Kantian categorical imperative). This is more than an ordinary wet dream; this is a deeply philosophical choice. Sade's ultimate desire is absolutely and resolutely intentional, embracing the purest impulse of destruction:

> Destruction being one of the chief laws of Nature, nothing that destroys can be criminal; how might an action which so well serves Nature ever be outrageous to her?
>
> (From *Philosophy in the Bedroom*)

So the 'nothing' we encounter here has a kind of vigorous, intentional, purposeful dimension, as opposed to the types of nothingness encountered in previous conceptualizations of evil. These are the concepts of evil considered in previous chapters that are based upon partiality (in both senses of the word), straying from the right path (Augustine, Kant, Ricoeur) or being in the grip of some external, (super)natural demonic force (Descartes, Freud) that results in a view of the human being as passive, docile and weak. Here, in Sade and Bataille, we encounter a reference to a species of 'nothingness' powered by the destructiveness of nature that is quite typical of the Romantics, using nature as the mirror image or ideal model of human or divine morality. But this is not quite the same as the death drive (*thanatos*) that forms an elemental part of the inner workings of the subject/psyche as in psychoanalysis. This is about evil as a—or for Sade *the*—source of *power*, not just some sentimental appreciation of nature or the self-actualization. As Carter (1979) observes, the characters in Sade's writings are remarkable by the absence of having any inner lives; theirs is not a sexual journey in terms of the development of the self or subject via eroticism, but one of extreme externality and materiality, founded on not just the human but the natural/corporeal world. In a reversal of the Cartesian fable of the Evil Genius, Sade looks to the natural, occasionally including the cosmic, worlds to vanquish through sex (as a form of revolutionary violence) the moral and spiritual realms of humanity.

And he goes even further, much further, seeking to turn the destructive powers of nature against nature itself:

> It's nature I wish to outrage...I would like to violate its plans, reverse its course, vanquish the stars that float throughout it, ravage whatever serves it...insult it, in sum, in all its manifestations.
>
> (From *Justine*, quoted in du Plessix Gray, 2000: 303)

It is the intensity and boundlessness of Sade's pursuit of evil in the violation of morality and the unleashing of suffering and destruction that contribute to his image as the monster he was known as in his own time and has retained ever since. He knew what he was doing was evil according to the prevailing moral codes, and he did whatever he could to make sure he could do it, and failing that, then imagine and write about it. This relentlessness and his wantonly unapologetic denial of his victims and of the moral codes of society make him into the monstrous icon of evil that he has remained to this day. It has also preserved his reputation as a figurehead of sexual depravity and rebelliousness in a more celebrated way; as the term 'Sadism' suggests, there are many who claim to follow him and want to imitate his example (as represented, for instance, by E.L. James' hero Christian Grey). But what does the case of Sade and his writings tell us about the nature of evil then and now, and to come?

We will return to the victim and her (or his) role in erotic literature presently. First, let us consider this destructive attitude toward nature; Sade's desire to want to destroy the destroyer. Does this render him one of the creative geniuses vis-à-vis the Romantic ethos? Does this make him the poster boy for the heroic, maverick rebel who rails against oppressive morality on behalf of a subjugated and inhibited majority? Is he, or his descendent Christian Grey, the sexiest thing to millions of women on two legs? Could Sade be a misunderstood artist/transcendentalist? Or a crass nihilist, someone who simply wills nothing but nothing?

In *Literature and Evil* (2006), Georges Bataille argues for the latter, pointing out first of all the creative stasis of arts during the French revolutionary period in general, and the sterility of Sade's work in particular (Bataille, 2006: 106). Here, the violence of the revolution is not deemed to be creative, generative or productive; it is not more than the sum of its parts, it is simply violence, destruction with nothing more to recommend it (apart from the sexual release), with no further symbolic or transcendent meaning. It is rather utterly literal and concrete, what it is and nothing more; from an aesthetic point of view, this equates to a form of nothingness that is hard to defend. And so it is with Sade and his work. Even Sade's request to be buried in a grave covered with acorns so that oak trees would grow and destroy any trace of his bodily remains is apt, Bataille states. The Sadean impulse is toward nothingness to the point of nihilism, rather than to creativity that is generative and life-giving, and it is this base nihilism that distinguishes Sade's work from the creative destruction of nature so loved by the Romantics.

Ideally, Sade's destructive impulse leaves nothing in its wake, not even justification for the evil that he claimed to love so much. This is the irony of Sade and his work, its ultimate sterility and repetition, even to the point of boredom. To this day, people say they admire him and that they want to follow or imitate him, but this not only unrealistic, Bataille argues, it is in actuality impossible, because of the literal quality of Sade's total obsession with the object of his desires:

> ...we talk about him, admire him, but nobody feels that he should be like him; we dream of other 'terrors'. Yet Paulhan has defined Sade's position admirably. He was not concerned with the possibilities or the dangers of language. He could not imagine his work independently of the object he depicted, because his object possessed him—in the devil's sense of the word.
>
> Bataille (2006: 114)

The implied contrast Bataille distinguishes here between erotic obsession and demonic possession is instructive, as is his reference to the dangerous qualities of language which Sade's work lacks. So we could say that Sade's work is not about the authenticity of self-creativity or self-expression and their attendant risks, but rather about the putative obliteration of the self in the absolute degradation and erasure of the other as the object of control and not desire, and that's it. Bataille compares this ironically to the annihilation of the self sought by some ascetic religious orders, branding Sade as more like a monk than a rebel or a modern maverick: 'He wrote lost in the desire for the object and applied himself like a monk' (Bataille, ibid.: 114). 'His books give us the feeling that, by an exasperated inversion, he wanted the impossible and the *reverse* of life' (Bataille, ibid.: 120): not sensual, not arousing or erotic, not life affirming.

Even his use of language is notable by its sterility and constriction; it does not lead the imagination or reveal deeper or secret meanings about the nature of human desire. It is not symbolic, literary or poetic, but

merely objective, concrete, dead. What is more, and of particular importance for Bataille, is that Sade's work fails to accord due significance to
sacrifice or the *sacred*, simply rejecting them out of hand, ignoring or
ridiculing them, as opposed to acknowledging their latent and deeply
ambiguous potential for the deepest fulfilment of erotic desire (see Hill,
2001). As any serial killer will tell you (as we will return to in the next
chapter), what erotic obsession requires is the presence of the *other*, the
object of desire; demonic possession that fails to accord due significance
to the sacredness of the encounter, as indicated by Descartes' fabular
encounter with the diabolical evil genius, is a desolate and isolating
business. What is also required, *qua* the sacred and even the evil of sacrifice, is the at least residual presence of the good, which as something to
corrupt must still, to some extent, meaningfully exist. This is recognized
in the anthropological research on taboo (e.g. in the seminal research of
Durkheim and Mauss). Notwithstanding his propensity for characters
with clerical or religious positions of authority, such notions about the
nature of the sacred and profane have little meaning for Sade.

There is thus what we would recognize as a strongly existentialist
strand to Sade's philosophy (and indeed Sade's work would influence
what would become known as existentialism). The closest Sade comes
to an existentialist declaration in his literary works is, again in a parody
of the Cartesian *cogito*, is 'I fuck therefore I am' (Carter, 1979: 26):

> From this axiom, he constructs a diabolical lyricism of fuckery, since
> the acting-out of a total sexuality in a repressive society turns all eroti-
> cism into violence, makes of sexuality itself a permanent negation.
> Fucking, says Sade, is the basis of all human relationships but the
> activity parodies all human relations because of the nature of the
> society that creates and maintains those relationships.
>
> (Carter, 1979: 26)

As a philosophical observation about the state of human social relationships, whether or not you agree with Sade, many will find (on some days
at least) that there is something to commend this polemical argument
that to some extent or another we are all basically fucked. But is this
empowering? Is it interesting or revelatory of what it is to be human?
Is it a path to revolution and/or liberation? Is it sexy?

As a libertine, Bataille recognizes Sade as a revolutionary against the
regulations and strictures of morality. But it is in Sade's rejection of the
sacred and the sovereign—i.e. the transgressive potency of morality and
ritual as constructed around sex, sacrifice and taboo—that, according

to Bataille, Sade misses or ignores their potential as foundational to the fulfilment of erotic experience (Roche, 2006). It is against these metaphysical-religious phenomena and their violent and visceral violation between sexual bodies that the utmost erotic pleasure is achieved, according to Bataille. So, while Sade advocates the total liberation from and annihilation of the rule of law (religious, moral, civil etc.) as the path to sexual fulfilment, Bataille points to the necessity of their existence and persistence as limits against which to resist and rebel against in the form of genuinely transgressive acts of sexual excess, now and again in the future. Where is the fun in violating a taboo without the possibility of being about to do it again? And what would be the sense in eliminating a taboo that you had a good time contravening on a previous occasion, enjoyment of (some) sex being as forbidden and desirable as it is? Sexual predilections being what they are, regardless of the content, generally speaking enthusiasts want to indulge more than once. Few fetishes involve singularities, and then nothing, on purpose. Again, as Bataille observes, this is the position of the ascetic, not the erotic; sex is, in a word, moreish, and to be really good it has to have something against which to struggle and subsequently refresh and revitalize itself.

Could it be argued that in his works Sade takes us to a point where the putative distinction separating natural from moral evil fundamental to modernity break down, and that this itself marks his contribution to modern philosophy and the study of evil? While it is true that nature encapsulates within it an inevitable and brutal impulse toward death and destruction that is at the heart of the most painful evils of human existence, it is simply not the case that nature and destruction are absolute categories (as noted previously, only God is absolute), nor are they synonymous. The Romantics acknowledged, and indeed revelled in, nature in terms of its cyclical and irrational drive toward death as an inevitable but not absolute destination, certainly not to the point of nihilism. Paradoxically, it is this very circular repetition of corruption and rebirth inherent in nature, sex and death that ensures regeneration and growth: in short, this *is* the human condition vis-à-vis evil; this is life. For there to be new life, transformation, change and renewal, there must be violence, suffering, loss and death. For Bataille, Sade's error was to overstate the case by focusing only or too stridently on the latter in his determination to 'master' and therefore obliterate and deny the former. Death may be inevitable, even desirable, but it is not the 'be all and end all'. Ultimately, it can't 'be' at all; without the conditioning presence of the sacred and sovereign, it is just 'end'. In the terms of its erotic and philosophical significance, the traumatic and deathly aspects of sex and the erotic are indicative of their deeply ambivalent, even paradoxical, nihilistic *and* generative qualities, positive and negative, good and evil, in ways that it is impossible to speak, control or fully comprehend. But sense and feel? Yes, beyond question. And this is true of language too, especially in terms of its risks and dangerousness. Such revelations are not conceivable in a litany of relentlessly tangled and rutting bodies overseen by a succession of powerful and corrupt tyrants. This is not a comprehensive narrative of erotic or evil, or if it is, it's a pretty pallid one, and very dull.

In *Evil and Literature*, Bataille draws attention to the monotony of Sade's work, the sheer limitlessness and repetitiveness of his destructive fantasies, making the analogy that his literary creations are more like a desert landscape rather than the idyllic vision of nature in rolling hills and streams as sentimentally envisioned by the Romantics. While it may be that we are not yet so attuned to the beauty of the barren landscape, Bataille opines, this still does little to lend much aesthetic substance to Sade's work. Sade, who cut himself off from humanity, only had one preoccupation in his long life which really absorbed him—that of enumerating to the point of exhaustion the possibilities of destroying human beings, of rendering them captive victims and destroying them utterly (particularly the most 'innocent' women and children) and of enjoying the thought of their death and suffering to the point of and in the service of orgasm (for an excellent précis of Sadean literature, see Neiman, 2002). Even the most beautiful description of erotic love would have had little meaning for Sade. The language of interminable monotony concerning the sex act alone functioned to present him with the void, the desert, for which he yearned, and which his books still present to the reader.

Boredom, not desire, seeps from the monstrosity of Sade's work, but it is this very boredom which constitutes its significance (Bataille, 2006: 115–116). So why then is he remembered, and why do so many consider him and the sadism named after his acts so fascinating? Many since Sade's time claim to admire or emulate this infamous libertine, but they do not truly know him or his work. The licentiousness Sade displayed is in the end simply too disgusting, even for the most depraved reader, to occasion the genuine sensual pleasure of the erotic. This is because the frenzy of Sade's encounters is so intense as to banish consciousness (Bataille, ibid.: 120) as well as any life-affirming impulse (which is, at least to some extent, contained in anything genuinely erotic) or the capacity to truly satiate human desire and subsequently arouse it again. Rather, the excess and disorder are simply sickening, the expression is concrete and lacking in artistry and his heroes, heroines and villains are cyphers, frauds, parasites and cowards, hardly warranting the literary designation of 'characters' at all, more mechanisms for propounding a philosophy (Phillips, 2005).

What the continuing popularity of Sade and his work confirm as much if not more than anything is that evil, pure evil on its own, is tedious, monotonous and dull. We like to maintain the pretence that evil deeds and those who execute them are somehow extraordinary and interesting, and those who do evil also like to think this—hence, the dark allure of the criminal—when, in fact, the opposite is usually the case (Eagleton, 2010). Evil of devastating gravity can, and often does, occur in the most unremarkable of circumstances, such as when a father exploits the sanctity and confinement of the private family home and cultural dependency and impotence of childhood to sexually violate his own child, or when children abduct a toddler from a shopping centre in order to obtain, torture and murder him in an out-of-the-way place. That such incidents often originate in private, secret or otherwise 'secure' family-friendly environments such as the family, consumer outlets (e.g. the shopping centre or Internet), home or prison and involve elements of sexual torture and extreme imbalances of power is no coincidence.

The role of prison

We may link Bataille's assessment of Sade's fantastic representations of sex to the terrible solitude of his imprisonment and the consequent obliteration of consciousness: 'Thus the Bastille, where Sade did his writing, was the crucible in which the conscious limitations of being were slowly destroyed by the fire of a passion prolonged by powerlessness' (Bataille, 2006: 125).

So we may ask, from a criminological perspective, is the real value of Sade's work in its exposure of the sterility and boredom of evil in the excess of human imagination as a consequence of the inhumanity of the prison regime that imposed upon him a solitude that obliterated his consciousness? Are the prisons of the penitentiary and nuclear-family home places where the monsters of evil are created and dwell? Or where 'animals' deprived of their humanity and compassion for the victims of their murderous crimes are hatched and housed? To return to Ricoeur's onto-theological logos of theodicy, is punishment always about healing and rehabilitation? And if it isn't, in an age of Enlightenment, what happens when we punish even the most vicious offenders too harshly, or when victims are born to endure their pain in secret only to repeat this cycle of evil across the generations? How do we 'rational-ize' such (in)human deviations in modern institutional regimes like the legal-judicial and prison and social systems?

These are questions that in many ways expose what writers and thinkers like Bataille and Sade were really getting at, in terms of their understanding of evil. And again, what this relates to fundamentally is not knowledge but its *limits*. And sometimes these limits can only truly be known when they are exceeded and transgressed. Not just limits of morality, decency and pleasure, but more significantly the limits of rea-son, of human rationality, human endurance and of the Enlightenment project itself. These limits shape and determine the human condition as we know it in ways that those living in other historical periods could have never conceived. The human being and the human soul are irre-vocably affected by these new possibilities offered by modern science and technology, and the postmodern cultures of moral relativism; what thinkers like Sade and Bataille argue is that these changes with respect to the manifestation of evil are uniquely present and observable in erotic and sexual experience.

As humans, we are not just rational but also animal and (for Bataille) even partially divine as creatures created by a loving and living God. In previous encounters with evil, rationality dominated as the distin-guishing human attribute; not here. While theologians and philoso-phers of previous eras recognized our sensual and quasi-spiritual natures, these were typically dismissed as either not up to the task of making sense of evil or even the source of evil itself (as in the Gnostic and ratio-nalist traditions). But the Romantics and thinkers like Bataille and Sade turned to the body, sexuality and the erotic sensuality as not just mean-ingful but crucial sources of understanding and inspiration. As anyone who has ever been in love knows, love encapsulates many urges, toward life, joy and unity but also toward rage, destruction and death:

> Bataille also credits Sade for revealing a link between sexuality and a wish to destroy *oneself*; 'this tormenting fact: the urge toward love, pushed to its limit, is an urge towards death' (*ER*: 42). (One could perceive here a hint of the Surrealist's interest in love, and sexuality, as rendering asunder of the categories of the 'reasonable'.)
>
> (Roche, 2006: 164 [original emphasis])

This death wish or wish to destroy the self (or even the beloved) could be understood as suicidal, murderous or nihilistic, or could be seen in the context of a wish to lose the self, to dissipate and disappear into the union with the beloved or achieve liberation through the elimination of the object of erotic desire. And as much as modernity is invested in the creation and development of the 'subject' (philosophical and otherwise) and maintenance of the 'self', who doesn't want to chuck these into the flames of hot, passionate sex from time to time, to lose themselves, to lose track of time, in that most delectable congress with another? To be lost, to give way to, to be *present* in a manner that evades the demands of temporality and selfhood in the form of things like career, duty, selfhood, responsibility and the cares and anxieties of everyday life, even if just for a little while? To sacrifice and be the sacrificial object; to dwell in the sacred and profane in one act and moment by the act of surrender and relinquishment, together. To be free to utilize the body to achieve this *jouissance*, this exquisite and supremely human joy, an element of which is contingent upon some sort of *loss*, a rapturous stillness or sublime nothingness (the Romantics loved the sublime!) that shatters and empties time of its linear chronology and blurs humanness. Orgasm, that elusive and, in capitalist modernity, that much sought-after prize that is infamously difficult if not impossible to capture in language, but for which modern literature—elite, romantic or pornographic—is an obsession, the ultimate goal. When the possibility for this rapturous and vertiginous experience presented by erotic desire is denied, as in unrequited love, then the passions of desire can take more negative and darker routes toward obsession or obliteration of the (once) beloved object of desire. If I can't have her/him, then nobody can.

Loss, emptiness, nothingness, death, abjection, want, privation... these are all elements of the philosophical theories of evil discussed in the previous chapters. In this chapter, we may add to this list the embodied and romantic emotions of passion, delirium, obsession, transgression, excess and the external sociocultural restraints of taboo, gender and family norms, sexual morality as well as the burgeoning influences of new digital technologies, social media, market economics and crime. In a couple of sentences, we have mapped the terrain of evil and modern erotic/pornographic literature (note: I am not interested here in contesting or interrogating this distinction; this is a perennial and contentious debate in its own right that is not strictly speaking directly relevant here). What I do wish to focus upon is the encounter with evil through popular erotic literature (in this instance those texts mainly written for women) that encapsulate the longing of women to be 'annihilated by love' in the words of Erica Jong's heroine Isadora Wing in *Fear of Flying* (1973: 10). This apparently perennial trope hinges on the equally durable chore of finding a man wealthy, handsome and otherwise sufficiently eligible enough and up to the job. And this is achievable only if a woman is vain, rich and persistent enough to be able and willing to engage in the enormously self-conscious, painful, expensive and time-consuming work of exfoliation, depilation, sanitation, augmentation and so forth, in the name of 'beauty'—as well as creating the perfect 'profile' and searching the Internet and going out to what are considered appropriate social spaces, activities and events; again, very self-conscious, costly and time-consuming. For all this effort, the reward is the ultimate sexual fantasy, to dissolve any vestige of self-consciousness in the orgasmic miasma of the luscious, politically incorrect abysmal absurdity that is that most seventies of feminist-inspired popular cultural inventions, Jong's eponymous 'zipless fuck'.

As in Sade's writings, the zipless fuck is (probably) impossible to achieve, but unlike in Sade's work, this doesn't mean a girl can't have fun trying. Sade's world is a scary and humourless place, where to absolve and give up oneself, willingly and wantonly, equates to a headlong leap into the abyss of sex in the form of endless gurning and physical rutting. The aim is not to gain traction on reality as an individual subject or self-knowledge or growth, as in philosophical or therapeutic psychoanalytic discourses, or to escape or have fun as in Jong's iconic novel. But while (even for Jong's heroine) to be 'annihilated by love' is a daunting prospect, it is also infinitely pleasurable and desirable, and for writers like Jong, it is, or can be, funny as hell, and in this sense liberating in a way that Sade would never have countenanced. What Jong advocates is a sort libertinism with a difference. The zipless fuck is the ultimate in (female) sexual fantasy, mainly because it doesn't happen. But not because, as in the case of Sade, it is just too violent, extreme, deviant and physically untenable to be possible. Jong describes it as pure, uncomplicated, fantastic sex between strangers with no external influences, limitations or agenda; zipless because

> ... the incident has all the swift compression of a dream and is seemingly free of all remorse and guilt; because there is no talk of her late husband or of his fiancée; because there is no rationalizing; because there is no talk at *all*. The zipless fuck is absolutely pure. It is free of ulterior motives. This is no power game. The man is not 'taking' and the woman is not 'giving'. No one is attempting to cuckold a husband or humiliate a wife.
>
> (Jong, 1973: 12)

[W]hen you came together, zippers fell away like rose petals, underwear blew off in one breath like dandelion fluff. For the true ultimate zipless A-1 fuck, it was necessary that you never got to know the man very well.

(Jong, 1973: 14)

It is worth noting the (comparatively speaking) light-hearted and ethereal references to the symbolism of nature, of privation/lack and the irreverent attitude to 'knowledge' deployed by Jong in this text, allied to a realism among women of the impossibility of such a thing, sex being as it is mostly a disappointment: 'Note that I said "female fantasy". The sexual *acts* in *Fear of Flying* are neither very many nor very ecstatic. They tend to fizzle in disappointment. The bedroom becomes a stage for a comedy of errors' (Jong, 1973: ix). Not for her the po-faced *thanatos* or nihilism of Sade or Bataille, nor the notion that such ridiculous fantasy could or possibly should ever be fulfilled. There is really no need for 'philosophy' in this bedroom; such a thing would be absurd, though Jong's prose suggests she would be up to it if such intellectual exertions were required; they are not. It's just a bit of fun, or it would be!

In contrast, sex for Bataille and Sade is a seriously and philosophically 'seminal' matter, not so much about joy, fun and laugher as about pain, depression and death. It is orgasmic as encapsulated in ' ... the French expression for orgasm *"la petit mort"* ("the little death") ... Bataille also notes that ... "depression following the final spasm [of orgasm] may give a foretaste of death" (ER, 102, 232)' (Roche, 2006: 164). But it would be overly simplistic to portray Bataille's erotism as entirely joyless. After all, what is true, what is not just possible but undeniable is that we are all going to die. This evocation of depression and the dread of death is somewhat different that than found in the writings of Julia Kristeva; here, depression is considered not so much a malady or social-psychological problem calling for therapeutic resolution as it is a delectable foretaste of death that is *coming* to us all, just a *soupcon* of which can paradoxically make us want only more, to do it again and again, as per the impulse toward sex. This repetition, this animality, this insatiable, lustful appetite that not only incorporates but is founded upon the lure of aggression, submission, violence, destruction and death and the willingness to abdicate and annihilate the self in the orgasmic encounter that are elemental to human sexuality and the human condition according to this view. This ethos completely turns the tables on Enlightenment thinking and the will to civility, morality and rationality—or to the putative decency of nuclear-family life as the pinnacle of modern human sexual morality. Similarly, in pornographic and popular romantic literature such as *Fifty Shades of Grey*, elitist standards of literary excellence are derided and turned on their head, as any pretence to artistic merit is dissolved in the turgid repetition and cliché, these being instrumental texts for more banal and basal instincts.

But to be devil's advocate for a moment, what is the point of life, what do we all yearn for, if not the erotic, whether in the form of love, sex and/or (sometimes) even porn? Certainly, many ideological debates around such a question have caused consternation among feminists since the 1970s and into 'post' feminism. So, against this background, and the female streaming of sex into popular pornographic romance, product placement and porn (again, see *Fifty Shades*), whence evil, sex and literature now?

As Sade recognized, for the most depraved, lust is not just useful for rape and murder but also for money. Even the great Immanuel Kant could not win this argument. Evil here is very much the way to human fulfilment by way of humiliation, corruption, destruction, domination, submission and death toward a further end of not just getting laid but, more to the point, getting filthy rich in the process. While Sade achieved notoriety through his literary explorations of these timelessly appealing themes, he was never able to convert this into cold hard cash, just hard time. Sade's obscene tales of two sisters describing the 'misfortunes' of virtue as recounted in his novel *Justine* (1791) or the 'amply rewarded' path of vice as expounded at length in *Juliette* (1797) contrast starkly to the astronomical success of other controversial texts such as Samuel Richardson's bestselling epistolary novel *Pamela or Virtue Rewarded* (1740). Though admittedly there are substantial critical differences between these texts, in many ways, as recognized by Lewis (2012), the publishing phenomenon that was *Pamela* marks the eighteenth-century predecessor to James's *Fifty Shades of Grey* (2011). Both were written by outsiders, literary unknowns; both were about the sexual awakening (and in Pamela's case eventual love) of an innocent, beautiful young ingénue at the hands of an older, more sexually experienced, predatory, socially enfranchised male who incarcerated her for the purpose; both were intended for and/or consumed by the female readership and inspired a general moral panic about women's appetite for 'obscene' literature; both spawned a plethora of imitators, sequels, parodies and tacky merchandise (Lewis, 2012). Pamela's story is told via letters to her parents; much of Anastasia's is recounted via email exchanges with Christian (who gives her a then state-of-the-art laptop for the purpose, Ana being a university student who has never owned a computer). Richardson, a printer by profession (like his near contemporaries and fellow very popular writers Daniel Defoe and William Blake), *Pamela* changed the publishing industry. Uncannily, though James's previous profession was in the media, the impact of *Fifty Shades* has also changed the face of publishing as we know it, severely testing if not eroding the editorial authority of traditional gatekeepers to the market in the publishing industry and shifting the balance of power to word-of-mouth recommendations facilitated by e-readers, personal and social networks, online book retailer reviews, blogs, fan fiction websites, and in the process overturning the tarnished and shameful reputation of self or 'vanity' publishing.

These transformations to the publishing market, consumption patterns, reading and writing technologies and subjectivities are reflected in the bottom line and influence in popular culture. Both Sade and even Richardson would have been dumbfounded by the revenue generated by the originally self-published *Fifty Shades of Grey*. In a somewhat reflexive move, filth, sex, obscene wealth and high-profile product placement of old (e.g. first editions of famous eighteenth-century novels, the likes of which somewhat ironically feature as gifts from Christian to Ana in *Fifty Shades*) and new technologies (e.g. mobile telephones, laptops, e-readers, helicopters, BDSM accoutrements etc.) and conspicuous consumption of all sorts (from the ultimate bachelor pad to designer wardrobes, personal trainers and 'red rooms of pain') are elemental parts of what is in essence a conventional romance narrative (Lewis, 2012). All find their apotheosis in E.L. James's eponymous anti-hero Christian (or maybe not so 'Christian') Grey, the handsome, young, sadistic and damaged 'frillionaire' (Parker, 2012: online) hero of *Fifty Shades*. Unlike Isadora, the heroine of *Fear of Flying*, James's heroine Anastasia wishes most of all to 'know' her man, primarily with a view to changing him; in popular romantic fiction, this is key to the formula and the fanatical impulse driving women's erotic love: finding the rich, powerful, sexy yet emotionally damaged man who is above all in need of female repair, the ideal perfectable erotic object as 'fixer-upper' (Erika Leonard quoted in Memmott, 2012: online). It is this underlying spirit of optimism, agency and future-orientation that to a very considerable degree, verging on fantasy, propels the narrative formula or romantic-erotic fiction and inscribes the female discourse of (erotic) Enlightenment. This inscribes the theodicy of erotic love many women are socialized to pursue: healing and closure (ideally through marriage) of the damaged, bad boy hero who needs fussing-over and sorting out.

In a perversion of the famous Augustinian dictum 'Give me chastity, but not yet', the extravagance of human desire converges around sexuality and gender norms in relation to crime, punishment and deviance. We want orgasm vis-à-vis the 'little death', but as for the big one, unlike Sade, definitely not yet. While Jong's and James's heroines lust the traumatized little-boy-lost-Master turned frillionaire, for Sade's women, this is characterized in the discomforting and highly controversial feminine desire to be dominated, victimized, damaged, destroyed, even murdered:

> Bataille takes the character Amelie (in *Juliette*) to be representative of this association of sexuality with the will to self destruction. Amelie, an impressionable young woman, tells Borchamps that she wishes to be killed as the 'victim of the cruel passions of a libertine.' She adds: '[n]ot that I wish to die tomorrow—my extravagant fancies do not go as far as that; but that is the only way I want to die; to have my death the result of a crime is an idea that sets my head spinning'
>
> An impersonal denial, an impersonal crime!
>
> Tending towards the continuity of beings beyond death!
>
> De Sade's sovereign man does not offer our wretchedness a transcendent reality...But in [the character] Amelie de Sade links infinite continuity with infinite destruction (ER: 176).
>
> (Roche, 2006: 164–165)

Such thorny themes of the evils of sexual violence, erotic love and female fantasy are explored in 'Every Woman Adores a Fascist' (Frost, 2000), where the complexity and ambivalence of such desires reflect the 'voluptuous' sexual dissolution into violence and brutality are often inculcated in women's erotic fiction. In her analysis of the works of Sylvia Plath, Virginia Woolf and Erica Jong, Frost considers the problematic desire for the fascistic and incestuous figure of 'Daddy', and how for writers like Plath the surfacing of these putatively latent urges were inflamed by that most public and socially constructed of feminine ideals: the icy and frustrated perfection of the 1950s white middle-class housewife:

> Dissatisfied with their culture that shuts them out of opportunities, these women savor and theatricalize their abjection and revenge. They replace romantic myths of love with a carnal imbalance of

powers where the torturer and his victim ('Daddy,' 'Rabbit Catcher,' 'Jailer') are bound together by hate, resentment, and lust. Daddy's love and the security of marriage are dissatisfying compensations for limited horizons; the female speakers' long-delayed rebellions against 'Daddy' arouse stiltifed desires for social power and sexual liberation.

(Frost, 2000: 51)

Plath, at least as much and perhaps more than any other writer of her generation, struggles in a very different way to Jong with what are the uncomfortable murderous desires of aggression and revenge toward the fascist patriarchal (and her own German) 'Daddy'. For Plath, in the end, these literary and sexual imaginings result in a desperate recapitulation and turning of this homicidal aggressive longing back upon herself throughout her work and in her life, culminating in this instance in the act of suicide (Frost, 2000). In *Fear of Flying* (1973), Jong cites lines from Plath's poem 'Daddy' in her sexual picaresque narrative. Both Jong and her semi-autobiographical heroine Isadora are Jewish, and Isadora's Jewishness is a prominent aspect of her identity and character in the novel; like Plath, she repeatedly encounters the fascist 'Daddy' in her picaresque journey between the various 'concentration camp' (again, American and German) dwellings that map the female landscape, responding like Plath with horror, shame and anger, but also with consummate humour, sarcasm, irreverence and insolence. Similar textual connotations linking the Nazi fascist and the life of a woman imprisoned in the 'comfortable concentration camp' of the middle-class home abound in that other classic and so-called 'instrumental text' of the generation of 'women's liberation', Betty Friedan's *The Feminine Mystique* [1963] (1992). What are we to make of such alignments of (women's) sexual desire with confinement, violence, submission, aggression, depravity, murder and death in the distinctive evil of modernity enacted in the public and private prisons spanning domestic landscapes of the penitentiary and (middle-class) family home? And what do we make of such representations of heinous sexual abuse in popular cultural texts such as these compared to others created by men such as Oliver Stone's *Natural Born Killers* (1994)? And, indeed, of the 'instrumentality' of texts, feminist and/or pornographic in terms of their representation of (female) liberation and sexuality, and the politics of identity and (domestic) violence and sexual abuse of women and girls? And how do we relate such fraught if not tragic themes to a popular pulp fiction text like *Fifty Shades*, if indeed we can or should, as a way of making sense of evil and desire for us today?

As Turner (2002) argues, female sexuality has provided a potent site for the contestation of politically radical and conservative struggles over power, deviance and identity since initial cultural convergence of sexual libertinage, extremist propaganda and pornography in the early modern period. The consensus among scholars is that such ideological, psychological and material alignments vis-à-vis female sexuality in narratives of subjectivity, crime, deviance, moral outrage, violence, fear and death in such 'obscene' texts are emblematic of the state of modern culture more generally:

> Sadism, suggest Michel Foucault, is not a sexual perversion but a cultural fact; the consciousness of the 'limitless presumption of the appetite'. Sade's work, with its compulsive attraction for the delinquent imagination of the romantics, has been instrumental in shaping aspects of the modern sensibility; its paranoia, its despair, its sexual terrors, its omnivorous egocentricity, its tolerance of massacre, holocaust, annihilation [these being topics we will return to in the final chapters of this book].

> It was prison, the experience of oppression, that transformed the rake into the philosopher, the man of the Age of Reason into the prophet of the age of dissolution, of our own time, the time of the assassins. Deprived of the fact of flesh, he concentrated his notable sexual energy on a curious task of sublimation, a project that involved simultaneously creating and destroying that which he could no longer possess, the flesh, the world, love, in a desolated charnel house of the imagination.
>
> Carter (1979: 32)

Carter goes on to argue that it was punishment, not taboo, that 'inflamed [Sade's] imagination to the grossest extent' (1979: 33), and that it is no accident that the infamous Marquis was produced by a society that practised punitive justice so harshly, flogging, mutilating, torturing, isolating even legislating murder. All that distinguished Sade from his male counterparts of '... the hanging judge, the birching magistrate, the military torturer with his hoods and his electrodes, the flogging schoolmaster, the brutal husband...' was that he did not have a licence to torture by his affiliation with the security apparatus of the state, notwithstanding the enabling functional role played by his membership of the aristocracy. And as noted in the previous (and following) chapter, torture and the body in pain are the most perniciously isolating and persistently modern of institutionalized legislated forms of suffering overseen by the penal regime of the state. That this converges, in Carter's assessment, in the isolated body of the Marquis de Sade alone in his cell with his perverted, lustful, angry and violent imagination with the return of the diabolical figure of Satan as cultural anti-hero is one of the primary paradoxes of Enlightenment and the pathetic faith it has placed in the salvific powers of reason as a way of dealing with evil manifest in the literary text:

> His solitude is the perpetual companion and daily horror of the prisoner, whose final place of confinement is the self . . . Sade projects this diabolic solitude as an absolute egoism; that is the result of thirteen years solitary meditation on the world. The desires of his imaginary libertines may no longer be satisfied by flesh; flesh becomes an elaborate metaphor for sexual abuse. World, flesh and the devil fuse; when an atheist casts a cool eye on the world, he must always find Satan a more likely hypothesis as ruling principle than a Saviour. Criminality may present itself as a kind of saintly self-mastery, an absolute rejection of hypocrisy.
>
> Carter (1979: 33)

In a canny and irreverent inversion of the Christian *logos* in which Jesus's divinity as human and divine are declared as 'word made flesh' (John 1:14), in pornographic/erotic literature, flesh is made word. And then it is used, crumpled up and discarded, like yesterday's news/today's chip paper as rubbish, worthless, used, nothing. In some ways, this represents through the body-written word the ultimate postmodern riposte to Enlightenment optimism, in that modernity becomes the most blatantly, shamelessly and recklessly nihilistic—if not outrightly evil—age of all, epitomized in dehumanizing process of the penal-security state. Sade merely personifies our atrociousness, albeit in a less hypocritical way. 'If Sade is the last, bleak, disillusioned voice of the Enlightenment, he is the avatar of the nihilism of the late twentieth century' (Carter, 1979: 34).

Carter's final polemical analysis concerning Sade relates to the recurrence of another popular metaphor of Enlightenment: glass, or the mirror. But this time, with respect to women and their knowledge about their place in modernity, and again in an echo of Pauline gospel and the 'looking glass' trope of the romantic fairy tale, what we perceive is 'through a glass, darkly' (1 Corinthians 13:12). For Carter, the mirror of modern erotic literature is more of a hole, an aperture onto darkness and torment torn open by the speculum of violent pornography as written by the likes of Sade, among others. This hole is wide and gaping enough to afford women a view for themselves of the true reality of the modern world around them and the absurd and paradoxical necessity of their narrowly confined roles within it. Penetration of this mirror/hole as a portal for women to gaze into the abyss of their own torn bodies as sexual victims, potential survivors and/or themselves at least temporary purveyors of the 'male gaze' is afforded by many popular cultural genres, including romance, erotic/pornographic literature (Sonnet, 1999) as well as the most gruesomely popular true crime of which women are the main consumers (Browder, 2006; Dobash et al., 1998). These texts are increasingly popular among female readers for a complex variety of reasons explored in a vast research literature, among them the use they make often of extreme sexual violence against women (and children) to convey to largely (but not exclusively) female readers a sense of empowerment, in the form of:

- *liberation* (whether as freedom to consume pornography and engage in what was previously male-only sexual fantasy);
- *survival* (to resist identification with and as victims, thereby gaining an epiphenomenal sense of agency and also 'infotainment' in terms of knowing the 'true story' and being able to avoid such a fate); and
- *courage* (being able to stare into the abyss of sexual violence and abuse) (Browder, 2006; Dobash et al., 1998).

'Power', 'freedom', if not 'liberation', are terms we have encountered in previous theories of evil, specifically the anti-theodicy of Immanuel Kant. To briefly reiterate, Kant's view was that human beings are moral agents who are uniquely *free* to choose how to act due to their distinctive rationality, whether for evil or good. However, his view of freedom and agency from the perspective of humans as moral beings was emphatically linked to the implicitly 'rational' choice for individuals to act in a way that conformed generally speaking to the moral law, or in circumstances where the prevailing moral law was in crisis, that other limiting principles in the form of categorical imperatives that undercut selfish behaviour and choices should be deployed and adhered to. For Kant, this marked the limits of metaphysics as much as individual freedom, and for many (if not most) people these days would result in a pretty insipid route to personal liberation. To put it another way, in contrast to some of the writers referenced in this chapter, Kant was by no means disposed to turning the spotlight onto human freedom with a view to turning up the fun (at least for certain actors); actually just the opposite as Kant's injunction was clearly to think of the 'other' and put the interests of others before one's own; this is the way to liberate not the self (certainly not from a venal perspective), but to facilitate the 'good', which is to be valued in and of itself. This is clearly not the ethos at work here. At the same time, there are similar limitations exposed in these erotic/pornographic works; many of these texts are regimented by a strict narrative formula founded upon a narrowly and conservatively defined conceptualization of a constellation of gender norms, social relations and socio-religious-political institutions, specifically the presumed submissiveness and the toleration of the victimization of women and girls. These include the rather useful normativities of heterosexuality, the patriarchal family, the public–private divide and the material, political, social and cultural capital of elite white men.

In her article ' "Erotic Fiction by Women for Women": The Pleasures of Post-Feminist Heterosexuality' (1999), Esther Sonnet explores many of these issues. While it is not possible (nor indeed necessary) to provide a full rendition of Sonnet's analysis, I will strive to briefly relate her main points to a more recent phenomenon in popular erotic literature marketed for women readers by returning to the narrative of *Fifty Shades of Grey* (2011), specifically the commodification of (sadistic) sex and the ambivalent pains and pleasures of sexual domination and identity (politics) for women in contemporary society based on the consumption of such texts.

The basic narrative of *Fifty Shades* conforms to that most popular and perennial genre of book publishing, the romance: 'Despite its scarlet reputation, the series is an old-fashioned love story with some odd sex toys, riding crops and mild bondage tossed in. It's the classic boy-meets-girl, boy-loses-girl, boy-gets-girl-back plot that has fuelled an infinity of romance novels' (Donahue, 2012: online). That is it written by a woman, Erika Leonard, albeit under a distinctively androgynous pseudonym E.L. James, is significant. As Sonnet (1999) argues in relation women's erotic fiction generally, the designation of female authorship conveys important ideological and cultural connotations to its audience. Chief among these is its valuation as permissible, that it is 'okay' for 'normal' or decent women to purchase and consume such erotic texts. Hence, *Fifty Shades'* famous designation as 'mummy porn', that is to say, pornography that is not written by 'men for men', but by a woman *for* women and that these texts are different, and women are thus permitted to enjoy without appearing deviant or depraved. At the same time, the androgynous pseudonym that is widely known to mask a woman author provides a frisson of tension and possible danger—it *could* be written by a man, but we know it's not, so that's okay, but it's kind of sexy to imagine that it might be. The cover imagery of the book is suitably neutral, a simply patterned man's tie, which does cohere to the 'by women for women' marketing stratagem. And this is important, as conventional porn (i.e. for men) is highly reliant on the visual and hence male-oriented porn magazines and videos tend to have much more graphic and explicit images of (semi-)naked women on their covers and packaging. The neutrality and restraint of the *Fifty Shades* cover art enables women readers to convey a sense of decency while still being able to read an erotic/pornographic text in public, as the cover doesn't shout 'I'M READING PORN!' More to the point, the emergence of tablet-based technological devices like the e-reader have in the event made this issue redundant, as this particular publishing technology makes identifying what one is reading virtually impossible to onlookers. 'Ebooks are today's brown paper wrapper' (Donahue, 2012: online). Hence, the 'gaze' in terms of seeing and being seen retain their potency with respect to the social construction of feminine sexuality, and the lack of visual clues that advertise (e.g. the conventional male porn magazine) or indeed hide (the brown paper cover) this to the public at large are factors enabled by new technologies—opening new markets and modes of consumption for erotic fiction and/or porn.

This, again, is a significant element of the *Fifty Shades* phenomenon, and indeed a symbolic manifestation of the values and purposes of modern science as shaped by capitalist market economics: that, from an economic-cultural standpoint, a pinnacle of our technological innovation in reading and publishing is to enable and make it acceptable—or even 'culturally compulsory' (Parker, 2012: online)—for women to access porn freely at all times and in public as an act, if not of sexual liberation, then of consumer choice. As in many online activities, 'people [are] able to indulge their curiosities anonymously . . . the taboo has been removed' (Donahue, 2012: online). But where one taboo has been eliminated, it seems that this is only to make way for repetition and/or more to take its place and be similarly violated, marketed and dispelled; Naughton (2012) observes the increasing incorporation of BDSM, LGBT, multiple partners and polyamory into mainstream romance publishing in the wake of *Fifty Shades*. As one commissioning editor of a major publishing house lamented in the wake of the phenomenal *Fifty Shades*, 'We are awash with porn.'

I think I am justified in surmising that such a phenomenon would not have been among the predicted benefits of science, technology and global market capitalism as envisaged by the early modern philosophers whose works inaugurated such a nexus that is modernity, not least in their advocacy of literacy and universal education (to include women and girls) and the expansion of scientific knowledge as remedies for the social evils of their time, as for instance in the notable case of Descartes. That such a device as the e-reader is yet another example of the little hand-held glass screen that was discussed in the previous chapter puts yet another spin on the anxiety of the 'glass delusion', and the capacity of women (and the market) to exploit these fears and fantasies with spectacularly profitable results, and all in the name of 'freedom', 'liberation', 'desire' and 'choice'.

The upshot in terms of evil and its liberating potential as manifest in erotic literature? The media commentary on *Fifty Shades* has been extensive, but here is a taste. 'S&M has gone mainstream ...' unleashing '...a deluge of literary smut' (Arnold-Ratliff, 2012: 54). The apparent removal of taboo is instructive. While the derivative imaginings of Sade have become acceptable, even the norm, what was previously normal among women readers has become even more so: the entrenchment of gender roles (i.e. male/dominant, female/submissive); the desire for romance and love especially as enshrined in the institution of marriage and romance. And this desire as an instigator for the publishing market is conveniently retrospective in its reconstituted nostalgia for the era of romanticism itself:

> The search for strong stories and characters has led some writers to spice up out-of-copyright classic novels. November brings the publication of [sic] one but two erotic versions of Charlotte Bronte's *Jane Eyre*: Eve Sinclair's *Jane Eyre Laid Bare* (St. Martin's Griffin) and Karena Rose's *Jane Eyrotica* (Skyhorse). 'In July of this year, we launched a new line called Clandestine Classics,' says Claire Siemaszkiewicz, the chief executive officer of Total-E-Bound Publishing...

What is interesting is that such classics are currently being read and re-written and re-read as if such sexual 'tensions' were already there, and that contemporary readers are now in the fortunate position to see these (quite literally) sub-narratives finally exposed:

> Whenever I read classics from authors like Charlotte Bronte, I was drawn to the underlying sexual tension between the characters. Readers will finally be able to read what the books could have been like if erotic romance had been acceptable in that day and age. And if venerated works of literature can be reinvented as vehicles for erotic fantasy, truly no taboos may be left.
>
> (Naughton, 2012: online)

The outcome would seem to be that 'Sex sells, but what women really crave is love' (Donahue, 2012: online). It might also be said that what women also really crave is stuff, given the prominence and proximity, even amalgamation, as in *Fifty Shades*, of sex with shopping and consumerism. Donahue (ibid.) calls this the 'lifestyle porn' element of the book and a noteworthy contributor to its success.

As we have also observed previously in relation to female sexuality and evil, levity and ridicule are time-honoured ways of neutralizing any potential revolutionary or liberating aspects of such discourses, and in this respect, regardless of its revolutionary or reactionary connotations, *Fifty Shades* has certainly received its fair share of satirical attention in the form of numerous parodies. Andrew Shaffer produces one such text 'Fifty Shames of Earl Grey' on his blog *Evil Reads*, re-establishing the link between such texts, the act of reading, writing and evil.

Summary and conclusion

By way of a summary of main themes of narrative and evil addressed in this and the previous two chapters of this book, I would highlight these main points with respect to evil and narrative. The human condition, notably in the face of evil and suffering, demands narrative and its components (e.g. language, symbolism, imagination, genres, therapies) as primary sources for dealing with and making sense of the chaotic raw experience of evil—whether from the inner, outer, intimately shared or cosmically transcendent worlds. With the inauguration of ever more highly mediated communications technologies and politically and ideologically contested virtual realities, the importance of narrative becomes ever more amplified as people struggle to 'tell their stories' in a manner that will capture the public imagination. Narrative, and narratology, focuses on how we make sense of the world around us, ourselves and our past and imagined futures through the subjectively active and socially engaged acts of storytelling. It is concentrated on the richness of (inherited) genres and the innovative creativity of new generations of storytellers, as for example with *Fifty Shades*, the melding of pornography with the fairy tale and romance. While there is the widespread temptation to label such phenomena as something radically new, it is in all likelihood that much of the source of the popularity of such texts is their utilization of what are basically conventional generic norms based on gender and sexuality (as well as class), albeit with a twist (such as BDSM, or in Jane Austen period dress etc.). When it comes to producing and consuming both popular and elite texts purporting to explore the boundaries of sexual freedom and/or erotic love, the all too familiar tropes of (masculine) aggression and violence and (feminine) submission and victimhood are often referred to as frameworks. However, as many writers such as the Marquis de Sade, Georges Bataille, Erica Jong and Sylvia Plath illustrate, such well-worn conventions of literature, philosophy and culture can be seriously and even gloriously explored and contested, even as they fuel further controversy, or even incite personal psychosis or moral panic.

The title of this chapter, 'Evil and Literature', is taken from Bataille, who accused literature as being guilty in its intimate proximity to evil. Literary writers know about evil, and they communicate this precious and dangerous knowledge through their work. This is what readers/audiences want. Such communication is necessary through the art of storytelling because reason and rationality have, as the Romantics and writers like Bataille, Sade and others insist, singularly failed in their ability to live up to Enlightenment claims. This is not an immoral task, but just the opposite, amorality being the new morality in this construction of moral relativity and freedom as liberation from any and all restrictions to pleasure and erotic fulfilment. Bataille, like Nietzsche, states that the need now is for 'hypermorality': morality beyond rules and the moral law. 'Literature is *communication*. Communication requires loyalty. A rigorous morality results from the complicity in the knowledge of Evil, which is the basis of intense communication' (Bataille, 2006: ix). Communication between human beings as more but also less than rational, that is to say, emotional, sensual, brutal and animalistic beings connected to a long and verdant past is the main theme of this chapter. It differs from the approaches in the first section, of course, by its (partial) departure from the orthodoxy of religion and philosophy, and in particular its increasing concentration on the self as an emotional and embodied, and sexually active, pain-inducing and abuse-suffering being.

So where does this leave science as the source of knowledge about evil, about actually *doing* it, for instance in the form or real-life crime and social deviance beyond the realms of literature and storytelling? This is the question that will guide the next and final section of this book, devoted to the social scientific approaches to evil. In these chapters, we will encounter real 'ordinary decent' criminals as well as the monsters and villains of history, and also the odd witch and serial killer, as a follow-on to our mothers, monsters, zipless fuckers and whores.

Part III
Evil and the Social Sciences

7
Doing Evil: Crime, Compulsion and Seduction From the Standpoint of Social Psychology and Anthropology

This chapter is the first of three in the last main section of this book, each focusing on the treatment of evil in the social sciences, including psychology, anthropology, sociology, history and politics. Like previous chapters, this section anticipates the final chapter by asking whether or not criminology should begin to reconsider evil and take the possibility of evil as a criminological concept and its study more seriously. In this chapter, we will pose the simple question asked by many if not all people in the wake of terrible (often but not always criminal) acts: why do people *do* evil things? Are they mad, bad or just in the wrong place at the wrong time? As many people often ask me, are some individuals born evil, do they become evil or is this just a convenient category for the rest of us to label criminals and deviants as 'other'? Why does evil happen, and why are 'ordinary' members of the public and the media—along with judges and police officers—so eager to denounce those who are responsible as 'evil', while academics and other such as parole and social workers are so resistant to use such language? And is it, in the final analysis, either useful or advisable for the public, the legal profession or academics to resort to such themes, categories and behaviours when things go so terribly wrong? In other words, does branding serial killers, paedophiles, rapists, dictators etc. as evil do anything to protect us from future atrocity and victimization? If so, how? And if not, why not?

In many ways, these questions get to the heart not just of criminology but contemporary theodicy, the 'problem of evil', for our times (e.g. what it means, whether we should apply or jettison the notion, and how scholarly research and higher education should treat a concept that has such currency in the public sphere and popular imagination). In delving into these questions, I will refer to theoretical concepts and frameworks considered in previous chapters. The examples I have chosen here are selected from some of the classics of social psychology, landmarks in the study both of evil and social anthropology and psychology that are still powerful and affecting projects, which raise many important issues and vital questions: these are Stanley Milgram's obedience experiment and Philip Zimbardo's Stanford Prison experiment. To these two classic studies in social psychology (and their recent updates) I will also consider a third landmark work published in the 1980s by Jack Katz, taken from the criminological canon, which uses ethnographic methodologies derived from anthropology to explore and analyse why people do such terrible things, and why these behaviours and narratives about them are so seductive.

As Katz explains in his landmark book *Seductions of Crime: Moral and Sensual Attractions in Doing Evil* (1988), criminology (along with most if not all of the other social sciences with the possible exception of anthropology) has so far been singularly neglectful of the significance of evil and its influence on crime, criminality, deviance and social control. Why? This is generally put down to the predominance of theoretical frameworks such as materialism, structuralism and positivism in the social sciences prior to the 'cultural turn' of the 1960s, which affected all the social sciences, criminology arguably more than most. This comparatively 'hard' science approach that dominated the interwar years focused overwhelmingly on the need to identify the scientifically proven and empirically observable and verifiable *causes* of criminal behaviour. Depending upon the theoretical position adopted (e.g. biological, psychological, sociological), such 'causal' factors had the epistemological characteristics of being isolated and determined outside of the criminal him- or herself (e.g. in sociological theories, as a result of poverty, social exclusion, marginalization, poor educational attainment and so forth); in a psychological abnormality within personality (such as a personality disorder or some other form of mental illness in psychological theories); or alternatively in a biological fault or predisposition (the much sought after criminal genes in biological theories). Generally speaking, these can be mapped according to Zimbardo's (2007) *situational* versus *dispositional* paradigms—that people are bad because of their surroundings or inherently bad in themselves. Or as Zimbardo put it even more succinctly, this equates basically to the 'bad apples' versus 'bad barrels' divide.

It is such causal factors of social and/or individual pathology that have been accorded status within the social sciences as key variables in the phenomenology of crime, to varying degrees of emphasis in the history of the social sciences (as we will see). However, the impact of other influences such as the sensual or emotional payoff of actually *doing* crime have been notable by their absence from the criminological literature—the fact that some people break the law or do what they know is wrong because they actually enjoy it or get a buzz out of it, or for some other reason *feel* compelled to do it. It is these motivational factors—e.g. emotions, seductions, passions, compulsions, bodily responses etc.—that Katz considers key to the ontological and qualitative realities of crime that he observed in his ethnographic research have been overlooked, and hence focused on in his work. From his research, Katz claims that people do evil and commit crime because they get something out of it, whether it is a sense of empowerment, pride, pleasure, arousal or some such emotional or corporeal reward. Those who commit criminal acts speak (when they do) of these motivational factors as key to their actions all the time; ignoring these as irrelevant or spurious leaves criminological theories that focus on too narrow a view of rationality, psychology and/or social interactions missing important pieces of the explanatory puzzle.

Time to rethink crime?

One aim of Katz's theory is to reconsider the nature of crime altogether, recognizing (as did Durkheim before him) that however pernicious it is, like evil, crime is in some sense necessary to ensure the development and vitality—and indeed humanity and moral evolution—of real, living societies. Evil and crime will always be with us; no security or police regime will ever eliminate them, nor should they (apropos Durkheim's 'normality of crime' thesis). While this doesn't mean we should simply give up and passively acquiesce to criminality or the suffering of evil it entails, at the same time, as Katz insists, it is important to recognize that many of those who commit crime do so because for some reason they want to. In other words, there is a compelling reason for doing so, and this in itself is not always a completely negative thing; what is more, viewing crime as a completely negative phenomenon doesn't help us in trying to understand criminal behaviour let alone deal with it as effectively as possible. As in the previous chapter, desire features here—this is something I *want* to do, I *need* to do it at this moment in time, so I am *going to do it*—if not for reasons of liberation or freedom from repressive norms then for some other enticement or reward.

As in the previous chapter, this leads us to pose some uncomfortable questions: Is crime a form of creativity or self-expression? Is it a good thing that communities are (occasionally) outraged? Is evil/criminality a way of making sense of the world and one's place in it, like any other art form? Does crime differ from other forms of creativity only by its negative consequences (Cropley et al., 2010)? Is creativity always generative or 'good', or is there a 'darker' side to human creativity? And is the 'dark side' of creativity always 'evil'?

According to Katz, some individuals experience criminal behaviours as positively creative: 'As unattractive morally as crime may be, we must appreciate that there is a *genuine experiential creativity* in it as well' (Katz, 1988: 8, original emphasis). In other words, people may be doing crime and/or evil as a way of expressing themselves, using evil or criminality as anything from a way of making sense of the world and their place in it to regarding it virtually as an art form or a way of re-vitalising the common 'good'. In relation to a subject like creative writing covered in the previous chapter, critics and thinkers such as Susan Sontag considered the furtherance and possible refreshment of literary codes within pernicious territory of the 'pornographic imagination' (1983). While it is one thing to reconsider the value or otherwise of smutty books in the rarified atmosphere of literary criticism, it is another thing altogether to convince the person who has had her car tyres slashed or been the victim of a vicious physical attack that these actions somehow comprise an advance in terms of the evolution of human creative endeavour. As we have noted, the real impact of evil on victims, their social networks and society at large is not to be dismissed, and to be fair that is what Katz or others considered here have in mind. This is what the social sciences are for, to realize and recognize these realities, and hopefully do something about it. What is being explored here are the phenomenal complexities of creativity and morality, which can, and do, occasionally go right, but also occasionally go wrong, sometimes spectacularly and catastrophically so. And it is important not to fall into the trap, when thinking of crime, of only looking at 'low-level' criminality or street-level interpersonal violence; corporate or 'white collar' criminals come very much to the fore in this arena, as demonstrated by the knowledge or technological breakthroughs made by academics or other 'pure' scientists that lead to the invention of weapons such as the atomic bomb. Or more recently the collapse in global banking and the apparent contributory factors of a range of 'creative' accounting practices, products and services that—up to the point of collapse—generated a great deal of profit based as a result of the abandonment of traditional principles of transparent and fair dealing in favour of the notion that the consequent 'risks' can somehow be managed or absorbed within the global financial system ad infinitum. But harking back to Kant's theory of evil in Chapter 3, are greed and selfishness merely manageable 'risk factors', or does such a view reveal severe faults in the prevailing moral law and norms of personal character? Some academic researchers in the field of business ethics are currently asking questions about whether or not the aspirational nature of 'creativity' in modern society and business itself can actually *cause* people to act in unethical, dishonest and morally reprehensible ways (e.g. Gino and Ariely, 2011), that these are either possibly elemental to the creative process or attributes of successful individuals (the trick being to be seen to be doing good, overall, or limiting the amount of harm you do to 'acceptable' levels), or both. Is evil about the abandonment of principles and personal integrity, or is it more about exceeding boundaries and getting caught?

Emotions, embodiment, social and institutional norms of status and morality, and the management of social and personal subjectivities all feature as primary issues across these very diverse types of criminal/deviant acts. To return to Katz's explanatory model of criminality, these are what he considers to be the necessary and sufficient joint causes of crime:

- *A path of action*—distinctive practical requirements for successfully committing a crime
- *A line of interpretation*—unique ways of understanding how one is and will be seen by others
- *An emotional process*—special dynamics of seductions and compulsions to commit the crime

(Katz, 1988: 9)

Central to all these experiences in deviance is a member of the *family of moral emotions*: humiliation, righteousness, arrogance, ridicule, cynicism, defilement, and vengeance. In each, the attraction that proves to be most fundamentally compelling is that of overcoming a personal challenge to moral—not to material—existence.

Katz (1988: 9 [emphasis added])

It is important to note that Katz's is not a deterministic model, merely claiming that emotions (these or any others) are on their own responsible for crime. Rather, there is an implicit critique here, pointing out how significant things like emotions, sensuality and the body are to how and why people (including but not limited to criminal offenders) who do 'wrong' or 'deviate', even when they know they are or that they shouldn't but *feel* they actually *should*. Katz situates his theory among the tradition of social interactionism, focusing on the 'foreground' issues that make people *want* to commit crime, which he opposes to the 'background' search for the *causes* of crime such as social deprivation, marginalization or individual pathology (we will return to this element of 'want' in our discussions of Milgram's obedience experiments). This latter approach he identifies with the positivist/empirical criminological theories which he claims portray the criminal agent as a passive 'black box' that is coerced by external forces to commit crime. From his point of view, it is these types of positivist/empirical explanations that are partial and unrealistic, not least, as with Kant's critique of the rational theodicy argument of evil, in that they tend to excuse the evildoer by placing the causes outside of him or herself in other external forces over which they have no control. In other words, explanation becomes tantamount to excuse, even excoriation, locating causes outside of the individual and hence making it at least look like it's not their fault; they are not morally to blame. It is this dynamic that tends to give the social sciences in general, and social psychology (and to some extent criminology) in particular, a bad name in the public mind as when obviously bad people do evil things and cause suffering to others people get upset and want, even need, to point the finger and denounce (Miller, 2005). More to the point, such explanations don't tell us why some individuals are affected in a manner that leads them to criminality, while others are not, making these 'hard' science theories rely on a kind of 'magic' that defines this transition. This is not to say that there isn't some type of sorcery going on in regard to explaining how and why crimes happen, a process often conjured by those who are doing it. Taking into consideration a wealth of information available on why offenders do what they do (e.g. biographies, news reports, interviews, court records etc.), when criminals talk about what motivated them to do what they did, often other rationales are brought to bear, as we will see.

This is what I understand Katz's view of the matter with regard to criminological theory to be. However, from a certain perspective, it is possible to detect elements of his approach in some of our most established positivist Enlightenment-based criminological theories, such as Rational Choice Theory and Routine Activities Theory, albeit with a difference (arguably of emphasis). While these other more conventional theories with their roots in early modern models of 'economic man' and the utilitarian calculus of risk and reward typically concentrate on the empirical nature of crime and criminality, embedded in the so-called 'pleasure' nexus is, naturally enough, the emotional payoff. Even the most 'economic man' weighs up among the potential costs and bene- fits vital elements such as feelings of self-worth, social status, the desire to be seen as 'strong', 'hard' or 'wanted' or to simply be entertained, excited and exciting, and fun. As Tremblay (2004) argues in relation to routine activities and rational choice theories, crime and criminality are often embedded in intensively complex interpersonal relationships, with particularly the search for 'suitable' co-offenders being key to con- structing the original motivation to commit crime; whether this relates to the capacity to bring together a diverse range of people (e.g. as famously described in *The Fence* and other narratives) or to appeal to a homogenous subcultural group (e.g. (ex)prisoners) for the purpose, what Bourdieu called the habitus of the body and emotions (especially those relating to attraction, competence and shame) are significant. A criminological theory like Katz's tends to elevate these less empiri- cally observable aspects in terms intimate/emotional bonds to a more prominent position as explanatory variables, compared with positivist theories like rational choice and routine activities theories, which grant these some limited, but less primary, status.

As with Routine Activities Theory, for those working in the phe- nomenological tradition of ethnography like Katz, the crucial site for observing the implications of these elemental aspects of criminal decision-making is in the micro situations and orientations of every- day life. So while the outcomes and implications of these theories may diverge wildly in terms of epistemological and methodological frameworks and conceptual focus, the significance granted to emotional life, identity maintenance, social interaction, corporeal habitation and moral values on the construction of criminal 'motivation' is still there (see, for example, Clarke and Felson, 2004). It's how these elements are *situated* and *interpreted* in their conceptual narrative stratagems that dif- fer. For Katz, the process of channelling a 'raw' emotion like rage and 'forming' it into more 'spiritual' or 'subjective' emotions like humil- iation so that people can justify and hence allow themselves to act violently that is central; again, this brings into question the function of factors such as impulsivity in criminality which tend to focus more on pathology and/or lack of control in the isolated individual who is perceived as comparatively speaking a passive rather than active con- tributor to making the motivation to commit of crime. On the contrary, what we see when we drill down to the nitty-gritty of criminal events and behaviours using more ethnographic methods like Katz's is that such episodes and experiences are far from thoughtless or impulsive as often depicted. Crime is thus not necessarily a consequence of lack of character or loss of control. Instead of reverting to empirically observable 'factors' or narrowly construed models of rationality, criminologists like Katz (and his heirs in cultural criminology) look to more qualitative and phenomenological epistemologies such as narrative, symbolic interactionism or ethnography as ways to represent, analyse and explain what's actually going on in these lived and felt processes.

In much the same was as Katz utilizes a range of secondary data, let us now utilize some existing research to explore these aspects of Katz's theory. Consider these examples taken from Shadd Maruna's *Making Good* (2001), excerpts from his interviews with persistent male offenders from Liverpool who had been rehabilitated who talked about their former behaviour and lives:

> I used to enjoy it, the offending. I would enjoy doing what I did, just burgling, joy riding, shoplifting... I enjoyed the rush... But I used to buy friends as well. I've always liked attention. I've always liked to have a lot of people around me, and again, if I had the money I would take me friends out for a drink. (Male, age 28).
>
> Maruna (2001: 82)

> I was starting to enjoy the sort of fame in school, like the big car thief. Everyone wanted to know me and find out what I was doing and that. We weren't even selling [the car parts] then. It was just the sheer excitement. The speed of the car. (Male, age 24).
>
> Maruna (2001: 82)

In their interviews, these young men describe first-hand how they find in criminality the pleasure and life-affirming joy of popularity, attention and excitement. Maruna finds many other examples from interviews with these persistent offenders to do with drug addiction and joyriding. Is this to stave off the alienation and fragmentation of modern social life they experience in Liverpool where they have little chance of living out these emotions in other more legitimate ways, or for some other reasons? Even committing a seemingly small and putatively 'victimless' crime like shoplifting something one doesn't need might serve the much more important purpose of the thrill of 'getting away with it', providing evidence of the personal competence of the perpetrator, especially if it is under the nose of the authorities.

But the importance of emotions doesn't just apply to the 'fun and games' of small-time crime. Katz continues:

> For the impassioned killer, the challenge is to escape a situation that has come to seem otherwise inexorably humiliating. Unable to sense how he or she can move with self-respect from the current situation, now, to any mundane-time relationship that might be reengaged, then the would-be killer leaps at the possibility of embodying, through the practice of 'righteous' slaughter, some eternal, universal form of the good.
>
> (Katz, 1988: 9)

With this in mind, let us consider another example from Maruna's interviews with another participant in the Liverpool desistance project:

> I said, 'Give me the fucking chain back,' and he pulled a knife out at me and his friend had got this baseball bat...I went home, and just couldn't sleep, you know. I kept waking up at, like, 2 a.m., saying 'I can't deal with this.' My girl was telling me to calm down, let it go. But I kept thinking to myself, 'This is going to have to be something big.' This isn't going to be just a fist fight. This is going to be big... Everybody in the scene knew I was looking for him... (Eventually) I met him at the pub. I brought this knife and I stabbed him... Unless you actually grew up in that situation, you wouldn't understand what I was going through. Common sense is just different in that situation. You just don't have the same common sense. Lying in bed, really, I think about it a lot. 'If this, if that,' but then the 'ifs' go away and you just have to say, 'This is the real you.' I had no choice really. You do nothing and you get written off the scene altogether. Street-wise, that's suicide—you're back to the bottom of the ladder, you're nobody. Sensible-wise, of course, that's the best thing that could happen to you. That means taking the alternative route with the suit and job and all. But I've got a rough streak in me somewhere... I had to do it. (Male, age 27).
>
> Maruna (2001: 41–42)

Here, we see a powerful and articulate account of the 'common sense' or even 'rational choice' explanation of, in this instance, violent or 'knife' crime and attempted murder, the kind of background context we don't often get from the news. Offenders like this young man have to assess the 'street-wise' rationality against its 'sensible-wise' counterpart when making their decisions about how to act on the ground, in their real daily lives in response to such situations. Clearly, his head, and his girlfriend, are telling him one thing while his heart and the 'street' are telling him another. In the end, dealing with the humiliation of having the chain taken from him in front of others was simply too much to bear, and he acted accordingly from this emotional and psychological compulsion to recover a sense of agency and respect. It may not be nice or legal, but it does in a way make sense and fulfil an emotional need to maintain a viable identity and personal and public self-esteem. The important thing to acknowledge is that while this might represent a deviation from 'normal' codes of morality, for the agent in question, it is nevertheless an action that is located in a moral sphere and the outcome of a reflexive process of moral decision-making. In his community setting, this is not a deviant or immoral act, though it might be technically a 'crime'.

Deviance is a major, and sometimes again often overlooked, consideration, this aspect of 'otherness' and departure from the normal path of righteousness that is so central to evil. Let's look again at what Katz says about the centrality of a 'family' of emotions in the compulsion to commit crime: 'Central to all these experiences in deviance is a member of the family of moral emotions: humiliation, righteousness, arrogance, ridicule, cynicism, defilement, and vengeance. In each, the attraction that proves to be most fundamentally compelling is that of overcoming a personal challenge to moral—not to material—existence' (Katz, 1988: 9). Note here the reference to 'defilement' as a symbolic category (echoing Ricoeur's theory discussed in Chapter 4). Clearly, the young man involved in the incident with the chain was struggling to deal with the damage and defilement to his identity—what the symbolic interactionist sociologist Erving Goffman would have termed his new 'spoiled' identity—and the consequences that would accrue to him in his everyday life in the aftermath. There is notably no expression of a desire to indulge in violent retribution on the part of this erstwhile victim and soon-to-be offender; on the contrary, if anything, he seems to be personally reluctant to commit a violent crime. But on his reasoning, weighing up the various options open to him (or those that he allows), the option of taking violent action himself is the best of a bad lot, and so he *has* to do it. On the other hand, there is the recognition that one alternative is to remove himself from this environment and get a proper job, an option he acknowledges but then quickly dismisses; reporting the incident to the police isn't even countenanced; in his moral sphere it doesn't even feature on the radar, and that says a lot too. Among other things, this assessment of the situation puts something of a different spin on the thesis that criminality is deterministically linked to social exclusion and/or marginalization; in this instance, at least, the prospect of gainful employment is a realistic if quickly discarded possibility. That the job in question might have been associated with a lifestyle that paled in comparison with life in a place where violent crime is an organizing principle is concerning, and we are apparently not talking burger-flipping here. This man appears to imply that obtaining a job that requires wearing a suit is a viable possibility. This raises a number of further and interesting questions about the personal motives and social situations of those who 'do' serious crime and consciously assume the identity of a violent criminal, even when that is not something an individual is particularly keen to do as a matter of impulsivity, aggressiveness or moral weakness, and even when they are aware they may have other non-violent and law-abiding options.

The use of language here is important; the words chosen by those who imagine and create the story of why they are compelled to offend. Katz invites us to consider the spatial metaphors of serious criminals, like torturers, Mafiosi and serial killers; they want to 'intimidate[e] others and take them into their world' (Katz, 1988: 9). Again, echoing Ricoeur, this mimics the behaviours of primordial gods, whereby serial killers flaunt their *senseless* (from a normatively rational standpoint) and often *motiveless* (in the Kantian sense of the diabolical) 'cold-blooded' killing. In other words, this is from a normal social and human perspective an irrational and pointless act; there is no obvious benefit accruing to the killer in any rational sense. The great thing about having a range of different 'worlds' on offer is that you can enter and leave them, and even populate and annihilate them, as the spirit moves you. As with the myths of primordial evil, the actions of such 'gods' and semi-human godlike figures are not constrained by the morality of what Nietzsche (and many serial killers) would denounce as the 'herd' mentality.

The narratives of serial killers evoke primordial creation myths by way of artificially manipulating and temporarily redrawing boundaries between the sacred and profane, not least in their symbolic transference of the victim from ordinary social counterpart to an object worthy of sacrifice. What is pivotal is the creation through symbolic rituals, actions and language of and control over new or alternative 'worlds' and beings, again, taking actions on others beyond the strictures of normative human moral laws in imitation of the myth of the primordial evil god. As a brief reminder, the myth of primordial evil as described by

Ricoeur (1967) is very ancient, with evil treated as being primordial and in existence before the creation of the cosmos as we know it. Prior to the creation, existence (such as it was, among the gods) was dominated by chaos, violence and conflict, and it is the remnants of those pre-human battles involving evil gods that are inherited by humans. In this type of myth, we see the emergence of hero, the god or demi-god who challenges the evil of the reigning god. These narratives are often shaped by tragedy. They contain a violent, simplistic and naïve conception of evil whereby ritual re-enactment of the original cosmic battle of good versus evil is required. Ritual functions as a way to redemption, and a way of managing or dispelling contemporaneous evil, but vestiges of evil always remain. Hence, the cyclical pattern, the need to replay tragic and violent events in the interests of maintaining the 'good'. Those whom Katz calls 'cold-blooded killers' want to evoke a sense of dread as described in the tradition of mythical narrative (Ricoeur), to create a place to act out their violent fantasies in the powerful, supra-moral, godlike role (psychoanalysis, Sade, Bataille), and have often spent time in institutions such as prisons, reformatories, seminaries or 'care' (Sade, Bataille). This constitutes a primitive rendering of evil in the form of a tragic narrative, with the attendant characterizations and role play many serial killers try to reproduce between themselves and their victims. It is constructed upon the narrative of a semi-private ritual that due to its fragile temporality and the persistence of evil as an original condition must be repeated time and again, and/or rendered reproducible for the killer via simulacral objects or 'trophies' that can evoke the original experience of evil and encounter with the sacrificial victim. There is a massive, diverse and seemingly growing appetite for books on serial and/or cold-blooded killers, so I will for reasons of space leave this figure here. But I include this here to gesture back to the chapter on Ricoeur's phenomenological hermeneutic theory of the narratives and symbolism of evil as a way of construing what is, for most people, that most prevalent of deviant and evil rationalizations in the current popular imagination. Like the young man with the chain, such offenders often go take great pains in creating a narrative justification and/or spatial and temporal arena for their actions, albeit one that is quite selective or distorted in what it recognizes and dismisses from the perspective of the moral hegemony. While this might still make it wrong, it doesn't mean it is mindlessly or diabotically 'evil' in the sense often conveyed in the media or in rational discourse.

Before moving on to the study of evil from the perspective of social psychology and two of the most (in)famous projects in the history of the social sciences, I would like to conclude this section with some general reflections on the study of evil from the social interactionist/ethnographic/phenomenological/hermeneutic tradition as exemplified in the work of Katz. As Macfarlane (1985: 58) says, 'One of the most puzzling problems for anthropologists has for a long time been why different societies should have opted for different sets of explanation [of evil] and also why such sets should change'. The search is then for a set of background factors that can explain these constellations of explanatory frameworks and the reasons behind them and mechanisms through which they are transformed. Generally speaking, Macfarlane (1985) finds that there is a generic link between the concept of evil in a society and its shifting relevance as an explanatory concept shaping and determining the 'world' as it is generally perceived by those who inhabit it. Evil is thus a fairly 'weakly developed or absent' (Macfarlane, 1985: 58) concept in 'primitive' or hunter-gatherer societies, being mainly applied to members of other communities or abstract, non-human entities who come and go as they please from these 'other' realms. The more densely populated and complex a society is, the more dynamic and morally relevant is their notion of evil, with the authoritative management of the 'magic' of religious-theological power and orthodoxy becoming more urgent and institutionalized. In highly complex modern industrial capitalist societies, we can say that what Max Weber called the 'de-magicification' or disenchantment of the world results in the reconstitution of evil, with the jettisoning of its supernatural qualities in favour of its potential for the purposes of fantasy (Macfarlane, 1985). If this is the case, then evil becomes a matter for social science, specifically the 'criminological imagination' (Young, 2011), a representation of the problem of evil that is (for most moderns) free of what is normatively deemed to be the outmoded constraints of theology, philosophy and religion. While this is a standpoint that results in an anxious and vertiginous postmodernist tendency to see evil as a matter of serendipity and chance (see Dearey, 2012), this anxiety is somewhat ameliorated by the repositioning of evil people and evildoers in scientific disciplines devoted to their study, such as psychology and social psychology, to which we will turn now.

Experiments in evil: The obedience and Stanford Prison experiments

In the remainder of this chapter we will turn our attention to two 'experiments' in why people do evil things are probably among the most (in)famous in all of the social sciences: Stanley Milgram's obedience study and Philip Zimbardo's Stanford Prison Experiment.

First to Milgram: Milgram's research was set against the background of an extremely violent and destructive twentieth century, in which things like institutional systems of governance, scientific and techno-logical advances and political ideologies were harnessed not to improve the quality of modern life (as the Enlightenment thinkers had so opti-mistically predicted) but rather to use such systems and technologies to put millions of people to their death in as efficient and brutal manner as possible as evidence by a seemingly endless number of genocides and in the Shoah or Holocaust. Clearly, as Milgram pointed out, the Holocaust could not be the work of just one individual, however diabolically evil, not even if he was working in league with a small cadre of his political supporters. For such massive and devastating destruction to take place on this scale, many, many 'normal' ordinary people, most of whom did not even ascribe to the Nazi ideology, had to be complicit if not actively engaged in these processes. And so, in the post-WWII period, the question presented itself to Milgram, why do people acquiesce to the inhuman, evil dictates of leaders like Hitler and the ideology of murder-ous hatred on such a massively destructive scale and with such frequent historical recurrence? Why do people obey such authority, even when they don't necessarily want to? Why don't they disobey more stridently and more often, why don't people stand up to corrupt authorities for what they know is right?

The details of Milgram's experiments are contained in his writings which he began to publish in 1963, and the many commentaries and follow-ups to the original study. But to give a brief summary, he pre-sented the study to potential volunteers as a project to do with learning and memory. The volunteer would be the 'teacher' who would work an impressive-looking but fake machine that would deliver a series of increasingly devastating electric shocks to the 'learner' strapped to a chair in an adjacent room with a glass window who was, in fact, an actor and was only pretending to be hurt by the shocks. The shocks on the machine ranged from 15 to 450 volts (labelled 'Danger—Severe Shock'). In the room with the 'teacher' was the person in charge in a white coat and with a clipboard who directed the 'teacher'/participant to deliver what he or she thought were actual shocks to the 'learner' when that person made a mistake in remembering matching pairs of words. The point of the experiment was to see how far volunteers would go in administering painful shocks to a defenceless, protesting person in the name of scientific experimentation when directed by an authority figure. The results astounded everyone. Despite the agonizing screams of the 'learner' at 285 volts and his pleading to be released, the majority of volunteers refused to respond to these entreaties and continued to deliver shocks to the distressed and apparently suffering 'learner', some going on to deliver the full 450 volts. Instead, the volunteers continued to respond to the comparatively mild prods by the experimenter, which included:

'Please continue'.

'The experiment requires that you continue. It is absolutely essential that you go on. You have no choice but to go on.'

Milgram began his experiment into the social psychology of evil by wondering how many people would refuse to deliver any shocks—and why would they do this? The surprising thing was how many people complied with harming another human being who had never done anything to them, and how much they were willing to harm them simply in response to what could only be considered to be mild prompting by an authority figure.

> Many subjects will obey the experimenter no matter how vehement or insistent are the demands of the person being shocked, no matter how painful the shocks to him, and no matter how he pleads, yells, or begs to be let out. This was seen time and again in our studies, and has been observed in several universities where the experiment was repeated. It is the extreme willingness of adults to go to almost any lengths on the command of an authority that constitutes the chief finding of the study and the fact most urgently demanding explanation.
>
> Milgram (1968: 3)

For Milgram, this finding explodes the 'monster' theory of evil, whereby it is the sadistic monsters that live on the fringes of society who are responsible for the great atrocities of modern history. Rather, what Milgram and others who have replicated his experiment found is that it is the banal faith in authority and their projects, and the ordinary inbuilt duty to obedience to these authorities that accounts for untold suffering delivered systematically to undeserving victims.

> This is, perhaps, the most fundamental lesson of our study: that ordinary people, simply doing their jobs, and without any particular

hostility on their part, can become agents in a terrible destructive process. Moreover, even when the destructive effects of their work become patently clear, and they are asked to carry out actions incompatible with fundamental standards of morality, relatively few people have the resources needed to resist authority. A great variety of inhibitions against disobeying authority come into play and successfully keep the person in his place.

Milgram (1968: 3)

The truth is, moral prescriptions not to do harm can be shunted aside with astonishing ease by careful manipulation of the social situation. Again, evil is not about mad or bad people, but bad situations. What Milgram's experiment, time and again, tells us is that evil, sometimes of catastrophic proportions, can be the outcome of how normal or decent individuals behave in certain social contexts.

So, why do people tend to obey the experimenter? Milgram says this is due to a complex of what he called 'binding factors' that lock the subject into the situation:

1. *Politeness*—a desire to uphold initial promise to help the experimenter and the awkwardness of withdrawal.
2. *Number of adjustments to the subject's thinking* that undermine his ability to break with authority, e.g.:

   a. The maintenance of relationship with experimenter and the reduction of 'strain' produced by the experimental conflict.
   b. This latter happens as an outcome of the tendency for people to become absorbed in the narrow technical performance of the task, so much so that they lose sight of the broader consequences of their actions.
   c. They also become immersed in the operation of the apparatus, the technology, operating the machine.
   d. Their desire to put on a competent performance overrides any moral concern.
   e. Significantly, they entrust the broader task of goal-setting and the assessment of morality to the authority figure, the experimenter.
   f. The most common adjustment for the obedient subject is not to see him/herself as responsible for their own actions, but rather to absolve responsibility onto the authority. The infamous Nuremburg defence: 'I was only obeying orders'.

3. *Context dominates meaning*—for a 'greater good' or 'noble cause', such as benefiting society or pursuing scientific truth, individuals will

override their moral sensibilities and absolve themselves of personal responsibility. So actions that might be construed as 'evil' in isolation will be seen as justifiable in their new contexts.

4. *Devaluing of the victim*—victims are less important than the overall goal.

5. *Systems*—the moral responsibility for evil is dissipated over systems and the involvement of multiple players, roles and layers of bureaucracy. No one person decides to carry out the evil act and is faced with its consequences, e.g. the pilot who drops the bomb, the inventor of Zyklon B gas, the mafia boss who orders the hit.

6. Therefore, the problem of evil is not merely a matter of psychology— i.e. of 'bad' or 'mad'—but rather of *situational* factors, the construction of social contexts within which evil can take place where it is unlikely that anyone will stop it. If anything, we are psychological disposed as social beings to do our 'duty' by following orders, striving to be seen as personally competent, and absolving ourselves of moral responsibility for our actions.

(from Milgram, 1968)

The Lucifer Effect

In many ways, Zimbardo's *Lucifer Effect: How Good People Turn Evil* (2007) is similar to Milgram's obedience experiment in that they both prioritize the notion that evil emerges from the dynamics of individual psychology and social situations, as opposed to emanating from the pathological core of the born evil or sick self. To use Zimbardo's analogy, evil is not so much a case of a few bad apples (as is often argued) as it is about bad barrels (or barrel makers and keepers, it might be more accurate to say).

The Lucifer Effect (2007) is itself the 'effect' of another notorious social scientific experiment on evil. This is the Stanford Prison Experiment (SPE) that took place in August 1971. Again, to briefly summarize, Zimbardo and his team initially wanted to research the effects of imprisonment and the mentality of prisoners and corrections staff. They came up with the idea of the 'Stanford Prison' where they would use a basement in a university building during a two-week holiday period as a makeshift 'prison'. For their 'subjects' they recruited two dozen 'normal' young men to take part in the experiment, randomly assigning the roles of 'inmate' and 'guard' to each half of the group. As with Milgram's obedience experiment, details of the SPE are widely available, and indeed are reproduced in *The Lucifer Effect*, so I won't go into much detail here. Suffice to say that the impact and outcome of this experiment were once again quite unexpected and shocking, as things started to go badly wrong rapidly. As Zimbardo himself states, within hours, the situation descended into conflict, chaos and sadistic punishment, with Zimbardo himself and his team finding themselves unwittingly complicit in the suffering of the 'inmates'. Everyone was shocked to see the speed and inventiveness of some the 'normal boys' into sadistic warders, and some of the inmates into passive victims. Even for those few 'good' guards, their goodness notably did not extend to being actively good; that is, intervening on behalf of the prisoners to stop the experiment or prevent the abuse meted out by the 'bad' guards by telling them to desist or reminding them that this was only an experiment. Instead, the 'good' guards mainly went along with the abuse, seeking to intervene only by the rather weak acts of giving someone a cigarette or a blanket in an attempt to ameliorate the inmates' suffering.

In light of Zimbardo's observations during the SPE and other notorious outbreaks of evil in the world since, e.g. the My Lai massacre in Vietnam, the abuse of prisoners at Abu Graib prison in Iraq, the sexual abuse of children within the Roman Catholic Church, the killing of more than 900 members of the People's Temple in Guyana, genocide in Kosovo, Rwanda, Burundi and Darfur, and so forth, he has developed what he calls 'The Lucifer Effect' thesis. This is a further development of Milgram's obedience thesis (in that he reiterates the above findings of Milgram). Like Milgram, Zimbardo challenges the 'dispositional thesis', the notion that that there is a separate species of evil, monstrous people who are bad to the bone and ultimately guilty of the worst atrocities that happen with astonishing recurrence around the world and throughout history, and that it is these 'other' people who are responsible for the atrocious evils that are apparently symptomatic of modern life. He also challenges the idea of the good/evil dichotomy, arguing instead that the evidence strongly shows that all of us are capable of evil, as well as good.

Instead, like Milgram, Zimbardo emphasizes the *situational* nature of social context and the systemic nature of sociopolitical organization over the dispositional factors of individual psychology in the manifestation of evil. This means that a whole dynamic complex of phenomena relating to social contexts and organizational structures can be identified in many if not all of the evil events listed above and more, and that they are not down to a few 'bad apples' in the army, police or prison service etc. In fact, when you take a closer look (as Zimbardo did in his role as expert witness for one of the defendants in the trials following the Abu Graib abuses), some of the people who are implicated in carrying out these evil acts are in actuality decent, even very good, people. What is 'bad' is the situations in which they find themselves in and are forced to act, where they are left to their own devices for the most part, where there is little or no oversight and rules are not enforced by those who are in charge, and the 'enemy'—the people who are on the receiving end of the evil—are systematically dehumanized and de-individualized, having their suffering denied or implying that they somehow 'deserve' what they get. Otherwise, it wouldn't be happening.

What is more, the stubborn persistence of the 'bad apples' theory of evil only serves to obscure the realities of good and evil, allowing those who hold the *real* responsibility—people in positions of power in organizations such as generals, politicians and so forth—off the hook from a moral point of view. These people benefit from their power and they should be held morally accountable when the systems for which they are responsible break down.

Summary, analysis and conclusion

What makes people do evil things, especially when they know they shouldn't and that others will be harmed because of their actions? The generic explanation from the anthropological and social psychology perspectives is that basically *context matters*. However, much as we may want to identify, isolate and denounce evil monsters, context still matters a lot. 'Context' here is no easy excuse; it is diverse and dynamic—taking in historical, emotional, physical, organizational, and ordinary everyday life. Whether this is broken down in terms of feelings and emotions or identities, relationships and social situations—these contribute to evildoing and criminality in very important and, in criminology at least, often not adequately recognized ways.

Evil does not emerge from a vacuum, and monsters do not arrive from another world, although this doesn't mean that such narratives and myths of evil are not somehow relevant (as, for example, in the rationales of serial killers). As Katz argued, criminals (whether serial murderer or 'badass') often do what they know to be evil in order to evoke these very fears and harness the sense of power that goes with it. According to Milgram and Zimbardo, situational as opposed to dispositional factors are often behind the most atrocious acts of depravity, whereby even 'good' people are complicit in the commission of evil. As with Kant's theory of radical evil, we all have the propensity to do evil within us; it does not emerge from a separate species of 'diabolical' figures. They argue that explanations which seek to distance or label others as evil does not reduce its devastating and atrocious nature, but it actually makes it worse. The truth about evil is both more disturbing and also more hopeful than we might have feared: that any of us, given the right circumstances, can be demons, but also heroes, as Zimbardo strongly argues. It is living with this capacity and its consequences that poses the real challenge for our collective future, and our contemporary global world.

While these represent important, even landmark, contributions to the social scientific study of evil, they are certainly not without controversy. As Miller (2005) records, many scholars who have addressed the thorny and vexed questions surrounding the causes and 'explanations' of the Holocaust have taken issue with Milgram's (and by extension Zimbardo's) focus on obedience and situations. Many critics contest the link between authority and atrocity, pointing out that it wasn't just 'ordinary' and 'decent' people who subjected them or their relatives to appalling, dehumanizing suffering of every conceivable kind, there were also some hateful, anti-Semitic, homophobic and otherwise bigoted sadists seriously at work as well, what about these individuals? Drawing on Katz, didn't they 'do' the torturing and killing because for some reason they 'wanted' to; they actually perversely desired it? And when we speak of such people, aren't we in a different territory here, at the heart of darkness and in the presence of real and true evil that while it may not just be down to context or situations, isn't reducible to this in a meaningful way either?

While these studies in social psychology give important insights into the significance of situations, for many scholars and 'ordinary' people, such explanations are unsatisfactory because, in essence, they let those who are responsible for the killing and other atrocities off the hook. To return to Kant, while evil may be 'radical' in the sense that we are all prone to do it, this does not mean that ' ... there is a Hitler in all of us' (Mandel in Miller, 2005: 222). However, it also doesn't mean that there isn't a Hitler in any of us. There are, sadly, some of them about, and some of those actors will actively seek or even create the social situations and enter the authority roles that enable them to carry out their wicked deeds. Sadism and personal intention, sometimes very highly motivated, comes into play here, at least sometimes and to some extent. While they may exploit their social capital and organizational situations to enable them to pursue their desires, this does not reduce their individual moral culpability for seeking out such positions, situations or roles; if anything, just the opposite. At the same time, the role of the state and its regulatory bodies in being complicit in enabling such people to wield power also requires closer scrutiny and critique. Social scientists are well placed to do this, and so they should.

To some extent, as Miller (2005) notes, the very idea of 'explanation' when it comes to an event as horrendous as the Holocaust is in itself offensive. We will return to this issue in the next chapter. But what most people want from their explanations of evildoing and evildoers is, at the end of the day, not excuses. They want reasons, certainly, and to know that measures will be taken to prevent such abuses in the future, but they also want—they *need*—to blame and condemn (apropos the theodicy), as much as from time to time they need their moral codes to be challenged and changed. These competing and complex needs constitute a recognition of the involvement of emotion, embodiment, identity, relationships and sociality from all sides, from the social collective of victims'/survivors' perspective and the wider public, to deviants and criminals. Evil, even just the word or the designation, seems to be useful in this process; somehow, it appears to deliver something in terms of offering the censure and hunger for justice or change required in such special instances and circumstances. Perhaps the complexity and slipperiness of all of these contradictory elements that lie behind the social and psychological designation of 'evil' is why so many social sciences have traditionally steered clear of it: we are to put it bluntly not normally in the condemning business, but in the fixing or, failing this, risk-management game. However, by disengaging from or ignoring evil, are we really doing ourselves and our disciplines, or academia in general, any real favours in terms of improving the quality of public understanding or debate about crime and atrocity?

What do you think?

8
The Banality of Evil: Genocide, Slavery, Holocaust and War

Chapter 7 addressed the question of why individuals actually *do* evil, focusing on a selection of theories developed from social psychology and ethnography which mainly concentrated on emotional, corporeal and, perhaps most controversially of all, situational factors that dispose people to indulge in such wicked and destructive behaviours, whether criminal, deviant or both. This chapter continues our explorations of social-scientific theories and concepts of evil by focusing on the phenomenon and consequences of what has been called *collective evil*, i.e. the manifestation of evil on a large scale involving and/or with the complicity phenomena such as complicity of many people, including but not limited to genocide, war, holocaust and slavery. Here, we consider the still controversial and challenging thesis about the nature and origins of evil in this atrocious arena as articulated by the philosopher Hannah Arendt, a thesis that she developed during her coverage of the Eichmann trial in 1961, contemporaneously with Stanley Milgram's initial obedience experiments in the early 1960s. From my experience of teaching this subject and text, and indeed from reading the scholarly research on genocide and the like, part of the lasting legacy of Arendt's argument about evil is how it has itself suffered as a result of the need to shock (of more later). According to Arendt, evil is not the result of the exceptional feats of the diabolical monsters, but rather that it is characterized by the banality and ordinariness of its obscuring into daily routines and the thoughtless acquiescence of those who carry it out; or indeed, as Susan Neiman (2002) puts it, evil of this scale is characterized by, if anything, the *lack* of malicious intent. This is a very different argument from that put forward by the likes of Kristeva, Katz, Bataille and Sade in the previous chapters in which evil is construed as intrinsically linked to the deeply personal experience of strong, carnal,

186

sensuous and socially destructive emotions. We will consider Arendt's 'banality of evil' thesis and its relevance to the study of evil and atrocity today and how the legacies of these historical events are dealt with and managed (e.g. the vexed question of apology) within contemporary multicultural societies. We will also reflect on the influence of theories such as those devised by Milgram, Arendt and Zimbardo and how they have contributed to and have been further developed by scholars such as Vetlesen and Staub who have carried out more intensively comparative studies of genocide and developed more complex theories of its dynamics and causes.

The banality of evil: Eichmann in Jerusalem

In 1961, the first ever televised courtroom trial was broadcast to the world from Jerusalem as an Israeli court tried Nazi SS Lieutenant Colonel Adolf Eichmann for crimes against the Jewish people and crimes against humanity. This was not just the first televised trial; it was the first global television media event. Its explosive nature made the O.J. Simpson trial look pale in comparison. Israel's then Prime Minister David Ben-Gurion claimed that he wanted to broadcast the trial to the world in order to educate a generation that had come of age after WWII about the atrocities of the Holocaust, and to claim justice for the many voiceless victims.

The trial was an emotionally charged event that revealed for the first time to a shocked world audience the full horrors of the Nazi campaign to exterminate European Jewry (among the other victims of the Nazis). It followed a period of about 15 or so years during which the horrors of the Holocaust or the *Shoah*, as it is also known, were relatively rarely spoken about (Greenspan, 1998). This temporary silence, or more precisely narrative hiatus, and the eruption of survivor stories about the Holocaust itself and also using it to tell other stories about widespread collective suffering and oppression following the Eichmann trial and the Seven Day War in 1967 is itself fascinating, and will be returned to as a discussion point in due course. For the moment, the purported silence and policing of these particular survivor narratives has been interpreted as having to do with the implicit shame and guilt converging around the killing of 11 million people (at least 5 million of whom were Jews), and also because of the pain of remembrance and the unspeakable nature of these stories—the struggle to articulate on behalf of the individual, the trauma of incredulity and horror on behalf of audiences, and the irrefutable dignity and challenge to accepted moral codes of the nature of humanity and the complicity of modern social institutions and the modern state in the manifestation of such atrocious evil. For the first time, during the course of the Eichmann trial many harrowing personal and previously unheard stories of suffering and loss would be told (often for the first time) to a world audience. The effect was phenomenal; a major cultural event.

Adolf Eichmann's name first surfaced during the Nuremberg Trials in 1945. In 1950, he fled to Argentina with the help of the Nazi underground. The Israeli government sent agents from its secret service Mossad to hunt for him for ten years, eventually finding him living in Buenos Aires with his wife and three sons. In the May 1960, agents from Mossad kidnapped him and forcibly brought him to Israel to stand trial as a war criminal. Eichmann was put on trial for his role in organising the deportation of the Jews of Europe to concentration camps. His defence, like that of other Nazis at Nuremburg, was that he was 'just following orders' (an infamous phrase and rationale for this evildoing that as we recall first inspired the Milgram obedience experiments discussed in Chapter 7). Eichmann was the mastermind behind organizing and moving the Jewish people out of their homes into the ghettoes, and then into the concentration camps. Over the time of his employment, he proved to be the Nazis' foremost Jewish specialist. His ability to organize, categorize and supervise enabled him to achieve murder on a colossal scale. By corralling men, women and children in cattle train cars, he sent millions to their deaths. During the trial, Eichmann sat enclosed within the now iconic glass booth. The Israelis built the booth for his protection because they feared someone would try to kill him before the trial was over, but the staging of the event and the visual impact of his encasement in the glass booth itself have become enshrined in cultural memory. The effect was to make Eichmann appear like a sideshow freak, captured animal, culled vermin, sample virus or a 'clown' as Arendt called him, captive and decidedly 'other' as a species of evil villainy. Such imagery recalls the cultural anxieties involving glass and its brittle and precarious evocation of transparency and separation in the face of evil in modern society as explored in Chapter 2. More than 100 witnesses were called to testify against Eichmann. The courtroom was packed. After an emotional 16-week trial, Eichmann was found guilty on all 15 counts of the criminal indictments against him. He was hanged, his body was cremated and his ashes were scattered in the Mediterranean Sea (a great deal of the factual data regarding the Eichmann trial sourced from PBS Online, undated).

Hannah Arendt was a German-born philosopher who in 1961 covered the Eichmann trial for *The New Yorker* magazine and two years later published a collected version of these works in her book *Eichmann in Jerusalem: A Report on the Banality of Evil* (1977). Arendt's book is an immensely challenging and controversial account of the trial and its true purpose and meaning. For starters, she was sceptical about the Israeli government's real motivation for kidnapping Eichmann and putting on the trial as it was. Was this really about educating people about the reality of the Holocaust, or was it more like a public relations exercise in the form of a 'show trial' to publicize the suffering and victimhood of the Jews—and most of all to demonstrate to the Jewish diaspora how imperilled they actually were in their lives outside Israel and how they couldn't trust any secular government in the defence of justice. Was the Eichmann trial really about justice or was it actually about politics, namely providing fresh legitimacy of the new 'Jewish state' and establishing a narrative rationale of victimhood and peril that would be used to legitimize pre-emptive and ex-officio action by the state of Israel against any of those it perceives to be its enemies to this day? And how could such motives help in making sense of an event of such extreme, ineffable evil, or to prevent such atrocities in the future? What is more, have such politically expedient narratives of scapegoating established in the public imagination during the Eichmann trial actually contributed to the expansion of evil and violation of human rights fuelled by nationalism and the power of the state in the name of 'security', as argued passionately by Jewish intellectuals like Andrea Dworkin (2000)?

Arendt argued that the Holocaust marked—or that it should mark—a rupture in social and political thought, a 'gap' in human history that, while it might be emblematic of evil, was unfortunately not a singularity or unique event by any means (Fine, 2001: 131). What is more, the insistence of the absolute uniqueness and mysteriousness of the Holocaust as a manifestation of inseratable evil on a unique scale as the result of the actions of one evil monster did a disservice to the victims and survivors by obscuring the real truth about it—that it was indeed '... all too understandable, all too continuous with what we are—human, all too human' (Gillian Rose cited in Fine, 2001: 131). And that this very same mundaneness and humanity extended to Eichmann too. It is worth pointing out here that this thesis on evil as banal and on the Holocaust as in some sense not a unique historical occurrence is in almost direct contrast to the thesis she developed in her earlier work *The Origins of Totalitarianism* (1967). This is a live academic issue in itself, which is far from straightforward, but central to her apparent change of view on the matter was the experience of observing the Eichmann trial.

Eichmann: Man or monster?

In her correspondence with her friend the philosopher Karl Jaspers in the run up to the Eichmann trial, Arendt initially expressed her feelings of alarm and anxiety in the face of the extreme and incalculable evil perpetrated by individuals like Eichmann—how could she adequately express her thoughts about the deeds and guilt of this awful man, this evil monster? But Jaspers responded by challenging Arendt's assumption about the 'grandness' of the status she was implicitly according Eichmann in his role as monster or evil genius. Subsequently, and on reflection, she took a different perspective on the matter, and instead of regarding Eichmann as the great purveyor of evil in the form of a monster, she opened her eyes and looked afresh, and what she saw before her during the trial was a very ordinary, perhaps even slightly comical little man, a bureaucrat, bean counter and paper pusher who was nevertheless indisputably responsible for organizing the untold suffering and deaths of so many innocent people. And when you think about it, this is even scarier than the monster thesis. How so? Consider the following.

The fact is that Eichmann is far from an anomaly. The world is full of such ordinary people doing just such banal jobs in the manner of Eichmann, often causing or contributing to massive damage, suffering and harm in the process. For examples, we need look no further than those thousands of people who have worked in the tobacco industry, or, some would argue, the alcohol, fossil fuels or arms industries, or in the banking sector etc.—to some extent, a great many 'good' people going about their 'legitimate' legal daily business have to some extent contributed to some pretty awful outcomes. Following this logic, the same could be said about millions and millions of ordinary consumers buying goods that have been manufactured far away by children, or under appalling and exploitative conditions. The point is that Eichmann's part in the evil of the Holocaust was marked by his banality as a human being; in his particular case, the efficiency with which he could do his job as an organizer and also his ability to devolve himself from any personal moral responsibility for his actions.

It would be this linking of 'evil' with the 'banal' that would haunt Arendt for the rest of her life, as many people found this thesis of the banality of evil simply unacceptable and an affront to the Jewish people, survivors and other victims of the Holocaust. How could being beaten, tortured, raped and murdered by the SS possibly be 'banal' some asked? Had Arendt gone too far in her demythologizing of evil? Was she guilty of 'domesticating' evil (Geddes, 2003: 107) and thus adding insult to injury for the suffering victims? Or of trying to score political points in the highly volatile political debates surrounding the state of Israel?

Arendt's banality of evil thesis

According to Jennifer Geddes (2001), Arendt's banality of evil thesis is really about rejecting any notion of an 'essentialized' or abstract reality of evil. Eichmann is no monstrous demon reminiscent of the theodicy or evil genius of metaphysical origins. Encountering someone like Eichmann even in the context of the 'trial of the century' could happen to anyone anywhere at any time, and in this instance led her to the undeniable conclusion about the ordinary thoughtlessness of this particular man in this particular (though admittedly extreme) case. Rather than looking for or expecting to find devils, monsters, villains or evil geniuses, we need to examine evil as it comes to us and manifests itself incrementally and in the course of our daily lives, and to take cognizance of it in its particular dynamics and circumstances—the truth is that that is our only real hope against it, especially in our modern world. Moral outrage and the determination to detect monsters and slay these demons before they can do their evil deeds only makes it inevitable that such things will happen again, and again, because they are so easily hidden behind a plethora of organizational and sociopolitical structures. Even in these horrible circumstances, we need to encounter the real people responsible: human beings who are only too easily persuaded to act in thoughtless and immoral ways with potentially devastating results.

What Arendt faced full on was the ' . . . dilemma between the unspeakable horror of the deeds and the undeniable ludicrousness of the man who perpetrated them . . . everybody could see that this man was not a "monster", but it was difficult indeed not to suspect that he was a clown' (Arendt, 1977: 54). In fact, the absence of an overt intention to do evil was replaced with a thoughtlessness that enabled him to achieve a level and amount of evil he never would have been able to accomplish as a lone actor, however well motivated, under the guise of doing his job. Arendt writes:

> Eichmann was not Iago . . . Except for an extraordinary diligence in looking out for his personal advancement, he had not motives at all . . . He *merely*, to put the matter colloquially, *never realized what he*

was doing...He was not stupid. It was sheer thoughtlessness...that predisposed him to become one of the greatest criminals of that period...That such remoteness from reality and such thoughtlessness can wreak more havoc than all the evil instincts taken together which, perhaps, are inherent in [humans]—that was, in fact, the lesson one could learn in Jerusalem...the strange interdependence of thoughtlessness and evil.

(Arendt in Geddes, 2001: 108, original emphasis)

It is important to reiterate that this 'thoughtlessness' Arendt speaks of is in no way meant to excuse him from his guilt. While he may have been just a guy who was motivated by the desire to do his job well rather than someone who hated and wanted to kill Jews, this is no excuse. While there is a recognition in Arendt's work of the significance of things like organizational structures and the personal desires and motivations for identity and role fulfilment as in the theses developed by Zimbardo, Milgram and Katz, it is important to note that there are distinct differences between these theories and the thesis put forward by Arendt. Arendt's thesis is not *deterministic*; it does not allocate the blame for these events in their external situational frameworks, but rather insists on locating the personal responsibility of individuals for their moral actions, not in authority or other situational factors. While Eichmann may have been thoughtless and deluded, he was nonetheless still morally responsible for his actions. And it is here that we find the real source of Eichmann's fault and his guilt, and moreover the origins of evil in modern society and its reliance on the rationalized bureaucratic state.

In his defence, Eichmann insisted that he was 'just following orders' and that it was his superiors who were really morally responsible for the consequences of his actions. In this, he evokes the Kantian concept of the categorical imperative we discussed earlier in Chapter 3. By way of a brief reminder, Kant's deontological or duty ethics is based on the root of the Greek *dei*, or 'one must' and *deon* meaning 'duty', hence its common designation as duty ethics. Human agents are free to choose their actions—but according to the exercise of their reason and duty, as opposed to the immutable principles of theological or ontological laws. Consequently, they are also fully responsible for their choices and subsequent acts. But in the cut and thrust of daily life, in this case working in a large and efficient organization and trying to pursue a career, it turns out this sense of individual moral responsibility is extremely fragile, and the recursion to 'duty' as a justification for action a tempting moral option. Kant's analogous notion of freedom and responsibility in modern liberal societies didn't seem to take sufficient account of the power of organizational structures and personal ambitions to override, or even pervert, this individual moral imperative, or the implications of 'duty' in the pursuit of a career in an ever more precarious modern marketplace.

Eichmann's defence

What Eichmann did in his actions and in his defence was to pervert the categorical imperative by focusing too narrowly on the issues of *duty* and *reason* in terms of carrying out the tasks of his job as efficiently and rationally as possible according to the law of the time. In addition, another significant factor in the manifestation if not inevitability of the great evil that took place was the analogous perversion of the prevailing (moral) law, influenced as it was by the prejudicial and malevolent will of the political leadership of the Third Reich and the personal hatred and vendetta of the Führer against Jews and other groups. While Kant recognized that such an overt perversion of the law at its highest level negated its legitimacy and the duty of moral agents to follow it, the fact of the matter is that this outcome is in practice far from straightforward. It turns out that an overriding moral imperative to civic duty persists, often regardless of the legitimacy of the moral authority in power, and that Eichmann, and many others before and since, have and continue to conveniently exploit and ignore this vital link. If anything, any genuine efforts on behalf of ordinary citizens to resist illegitimate or contested political regimes are in the post-9/11 global environment even more severely tested with the development of surveillance networks and the strengthened security apparatus of the state.

Arendt argues that this perversion of the law was consummated by the perversion of individual desire in that Eichmann actively used the excuse of duty, career and the need to follow orders as a way of *resisting the temptation to do good* (Birmingham, 2003: 85). *Desire*, as a source of motivation for action, was itself perverted. Hence, evil under the Third Reich had lost the intrinsic quality by which most people recognize it— the quality of temptation (something we will recall from many if not all of the previous theories, from theodicy (the seducer) to psychoanalysis (the lure of violence, aggression and sex)). Many Germans and possibly some Nazis, probably an overwhelming majority of them, must have been tempted *not* to murder, *not* to rob, *not* to let their friends and neighbours go to their doom. But, as God and everyone else knows, they had learned how to resist this temptation to do the right thing in very wrong circumstances (Arendt, 1977 in Birmingham, 2003: 85–86, original emphasis). Is this the same as a situational argument as put forward in the previous chapter, and as argued by researchers such as Milgram and Zimbardo? Not exactly.

In this regard, Arendt reiterates the importance of individual moral responsibility even within powerful organizations and social systems, *and* also within the human heart and conscience that are so prone to being manipulated to tell us otherwise. So, while Arendt rejected the notion that Eichmann was 'radically evil' in the sense that he was a not a monster, she implicitly accepts that he was *radically evil* in the strict Kantian sense, i.e. that we have the *propensity* for being good or evil, and that we are ultimately responsible for the choices we make. But, here again, we note the tension between the human susceptibility to evil that is intrinsic to the human condition, and the responsibility for evil actions that are a consequence of a person's free will or choice according to the prevailing moral law. For Arendt, the Eichmann trial demonstrated that it was a mistake to consider evil 'radical' in the sense that people who carried out evil acts were somehow qualitatively different to the rest of us, or possessed by some demonic power. The truth is much more disturbing, that we are all capable of doing great evil and that this can happen quite easily and without 'malice aforethought'. Evil as such doesn't have the metaphysical reality of demons or wicked gods; it has no depth and at its basis is nihilism or nothingness, so it can't be 'radical', only extreme. Only good has this capacity, and so only good can be 'radical' in the sense of having substance (Arendt in Bernstein (1996)). To put it another way, the extreme character of evil in relation to an actor like Eichmann is not real but hyperbole, an exaggeration for rhetorical effect. Sadly, evil is not fictional, but in its factual manifestation clearly worthy of a fable or cautionary tale with moral content. If good is the truth, evil is a lie. It lacks substance and depth. It is, in epistemological and ontological terms, nothing, and morally worthless, nothing more. Its radicality resides in this, not in some inherent 'badness', nor in the (mal)functioning of some external systems. It is in us, and in us all, and we are morally responsible for choosing it, whether by omission or commission.

'Simply put, [radical evil] refers to our propensity knowingly to choose maxims contrary to the moral law' (Louden, 2000: 138). Radical evil is the (occasional) deviation from the moral law, even though we know what it is and what we should do. This (sometimes) happens because of three factors: frailty (or weak will); impurity (lack of integrity of our actions, deviation from the categorical imperative); and, finally, wickedness or perversity (this being the most serious because it implies not just weakness but forethought). But at the end of the day these three have one common root: selfishness or self-love, and ultimately this accounts for our inability to put the moral law and the universal good first over our own interests. In this regard, it is the selfishness of someone like Eichmann that while it by no means negates the other external influences trumps them as a mechanism for generating great amounts of evil. He was open to the pernicious influences of the Nazi ideology because it suited his own selfish desires for power, wealth, status and the many other perks. For this he is morally responsible. Not being a person who hated Jews does nothing to absolve him of his guilt, though there were these people at work, too.

We will recall that Kant suggested that the propensity toward evil can be negated through the exercise of good moral character as a kind of 'filter' separating out the evil before it becomes manifest in our actions. We can be disposed toward evil by nature, but this can be overcome through our exercise of moral disposition, preventing evil actions being chosen in the first instance, primarily through our conscientious relationship with the principle of moral law. On this reasoning, Eichmann was guilty by virtue of his acquiescence to selfishness (in his career ambitions) and in his acceptance of perverted moral law under the Nazi regime. Was it bad character that was ultimately to blame, rather than organizational structures and systems? Or if a combination, where does the balance of blame lie, and what should be done to address it, as Hitler and the Nazis were by no means the last of their kind?

Bosnia, Kosovo, Rwanda, Burundi and Darfur: Evil linked by banality?

Part of the 'gap' identified by Arendt marked by the genocide of the Holocaust is foregrounded by the context of the legal trial; that is, the need to establish a link between the awful suffering visited on the victims as a result of criminal activity by others and the imputation of responsibility and guilt (and subsequently punishment—and/or the need to make reparation or apology; we will return to this issue presently). This leads to a number of difficult questions. Ultimately, who was responsible for the Holocaust? Who is responsible for any genocide? How do they happen and can they be explained, predicted and/or prevented? Are the guilty parties the aggregate number of individual bureaucrats like Eichmann? Are all members of the society in question to blame? Or are we all somehow blameworthy; do we all carry with us the implied guilt of collective evil carried out in the name of the modern nation state in an age of global capitalism? But if it is the case that we are all to blame, then pragmatically isn't it the case that no one is guilty or held responsible? What is meant by the phrase 'collective evil'? Is it qualitatively different from evildoing by individual actors? And how can our criminal justice system and/or (inter)national political organizations deal with imputing guilt and punishment on this sort collective level? Finally, is Arendt's thesis on the banality of evil developed during her observations of the Eichmann trial universally transferable to other and more recent atrocities? In other words, is it accurate to say that what links the genocides like the Holocaust with those in Bosnia, Kosovo, Rwanda, Burundi and Darfur is their 'banality' in terms of the evil that took place?

Assignations of blame and guilt for evil of this type are extremely troublesome. In 1945, posters were put up in many German cities emblazoned with the words 'YOU ARE GUILTY', accompanied by images of Buchenwald and a finger pointing at the viewer (Schaap, 2001). This charge of collective guilt was met by those who were greeted by these posters with widespread indignation and cynicism; how could ordinary people be charged as collectively guilty of the atrocities of the Holocaust? And what did this accusation of 'guilt' mean anyway? According to Schaap (2001), people typically respond to such allegations with either denial or sentimentality—neither of which really does anybody any good. Do such collective accusations achieve anything in terms of advancing the cause of justice or ensuring the promise 'never again'? Do they actually play into the hands of those who strenuously deny that any such atrocity ever took place? And if we are all guilty, what do collective expressions of sorrow or regret actually mean, such as when those alive today or their political representatives say sorry for past historical wrongs such as slavery? How do we, using political science, understand the impact of the past evils on political agency, national identities and international relationships today and in the future?

We've all seen collective suffering and know what it is. So, what is collective evil, and what do we do about it?

Collective evil

In his book *Evil and Human Agency: Understanding Collective Evildoing* (2005), Arne Johan Vetlesen takes up this issue of collective evil in his efforts to try to address many of the questions posed above. Drawing upon the theories of Hannah Arendt, C. Fred Alford and Zigmunt

Bauman, Vetlesen develops a theory about the nature of collective evil based on a triad of causes involving *character, situation* and *social structure*. I will now integrate this theory with Evrin Staub's (1989) thesis on the origins of genocide and other atrocities.

So, what is collective evil? Like individual evil, Vetlesen defines it as sharing the same generic qualities of intentionally inflicting harm and/or suffering on another person or persons. But unlike other theorists like Alford and Arendt, the key motivations for doing collective evil are not limited to the lack of empathy, or thoughtlessness or indeed the simple vindictiveness that characterizes individual evil acts, i.e. evil acts done by one person against another person for whatever particular concrete reasons to do with those specific relationships or circumstances. Neither is collective evil simply the aggregate sum of the evil actions of individuals against one or more other collective groups, such as might be assumed by the question developed above about extending Arendt's thesis about the banality of evil from the agency of one person to the collective of whole bureaucracies. This would be the erroneous application of methodological individualism to the phenomenon of collective evil, such as genocide. Collective evil is not simply a crude accumulation of individual evil(s). It is more than this, and different and distinctive to evil carried out by individual actors, as described for example in chapters 5 and 6 by theorists such as Kristeva, Bataille and Katz (among others).

Key elements of collective evil (combining Vetlesen and Staub)

- Differs from individual evil in terms of *proximity*
- Group-oriented, 'us and them'
- Cultural concepts of the self, values and goals—the idea that some people are superior to others
- Devaluation of subgroups
- Charismatic leaders
- Obedience to authority—totalitarian ideologies
- Collective evil more formulaic, distinctive 'absolutizing' logic
- Requires significant amounts of planning and imitation
- Reactive, retaliation for past wrongs, self-defence
- Mythologizing of the past
- Necessary steps along 'continuum of destruction'

Collective evil differs from individual evil in terms of a number of elements and dynamics. According to Vetlesen (2005), the first is that of *proximity*. Acts of individual evil tend to be psychologically and emotionally as well as spatially and (sometimes) temporally proximate in terms of the closeness and intentionality of the actors; most actors will want to hurt particular known individual(s). This is the kind of close, intimate, interpersonal evildoing that Alford (1997) discussed in his book on evil, as did Katz (1988). Collective evil doing is fundamentally different in that its basic component is the *group*, as opposed to the individual. Hence, these are cases where individuals act not as individuals but *as members of a group and on behalf of the group*. Similarly, the victims of evil acts will typically be selected not as individuals who are necessarily deserving of suffering as individuals (in many if not most instances, these victims are individually completely innocent), but rather *because of their identification as members of other group(s)*. We may recall here the example given in Chapter 6 of the young man who decides to stab the man who stole his necklace; retribution of this type against this particular individual was elemental to the meaning of this act of violence as an act of individual vengeance. However, we may surmise for the purposes of illustration here that the original crime of stealing the necklace may have been individually or collectively oriented; this first act of evil may have been committed as an act of robbery because the offender coveted the item or had a grudge against the owner (as an example of individual evil), or alternatively because the necklace wearer was the member of a rival group, such as a gang. In the latter case, this act would be an act of collective evil, as it was taken primarily as an act of one person acting as a member of a group against another person who represented another group.

This type of evil typically involves the application of distinctive ideologies and the identification of victims by symbolic or narrative means, such as group membership by nationality, sexuality, race, disability, gender, age, class or ethnicity. This gives collective evil its essential '*us and them*' dynamic.

In his book *The Roots of Evil: The Origins of Genocide and Other Group Violence* (1989), Ervin Staub (1989) points to the additional dynamics of *cultural concepts of the self* and associated *values* and *goals*, and their role in the origins of genocide and other atrocities. According to his analysis of multiple genocides, it is not only that there is a qualitative difference between individuals and groups in terms of the generation of collective evil (e.g. in terms of physical or spatial proximity), but rather that shared ideas about the nature of what it is to be a person or self has massive consequences for including people in or, to paraphrase Hollywood mogul Samuel Goldwin, 'including people out'. This is observable in certain cultural contexts where people feel they are somehow intrinsically superior to others in terms of their ethnic or national identities, even to the point of denying that members of the 'other' group are human, and that it is one's own group that is exclusively human. In practice, this often happens among those who are very close in terms of proximity and/or highly integrated within social communities in crisis or conflict, as was the case with the Jewish people in Europe before and during WWII. Sometimes, this feeling of self-superiority mixes with nationalistic values and aspirations in the wake of socio-economic or other crises that can result in heightened levels of anxiety regarding the durability of this sense of self-superiority and capacity to expand and control the destiny of the legitimate and soverign nation. Staub (1989) argues that this was the case in Nazi Germany but is also observable in genocides that have taken place in Turkey, Argentina and Cambodia, with devastating consequences. This influence of a culture of self-superiority is particularly dangerous in instances when the culture in question is in crisis from events (real or imagined) such as public humiliation or climbdown on the world stage, and its feelings of superiority are under threat (possibly analogous to the 'family of emotions' that includes humiliation as identified by Katz (1988) as a cause of individual evil). Dominant or majority groups can then turn on their weaker or minority 'enemies' in these circumstances as a way to reinstate their intrinsic feelings of 'greatness' and restore their power and control. Staub (1989) adds to this associated self-concept the *devaluation of subgroups*, such as long and embedded cultural histories of anti-Semitism or anti-leftism or -rightism that are latently preserved within societies and flare up from time to time, in the form of moral panics or pogroms (actual violence against these groups). These instances of violence may be sporadic or frequent, but they are often treated apathetically, tolerated or even tacitly condoned by other members of the society, bystanders and those in authority (such as politicians or the police).

Vetlesen claims collective evildoing is also distinctive in that it owes much of its vehemence to the manner in which *charismatic leaders* are present and able to activate, channel and exploit the latent psychic motivations of group members/followers. Here, again, we observe the aggressive and psychological motivations of individuals vis-à-vis their collective identities as members of groups, not as individuals or intimates. In this regard, and echoing Milgram, Staub (1989) concentrates on the strongly embedded cultural *obedience to authority*; for example, as seen in highly militaristic cultures (e.g. Argentina), very hierarchical social structures (e.g. Turkey), those with authoritarian parenting practices (e.g. Nazi Germany) or strongly traditional, feudal and monar-chical social systems (e.g. Cambodia). He also points to the tendency for such societies to be *monolithic*; that is, totalitarian and having a history of violent repression, lacking in real pluralism or valuing tol-erance in itself. *Ideology* also plays a key role here; for instance, in the Nazi ideology of racial superiority and 'purity' and its easy trans-lation into genocidal 'solutions' to socio-political-economic problems and defilement (again, real or imagined).

Collective evil differs from individual evil by being much more *for-mulaic* according to Vetlesen and characterized by its own distinctive *logic* in comparison with individual evil, which is much more specific in terms of the spectrum of motivations and acts at issue in partic-ular relationships, and hence more difficult to make generalizations about. In contrast, collective evil has its own distinct logic in terms of behaviour, whereby *agents act, think and feel in a manner that gives pri-macy to the relationship or bond with co-actors/group members rather than to the relationship to the victim(s)*. This means that things like moral duties, obligations, entitlements and so forth relate exclusively to these col-lective bonds within the group, with the victims regarded as devoid of any individual intrinsic moral status. This is of seminal importance: the notion that the priority of the moral bonds of the group actually can-cel out any need to recognize the moral being of or duty to the victims such as expressed in the Kantian categorical imperative. In the case of an individual actor like Eichmann, as Neiman (2002) argues, personal or private motivation to act against the victim strictly speaking doesn't necessarily need to be present at all. In many ways, this absence of motivation is reflected in the absence of ontological reality accorded to victims; from an ethical and practical point of view, they are sim-ply moral non-entities, not fully human; hence, acting against them would for many (though not necessarily all) be as absurd as acting in their moral defence. We may reflect here on the Augustinian conceptu-alization of evil as lack or privation, or non-being; a lack of ontological status that is actually being accorded to the victims of collective evil. Such complicity among the majority group, moral apathy and tolera-tion of harm to victims would seem to be as essential for collective evil as the active hatred of bigots and despots, possibly more so; counter-intuitively, rooting genocide in indifference and uncontested prejudice as much as to overt racism and hate, if not more so.

Vetlesen categorizes this relationship of one group over and to the complete and utter detriment of the other to the extent that the exclu-sivity of intra-group morality makes the denial of the other group itself a moral 'good' as an *'absolutizing logic'*. Hence, the elimination of the

Jews for the Nazis was a morally good act in defence of the fatherland and the Führer. In the cut-and-thrust propaganda of daily life under the Nazis, many would have even been compelled to regard it as being in the best interests of the Jews themselves. Indeed, it is arguable that we have encountered this sort of logic before, as in the case of some theodicies, such as of the Malthusian variety: those that take a logical train of thought to such an extent that what most people would regard as good and evil not only break down but are actually reversed. It is 'good' that members of an inferior/marginal/poor group expire, because they are faulty or poor or indulge in deviant or sinful behaviours and deserve all they get (as some viewed the emergence of AIDS in the homosexual community during the 1980s). Hence, the common pronouncement that 'some of my best friends' might be gay, or gypsies or Jews etc., and while I might have nothing personally against them, nevertheless I won't be taking any stands among my comrades in the majority to argue against their exclusion or victimization. Taking issue with Arendt's banality of evil thesis, it is this 'logic' that accounts for such collective evildoing at the level of genocide, not simply the thoughtless complicity of an amalgamation of office workers like Eichmann. Rather, as Vetlesen argues, other more intense psychological factors and fantasies relating to different and distinctive groups have to be mobilized, ideally by charismatic leaders who have a particular ideological vision to promote, one that is self-interested and invested in the fears of the 'other'.

Further key elements of this 'logic' of collective evildoing particularly in the case of genocide is the reinforcement of all of the above elements, with the added dimensions of *planning* and *imitation*. Genocide is not 'thoughtless' or spontaneous, but requires careful foresight and planning. It is *reactive* in its ideology in that it seeks to portray the violence and suffering visited on the 'other' as a retaliation for (often imagined) past wrongs done to the group now galvanizing itself for action. And these reactions have a paradoxical and chilling character in their practical manifestation and strategic justification and pursuit. 'If there is one *Gedankenfigur* that is common to most well-known instances of genocidal logic, it is this: the perpetrator group does exactly what it castigates the target for having done (in some remote or recent past) or for being now about to do against one's own group' (Vetlesen, 2005: 175). So 'past wrongs' are visited on the other group and are justified as *retaliation* or even pre-emptive self-defence, with this notion of *self-defence* most commonly providing an especially useful reference point for legitimizing violent action against others.

Not just space but also time is a key factor in collective evil. Spatial proximity in genocide and other forms of collective evil is often accompanied by temporal distance. Collective evil does not happen in a historical, social, political or cultural vacuum, but is carefully contextualized in these respects, especially in the contemporary *mythologizing of the past*. In other words, collective evil relies on narrative, or storytelling, in the form of myths about what makes the majority superior and the minority inferior or inhuman. These stories can go back centuries, and also extend to the future end of time. Hence, past acts and events are transformed into the collective dynamic of the 'us' and 'them' group relationship, against which all present and imminent events are narratively interpreted and within which all individuals are able or even encouraged to 'read' themselves and their own experiences into a temporality that collapses both history, destiny and everyday life. Thus, events of the imagined distant past (or anticipated future) can assume tremendous symbolic and emotional resonance in the present moment, regardless of factual accuracy or owing to paranoid flights of fancy, especially but not limited to those in positions of authority or influence (as in the role of the radio broadcast media in the Rwandan genocide). Once this is how history and the culture of the present and unfolding future are conceived, human agency can take on a distinctive group/individual dynamic, whereby individuals are compelled to be 'answerable' for everything there group has, may have, is or will ever be likely to do. This manipulation of *time* and obliteration of the distinction between individuals and groups in terms of moral responsibility is key to the logic of collective evildoing in genocide.

Staub (1989) emphasizes the necessary steps along what he calls the '*continuum of destruction*' that characterizes genocidal societies. So, for example, genocide doesn't suddenly emerge from out of nowhere, as Vetlesen states, but is typically preceded by other usually less extreme instances (though not necessarily; historically, there have been repeated instances of mass killings of Armenians by the Turks, according to Staub) of mistreatment or violence against other groups (e.g. Nazi pogroms against the Jews). These typically become increasingly frequent (even cyclical, as in instances of 'tit for tat' political violence) and escalate in severity, frequency and/or extent as those inside and also outside observers become ever more complacent about their detrimental impact and effect.

Summary and further questions

In the wake of WWII, Hannah Arendt stated that evil would be one of the major issues of concern during the twentieth century. While she was in a sense correct about the resilience and repetition of evil as it has since manifest in repeated instances of organized and horrific suffering at the collective level of atrocity, the philosophical discussions she called for have yet, or are only starting, to take place. However, among the social scientific community, particularly political theorists, attention to the study of evil of this variety and with these devastating consequences are being formulated. What these thinkers have stressed is the implication of rationality and efficient working of organizational systems that are embedded in the bureaucracies and systems of the modern nation state, on its own and in relation to international bodies. What we also see is not only a recognition of the role of charismatic leaders but also the persistence of Arendt's observation during the Eichmann trial that genocide is not the work of a single monstrous figure along with his or her minions, but is rather or also attributable to a range of many ordinary people. Contemporary theorists such as Vetlesen and Staub have developed the concept of collective evil as the convergence of a number of elements in the manifestation of atrocities such as but not limited to genocide. Drawing on the previous historical research on evil and genocide, these include situation, character, myth, logic and desire (all factors of evil we have encountered before) with the added dimensions of identity, nationalism, ideology, group, place and time. While contemporary theories of collective evil are more complex than Milgram's and Arendt's original theses on the role of authority and the significance of the everyday and banal, they by no means negate their seminal importance as causal factors in the emergence of such atrocious and horrific events. Rather, by having the advantage of studying more cases and in more documented detail, scholars today are able to make some generic observations about the nature of collective evil and also to contest and demythologize the 'singularity' of individual atrocities or other such historical events. This in itself tells us a lot about the nature and extent of evil in contemporary and future global modernity and puts in question the views of some agents who insist on the uniqueness of individual atrocities and the role of memory and morality in attributing guilt and blame, and the way forward to prevent such atrocities repeating themselves under the maxim 'never again'. This is a controversial debate, one in which both sides argue that the insistence or denial on singularity and uniqueness does a disservice to the victims.

Instead, what theorists like Arendt, Vetlesen and Staub advocate is a multifaceted perspective that stresses on the many and often little noticed practices and prejudices of daily civil life that are enacted in a way that legitimizes the victimization of the 'other' as dehumanized members of opposing groups. One way of ensuring this preventative stratagem is to strengthen the cultural and political role attributed to human rights within a society, even when that is hard or inconvenient, and to resist the temptation to fall into the trap of apathy, denial or sentimentality, whether by internal members of a society or external observers. As Arendt so powerfully argued, attributing blame for the Holocaust to one or a handful of actors might make people feel better in the short term, but it does little to protect us from the hazards of future suffering. What is needed is the development of an appreciation of the path to collective evil and the necessity for every member of society to develop a civic disposition to strive to be vigilant against the steps along this perilous way in the incremental unfolding of real time lived alongside real neighbours, even and especially when this is psychologically difficult or contrary to the cultural shaping of 'desire'. As Schaap (2001) argues, Arendt's vision of political responsibility would replace a simplistic and disincentivizing culture of guilt for the evils of the past with one of shared mutual responsibility by ordinary citizens for the past, present and future that could lead to a more mature and accepting spirit of tolerance and reconciliation.

9
The Axis of Evil—the War on Terror, the 'Enemy Within' and the Politics of Evil and the State

In this penultimate chapter, we will conclude the final section of the book dealing with social science theories of evil with an examination of an important contemporary issue involving politics, evil and the state: the so-called axis of evil and the war on terror. The main questions/themes addressed are what is evil at the state level, e.g. by and between governments, international agencies and political elites and their (perceived) enemies? What is the impact of these conceptualizations of evil from and among states, and what kinds of political realities, discourses and consequences do they generate from the perspective of non-state actors, such as 'terrorists' or ordinary citizens? How does studying evil with specific reference to the modern nation state in the wake of 9/11 shape our understanding of the term? And what do political science, cultural theory and feminist theories have to tell us about the gendering of evil in relation to the social institutions and the state?

Evil and the state after 9/11: The axis of evil and the war on terror

In the days immediately following the al-Qaeda terrorist attacks of 9/11, then President of the United States George W. Bush issued this statement:

> Just three days removed from these events, Americans do not yet have the distance of history. But our responsibility to history is already clear: to answer these attacks and rid the world of evil. War has been waged against us by stealth and deceit and murder. This nation is peaceful, but fierce when stirred to anger. The conflict was begun on

the timing and terms of others. It will end in a way, and at an hour, of our choosing.

(President Bush, 14 September 2001)

Bush clearly indicates in the above quote, even at this early stage, the approach the US would adopt and continue to pursue for some considerable time in terms of its strategic response to this seminal event primarily construed as evil. Even at this point, we see a determination that this would be accomplished in a way that restored the righteousness of the American nation—and the world—through a process combining moral outrage and military might of the US in an unfolding international drama framed as good versus evil. Central to this agenda, or pivotal to this strategy, would be the restoration of the agency and potency of the US as a nation state very much resuming control of this very disturbing and disruptive historical situation.

In his later prefatory remarks in the *National Security Strategy for the United States* (2002), George W. Bush returns to history, specifically the so-called Cold War, drawing parallels between the 'decisive victory for the forces of freedom' claimed as a result of the 'great struggles' of the twentieth century between 'liberty' and totalitarianism, and how the ideological victory of market (neo-)liberalism over communism paved the way for 'freedom, democracy, and free enterprise' (Bush, 2002: iv). Against this victorious background, Bush maps the current situation facing the US:

Defending our Nation against it enemies is the first and fundamental commitment of the Federal Government. Today, that task has changed dramatically. Enemies in the past needed great armies and great industrial capabilities to endanger America. Now, shadowy networks of individuals can bring great chaos and suffering to our shores for less than it costs to purchase a single tank. Terrorists are organized to penetrate open societies and to turn the power of modern technologies against us.

(Bush, 2002: iv)

The historical narrative against which the current crisis is read is the 'good versus evil' of the Cold War; the US has prevailed in its previous 'great struggle' against communism, and it will prevail again. However, in the meantime, a new enemy and a new set of threats have emerged, involving more 'shadowy' characters whose 'penetration' of American society and use of modern technologies has unleashed 'suffering' and 'chaos' sufficient to 'endanger' American civil society. The evil nature of these individuals and their use of widely available information and affordable market technologies intrinsic to Western global capitalism means that the US's new enemies no longer require an organized militia or even the backing of a state, just a computer and a relatively small budget. It seems that the great threat posed by the evils perpetrated upon the US and its allies primarily by terrorists and rogue groups/states presents a new but also in some respects familiar dichotomous political reality.

The good news

On the one hand, the Bush administration argues that there is the optimistic side that offers great opportunities in terms of enabling the US to fulfil its destiny as a force for good in the world, a shining example and beacon of strength and the force of right (as of old). This construal of the situation taps into what eminent American Professor of Political Science Robert Jervis (2003) identifies as a core belief common among powerful states generally but applicable to the US in particular, 'that its values are universal and their spread will benefit the entire world' (366). The main evil thus posed by the threat of terrorism is constituted by its challenge to the stability of the present prevailing political 'natural order' and the danger of abrupt shifts in power beyond the parameters of American dominance and control.

The argument put forward by British Professor of Political Science Stephen Chan (2005) would correspond with this conception of evil from the perspective of the modern nation state and the US government. But what Chan emphasizes in contrast to Jervis is the strongly Manichean conceptualization of evil that is foundational to such international foreign policy, what he identifies as 'Manicheanism in its crudest form' (Chan, 2005: 86). According to this perspective, much favoured by the 'hawks' of the US administration generally and then Secretary of Defense Donald Rumsfeld in particular, evil is located in the two original spiritual, moral and reality principles (maybe even two creators) of the cosmos: one of good, one of evil. Among powerful political elites like the Bush administration and its heirs, this crude Manicheanism is still evident today, despite centuries of Christian theology which has branded Manicheanism as heresy and sought generally to divest evil of its ontological substance and reality. Implicit to this 'crude' Manicheanism is the notion that some leaders are intrinsically good (Bush, Blair) and others are intrinsically evil (Saddam Hussein, Osama bin Laden). This dichotomy not only justifies the headlong pursuit and violent vanquishing of such evil leaders; it implies that their very absence from the political scene will enable the manifestation or 'spread' of the good, like some sort of cosmic margarine. This is why, Chan argues, it was not seen as necessary by members of the Bush administration (or by implication other allies such as the UK government under Tony Blair) to put in place detailed plans for Iraq subsequent to the campaign to remove the regime of Saddam Hussein. The absence of a post-conflict plan was not an oversight on the part of the US government (or its allies), but intrinsic to their understanding of the problem at hand. Rather, as a result of the excision of evil on a Manichean model, good would naturally prevail and become increasingly more evident in the absence of evil (hence what proved to be the rather fantastical predictions broadcast by those such as the Secretary of Defense Donald Rumsfeld of the welcome allied troops would receive from the ecstatic and grateful populous (for an illustrative example of which see Miles, 2003)). The Manichean myth of good vanquishing evil linked to a fundamentalist eschatological mythology of the state filtered through the 'end of history' thesis propounded by thinkers like Francis Fukuyama [1992] (2012) would reassert the ideological immanence of American nationhood as the supreme power and exemplar of goodness par excellence in the world by right.

Performative power: 'Shock and awe'

Chan (2005) argues that the Bush administration's initial military ventures in the aftermath of 9/11 would have the effect of pre-empting resistance or any further actions by terrorist groups or their fellow travellers as a result of the fear instilled by the performance of the sheer force of superior allied military power and righteous moral outrage. This in itself would provide a world stage in collaboration with the broadcast media to display the moral as well as physical power of the US not just as a potent force for good, but more to the point one not to be messed with ever again. This is what Chan calls 'Full Spectrum Dominance'. Thereafter, the removal or 'surgical' excision of evil will create a vacuum in which, as we have seen, good can then flourish and spread, without the need for prior planning or management by those who unleash such militaristic demonstrations of force. But as it turns out, there is always the danger of things not going to plan. Hence, we have the pessimistic scenario.

The bad news

On the other hand, there is the possibility that the US does not fulfil its role as an exemplary force for good (i.e. freedom and democracy) and the world is then in peril of becoming a more dangerous, chaotic and terrifying place. The rhetoric used by the Bush administration implies that the one thing that is worse than the fear generated by such rogue and terrorist forces is the *fear of fear* that is generated by the threat to contemporary (American) society in the wake of the war on terror (we may think here of Kristeva and the abysmal and irrational fear of abjection discussed in Chapter 6). This widespread public anxiety at the state level is so endemic and pernicious as to disrupt the very core values of political liberalism emanating from Enlightenment thought that the US claims to defend, such as tolerance, rationality, justice, restraint and secular pluralism. According to contemporary theorists, such as the French postmodern philosopher Jean Baudrillard (1993, 2005), this is explicable by the particular dynamic of evil at work in terrorism and the state; this evil is transparent and mirror-like, whereby actions, motivations and justifications of violence are reversed, repeated and reflected by each side onto the other (as observed by Vetlesen (2005) in his analysis of genocide in the previous chapter). While this evil lacks ontological substance (in the Augustinian sense of privation, and in the Cartesian sense of a reflection, fable or dream), in contemporary postmodern society, it nevertheless is massively influential as a *form*, as something that gives shape and the appearance of substance to the free-flowing and volatile power and aggression that drives global capitalism and its attendant technologies. It is its formative, formulaic and chimerical qualities of evil that accounts for this eruption into the manifold and cyclically repetitive types of violence that accrue under the umbrella term 'terror'.

What Chan and other political scientists argue is that the use of such political rhetoric based on a simplistic and recursive conception of evil results in important political questions regarding the legitimacy of such pre-emptive aggression by the state being are foreclosed, or deemed irrelevant, vexatious or even seditious. Consider also the quality of 'freedom/liberty' being exported by the 'West' in such campaigns; how realistic was it, for example, to expect that the electorate even in a democratic Iraq would vote into power leaders who reflected the image and values of Western political liberalism of the US? (We may consider, in passing, the electoral successes of what would be regarded as fundamentalist/extremist political parties in newly 'liberated' or freshly democratized states like Egypt, Pakistan, Libya and Afghanistan in the wake of the 'Arab Spring'.) Would a new democratically elected Iraqi government automatically have recognized Israel and renounced its claim to Kuwait? The fact that these events would not have been likely to play out as the US minders imagined, expected or perhaps fantasized, makes the use of this as a premise for justifying the declaration of war on a sovereign nation and implementing a strategy of regime change highly dubious, to say the least. In this respect, the Bush foreign-policy doctrine is not based on the Enlightenment principles of rationality and objectivity, but rather is essentially a faith-based foreign policy of right (Jervis, 2003). The emotive impact of such policies founded on faith that presume the rightness of one's moral authority, justification and probity in taking such actions have the effect of rendering the need for objective, rational justification less pressing (Chan, 2005).

Chan (2005) points out that by not responding to the initial 'shock and awe' bombing campaign in the way the US administration expected, the 'villains' in this story weren't following the script. Rather than submit obsequiously to the will of a superior moral and military power, the reality—or 'real story'—was and in many respects continues to be somewhat different. For starters, the attempt at making an example of Iraq on the international stage in the eyes of other 'rogue' states and political actors has not worked. As Chan (2005) perceptively observed, this means that the Bush administration and its allies are thereafter obliged to vanquish all of their enemies, one by one, thereby always being in the position of having to open up new fronts in the 'war on terror', potentially endlessly expanding its military operations abroad seemingly ad infinitum. The 'war on terror' is not a war in the conventional sense, with a defined enemy and a specific agenda, but instead a series of violent conflicts in an ever expanding and mutating series of cultural and geopolitical spaces—material, transcendental and virtual (Chan, 2005). Not just bodies but meanings, identities, histories, values and powers in this, the 'real' world, and all other worlds (theological, metaphysical, moral, virtual, mythical, eschatological etc.) are broken and exposed, to a barrage of external and cultural forces also 'at war', e.g. religious ideologies, ethnic identities and global market capitalism. In this highly gendered battle (see Dworkin below), it is presumed that it will be the most violent, ruthless and determined political and military actors who will emerge victorious from the cosmic chaos. This is what Chan identifies as the down and very nasty side of Full Spectrum Dominance situated as it is in a political discourse of evil.

As depicted in Cartesian themes of evil as represented in films like *The Matrix* (1992) (discussed in Chapter 2), while one evil regime may be conquered, new evils emerge in a Hydra-like fashion to take its place. In the current geopolitical climate, the vanquishing and removal of one regime, no matter how evil, doesn't seem to quell the emergence of new and even more pernicious evils. Often, these can be even worse, in that they can be more difficult to predict, mollify and control. They have the advantage of having studied their Western enemy, perhaps even to have been previously trained or armed by these same Western powers, while the allied forces do not benefit from such an incisive advantage. So, maybe the present situation is not really so unfamiliar, in the sense that good and evil are presented as being distinct and mutually exclusive, with the US (and its allies) standing at the crucible of moral as well as political reality, not just for its own well-being (though this is a primary concern) but also for the future well-being of the world. As those knowledgeable about the history of theories of evil will recognize, this is by no means a novel or very modern version of evil, but rather a distinctly ancient, pre-Christian, possibly even heretical one (from a Christian theological standpoint). Chan (2005) notes also that the term 'axis' itself used in a wartime context is also redolent of the massive moral victories of WWII, against 'The Axis' powers of Germany, Italy and Japan. It was the subsequent historical reading of the moral victory of WWII that would enhance the view of the war on terror as a *moral* war by the allied forces, in opposition to a *holy* war of Jihad (Chan, 2005). So while the overt reference made by Bush to the Cold War had the rhetorical effect of reinforcing the inevitability of American victory, the implicit evocation of WWII drew on a strongly moral narrative of 'just war'.

Political scientists like Jervis and Chan note how nation states such as Iran, Iraq (under Saddam) and North Korea have found themselves located firmly on the evil axis. Cuba, Libya and Syria were later deemed 'beyond the axis of evil' by then US Ambassador to the UN and well-known 'hawk' John Bolton. This geopolitical matrix was then expanded by a number of so-called 'outposts of tyranny' in the words of then Secretary of State Condoleezza Rice, also populated by Belarus, Zimbabwe and Myanmar (Burma). However, what has remained disturbingly and recalcitrantly unfamiliar is the 'shadowy' (we can think again of the psychoanalytic approach of Julia Kristeva here) and 'chaotic' (Ricoeur) nature of the evil predominant in this political landscape. This fear and anxiety is exacerbated by the fact that it is in practice not so easy to locate the terrorist 'enemy' by the coordinates of geographical areas or states, nor to always clearly recognize them by their physical attributes or identify who their 'fellow travellers' are. Some of them are even among us as we speak: our own 'home-grown' produce! What is more, they do not fight us with strange, alien weapons or ideologies, but rather turn our own technologies and values against us—again, confounding the faith in the Enlightenment-based capacity of science and technology to accomplish US aspirations in the region once and for all. This is a new and unsettling development; one that is potentially so disruptive to the stability of the American nation state that is calls for decisive and pre-emptive violent action on behalf of the American (and other 'willing') nation states.

And that's one of the paradoxical things about locating evil on a political 'axis' because it presents only two possibilities (Jervis, 2003), neither of which is very comforting:

- either you (being a political entity normally in the form of a state) are off the graph entirely and consign yourself to a version of political oblivion; similarly, one's place on this axis is unstable, as nation states can be added (e.g. Syria, Iran, Cuba) or removed (Libya, Syria) in response to a number of ever shifting circumstances; or
- you must also find your place on the graph delineated by the two axes, whereby the axis of evil by virtue of its opposition to the axis of good nevertheless is destined to 'intersect' at some point, potentially contaminating those located in the 'good' quadrants as a result.

In a fast-paced, ever-changing global environment, the stability and legibility of the shifting axes and the political agencies and alliances among the diverse actors are increasingly difficult to reliably discern, raising anxiety levels even more. Without the stabilizing factors of tradition and real, substantial guiding principles (e.g. Kant's categorical imperative), the faith placed in the righteousness of ideologies of evil, the utility of scientific technologies and the new frontiers of virtual realities are ambivalent—or 'flowing' or 'vertiginous' in the language of postmodern theorists such as Zigmunt Bauman and Jock Young.

Chan (2005) implies that one major advantage offered by the 'axis of evil' rhetoric is that it only recognizes nation states. This in itself provides a comforting diversion from the fundamental truth of the 'war on terror': that the US does not actually know how to fight the kind of enemy encountered on 9/11, the 'shadowy forces' Bush referred to earlier who are without a firm geographical location, governmental structure, systematic links or a coherent political ideology or conventional standing army (as would be the case with a state). But it does know how to fight nation states with organized militia. This is why, Chan argues, we find the war on terror being carried out primarily in places like Afghanistan and Iraq, rather than on distinct terrorist networks which are notoriously difficult to reliably detect.

Let's take stock here. In our excursion into the different languages, narratives and logics of evil, we see how two eminent political scientists make sense of evil from the point of view of the state, specifically in the war on terror and the axis of evil.

And what do they find in terms of the treatment of evil in relation to the state? According to cultural theorist Terry Eagleton, these are the central factors at work:

1. *Irony*—a strangely and perhaps ironically premodern and, indeed, ancient discourse of evil, referring to Manichean notions that construe evil as two separate and competing (and, indeed, conflicting) realities. This is quite unlike the Christian (e.g. Saint Augustine) and modern/Enlightenment concepts (e.g. Kant) of evil that actively seek to divest it of its ontological substance (in the first instance) and its meaningfulness in a conceptual framework that prioritizes the empirical, rational, scientific and objective over faith and superstition. Enlightenment political philosophy also urges dialogue and tolerance, factors that are not immediately evident in current political debates over the threat of terrorism.

2. *Contradiction*—the rather bizarre combination of realism with liberalism (as noted by Jervis) results in a number of contradictions in terms of policy based actions and decision-making processes. Rationality, objectivity and restraint would not be immediately recognizable as key principles to describe much of the political rhetoric and action operationalized in the war on terror. While not strictly speaking registering on the radar of political liberalism and the discursive structure of the modern nation state, nonetheless it turns out that evil is a primary factor invigorating political activity and policymaking (even at the very serious level of going to war against another nation state). But when the state is the victim, who takes over the objective stewardship of the criminal justice process on the state's behalf? International courts and other transnational bodies, in this regard, appear to have limited power and

success as regulatory or judicial forces. Given the nature of the harsh and sometimes extralegal punishments handed out to terrorist suspects and offenders (to include torture), it would seem that the state is a vicious and vengeful victim.

3. *Denial*—systematic denial of the suffering of the other and the implicit moral responsibility for causing such evil. The 'end' of history vis-à-vis apocalypse, or the temporal spirituality of 'rapture', the immanence of the US as a dominant world power or whatever does not negate or justify the suffering of so many blameless people and on the environment on such a massive scale (for studies of which see Roberts et al., 2004).

4. *Fear*—particularly fear of fear, or fear of contamination by placing 'others' on an opposing 'axis'. Fear of recognizing that evil is rife in modern global capitalism; the need to maintain a cultural climate of fear in order to legitimate the above-oriented policy decisions. As we know from our venture into psychoanalysis, fear is a potent and often unpredictable emotion, especially when it is at the root of violent crime.

> For some commentators, trying to grasp what motivates Islamic suicide bombers by, say, pointing to the despair and devastation of the Gaza Strip, is to absolve them of their guilt. But you can condemn those who blow up little children in the name of Allah without assuming that there is no explanation for their outrageous behavior— that they pulverize people simply for kicks. You do not have to believe that the explanation in question is sufficient reason to justify what they do. Hunger is a sufficient reason for smashing a bakery window at two o'clock in the morning, but it is not usually regarded as an acceptable one, at least not by the police. I am not, incidentally, suggesting that resolving the Israel-Palestine problem, or any other situation in which Muslims today feel abused and humiliated, would make Islamic terrorism disappear overnight. The grim truth is that it is probably too late for that. Like accumulating capital, terrorism has a momentum of its own but it is a fair bet that, without those humiliations, such terrorism would never have got off the ground.
>
> Eagleton (2010: 7–8)

> But it is precisely the fact that they are human that makes what terrorists do so appalling.
>
> Eagleton (2010: 9)

In his book *Holy Terror* (2005), Eagleton addresses these very issues pertaining to the war on terror and the cultural phenomenon of terrorism, revisiting the significance of evil as a key concept in the current political and cultural realities. Eagleton begins by contesting the utility of existing political discourses of 'left' and 'right' as being inadequate for discussing and making sense of the current global political climate. In particular, he claims that the challenge of terrorism makes it necessary to reconsider and revise conventional ways of talking about such issues. This doesn't necessarily mean finding an entirely 'new' political language to enable debate and dialogue, but paradoxically harking back in a new way to what is a range of very old concepts, among them, evil.

Part of the disruption to the established political discourses emanating from the Enlightenment legacy of secularism, rationalism, pluralism, tolerance and individual human rights with its rather disinterested, dry and abstract, objective character is to return to some older and less familiar notions to make sense of current events. These other notions include the thought of death, sacrifice, the sublime and evil (Eagleton, 2005: vi). The purpose of this 'return' to reconsider concepts such as evil does not mark a recourse to reactionary politics in the face of fear and loathing reignited by terrorism, turning for some kind of solace to the past. Rather, Eagleton argues, the return to such ancient concepts marks a distinctively modern desire to extend the discourse of the 'left' while also posing challenges to the 'right' in the wake of disturbing and puzzling political violence that doesn't seem to be alleviated by debates limited to such conventional language. What we need to do now is not just allow political elites to use terms like 'evil' uncontested, but to begin to take seriously such concepts and become more knowledgeable and critical about their usage and meaning.

To this end, Eagleton claims we can learn from the great dramas of ancient Greece—tragedies and comedies—(in this instance we will focus on Aeschylus' *The Bacchae*) as a way of comprehending contemporary forms of such political evil involving threats to the authority or sovereignty of the state. 'Reason, faced with libidinal riot, goes berserk, as one kind of excess (anarchy) provokes another (autocracy) into being. Pentheus, one might venture, reacts to the cult of Dionysus rather as the FBI reacted to the cultists at Waco' (Eagleton, 2005: 5). In the wake of the release of such disproportionate and indiscriminate violence by the security apparatus of the state, it is not entirely clear who is the 'terrorist' here, the 'cultists' or the state. What is clear is that neither party would appear interested in exercising rational, disinterested, restrained control over their actions, or in finding a non-violent diplomatic solution that spares the indiscriminate death and suffering of vulnerable and defenceless victims, including children.

In such classic dramaturgical discourses from ancient Greece, the evil of sexual transgression and excess (e.g. orgy, unrestrained female sexuality, maternal sexuality, incest) serves a distinct purpose in reaffirming the normative values of society as a whole, in part by emphasizing the 'interweaving of the alien and the intimate' (Eagleton, 2005: 8) and the disturbing proximity of intimacy and otherness that all of us share in our daily lives. This is the basis of the 'enemy within' narrative that while it is very 'shadowy', scary and anxiety-provoking, is at the same time fundamental to the idea of political society (e.g. civilization, and the collective values placed upon the social contract and following rules). Such is the basis of the public–private divide and the implicit role of child socialization and gender norms enshrined in the ideology of the conventional family as an intrinsic part of this civilizing process. The same lessons that make us upright moral citizens—e.g. regarding the dangers of murder, incest, rape and so forth—are ironically those that most threaten to shatter us as individual subjects (Eagleton, 2005: 8). 'This is one of several reasons why the authoritarian preserves a secret compact with the anarchist' (ibid.: 9). On the other hand, as we saw with Bataille, sexual transgression and excess can have their liberating and edifying aspects too; this is the basis of his ventures and explorations into the realms of sexuality and the erotic and his wanton violation of taboos (specifically around maternal sexuality). Similarly, as in *The Bacchae*, most mothers are not intent on sexually devouring their own sons. Though these stories still do shock, they also have the effect of teaching us humility, instilling a social ethos to resist the rigid intransigence of strident political authority, and to retain a healthy scepticism toward puritanical sexual codes, family structures and gender norms through which such political agendas are enacted.

Eagleton argues that myths and storytelling are key here, and central to constraining the evils that are in our midst and how we can better understand them, beyond and underneath the political rhetorics built upon their invisible foundations. Every fairy tale in which the rough beast becomes a handsome prince—and every beautiful virgin princess that becomes a wicked queen or evil hag—has its seed in this transfiguration. This means, however, that there is a secret affinity between what founds the state—violence—and what lays siege to it, and what it is possible for it to become, including the moral depths to which it could sink. This is not to claim a moral equivalence between the terrorist and the state: citizens do indeed need safeguarding, by force if necessary, from

those who threaten to destroy them. Terror (and indeed the evil of suffering as, for instance, in the pain noted by Ricoeur in punishment) has
its legitimate uses in civil society; but it is to be approached with rev-
erence, in fear and trembling. If the state is to deploy evil effectively
and right, it must acknowledge, respect and understand evil's duplici-
tous nature. Otherwise, as in the case of Pentheus, the sweetly seductive
unleashing of terror as an expression of moral outrage against evil by
humiliated state actors can result in the violence turning back on the
aggressors and tearing their own societies apart. Civilization must pay
homage to its other, not least because there is a sense in which it feeds
off it (Eagleton, 2005: 15). What Eagleton argues in *Holy Terror* is that
the sacred (good and evil) is a 'Janus-faced power' (115). It is vitality,
at once life-affirming and death-dealing. It is an awesome power that
should not be taken lightly, but approached with extreme trepidation,
and great restraint.

In this context, Eagleton is urging a more nuanced and inclusive
understanding of evil (and also of good in the sphere of the 'sacred'),
the opposite of the mutually exclusive Manichean version advocated by
the Bush administration. Modern civilization, including modern nation
states, have at their roots the kind of violence, fear and chaos they seek
to purge from their midst. While this undoubtedly constitutes a paradox that gives rise to supreme contradictions in practice (as the political
scientists recognize), this is nonetheless the reality of our human condition as historical and cultural creatures and citizens, who make sense of
experience not just through rationality but also through our emotions
and myths. This applies even to us moderns.

Does this recognition of evil and cultural relativism mean Eagleton
endorses the 'war on terror'? Not at all. Similar to Chan (2005), in the
so-called war against terror, 'evil' is used to foreclose the possibility of
not just political debate but also historical explanation. In this sense,
Eagleton argues, 'evil' has something like the function of the word 'taste'
during the eighteenth century. In the disparagement of rational analysis which it suggests, it reflects something of the fundamentalism it
claims to confront. Explanation is tantamount to exculpation. Reasons
become excuses (Eagleton, 2005: 116). In our analysis of evil and crime,
this is a familiar and pernicious conflation, and one which is, with a
better understanding of the concepts and theories of evil, possible to
overcome.

What Eagleton is doing in his analysis of evil is to utilize the methodological tools of narrative, cultural analysis and literary criticism to
expose the dangerous rhetoric of evil as deployed by the current political

powers that be. Paying attention to the ways in which they use language (specifically their strong reliance on metaphor and the implications of these modes of signification) is in many ways more revealing of the political reality we face than just taking what the politicians tell us at face value, which is frequently tautological and rhetorical in any case and offers nothing by way of real explanation. With alarming frequency and irony, the reality appears to be that such political discourses are used by state actors to violate, pervert or roll back legal regulations that protect the civil and human rights of individual citizens and communities. When it comes to primary reliance on the term 'evil' for political and military action in the real world, such outcomes are not surprising. What Eagleton is recommending is that in the modern world of *real politik*, it is wise and pragmatic to refer back to some premodern notions, ideas and ways of knowing that might actually help us to make sense of our world now, evil being one of them. Again, this isn't a reactionary step, but one that strives to interpret the world in a more nuanced, inclusive and intellectually mature and humanitarian way, one that doesn't depend on a reductive and simplistic identification of who the good guys and the bad guys are. The truth is much more complex than this and much more disturbing, but continuing to deny this is probably just guaranteed to make things worse.

Madness and irrationality of evil in terrorism?

Eagleton argues that if we insist on regarding terrorism as madness and its root causes are completely irrational, then what we are really doing is ensuring that we can never understand let alone defeat it. This is because this—along with our irrational belief in our own moral probity and adherence to reason—is a huge distortion of the reality. To say otherwise is to put too much store in our own propaganda, or to put it another way to believe in our own bullshit. The truth is, in contemporary global politics, neither 'side' is totally mad or totally sane. No political agent is totally good, or completely evil. It is only too evident in contemporary international politics that violence as a way of pursuing your political aims often (if not always) succeeds—look at the IRA (e.g. White, 1993) and the recent dialogues between the Taliban and the US. While it is morally objectionable to kill people more or less indiscriminately in order to achieve your political objectives, it is not irrational; as Eagleton puts it, it's not like thinking you are Marie Antoinette. The truth is that terrorists and the state use violence indiscriminately or at least disproportionately, and owe this to their power, and also to their problems in making political capital out of this brute exercise of power.

Eagleton advises us to ditch the war on terror and its construction of evil as a brush with metaphysical as opposed to historical actors and events. Even the SAS can't defeat Satan (Eagleton, 2005). The thing about metaphysical or diabolical evil (as we saw in chapters 2 and 3) is that it is totally inexplicable, from the human point of view, and hence open to utter speculation and manipulation by those who would use fear of the unknown for political gain. Perhaps the most unsettling thing about historical evil is that it is potentially all too explicable, and its consequences and justifications all too human.

Finally, before concluding our explorations of evil and the state, let us look briefly at a feminist interpretation of this thorny and intimately intertwined relationship. Andrea Dworkin (1946–2005) was a Jewish American and a radical feminist. She wrote extensively on physical and sexual violence against women, and was deeply committed to radical change of the current patriarchal social order. Her works are extremely interesting and challenging, but also very provocative and controversial. Here, we will concentrate on her polemical argument against the violent militancy and sexism of the Israeli state developed in her book *Scapegoat: The Jews, Israel and Women's Liberation* (2000).

Dworkin begins her analysis the modern nation state with a critique of nationalism. She is particularly concerned about the link between nationalism and sexism in the modern age. She argues that the modern capitalist nation state is built upon the largely unpaid and undervalued work and social marginalization or exclusion of women. The affective spirit of nationalism is suffused with feelings of romance, obsession, infatuation, love without condition and blind loyalty to one's fellows. This ethos is consonant with the erotic ideology of heterosexual romantic love and, like it, forms the basis of patriotism, citizenship and the social contract upon which the modern nation state is built. Liberty, equality and fraternity are not coincidentally bonded to brotherhood.

As we saw in the previous chapter, Hannah Arendt [1963] (1977) argued that the Eichmann trial and Jewish nationalism emerged from the establishment in the public mind of the linking of the Jewish diaspora, the Holocaust and the state of Israel. Subsequently, there was a new and strong sense of collective identify among Jews, as a diaspora and as citizens of a modern nation state, and that they (as well as the state of Israel) are constantly in danger of great evil, under siege no matter where they live, including Israel. Jewish feelings of nationalism and nationhood spread beyond the nation of Israel, and these feelings of fear and peril as shaped and experienced by the Jewish diaspora began to influence national policy of other nation states (notably the US). Consequently, according to Dworkin (2000), the realities and dynamics of Arab and Palestinian suffering took on a much less urgent tone in the public imagination, with a much lower appetite for subjecting the Israeli military-security machine to public criticism for the suffering inflicted on the Arab 'other'. The priority is to defend the state of Israel, at any and all costs. In these unfortunate incidences of abuse carried out by the Israeli security and military forces, the excesses of Israeli soldiers are often excused as 'just following orders', a chilling phrase used to justify the actions of any state, not least for a Jewish intellectual. As a Jewish woman in the aftermath of the Holocaust, Dworkin was deeply disturbed by this infliction of great suffering on 'a people' and the public and intranational tolerance of it and international indifference to it, as well as the ease with which Jewish soldiers are able to divest themselves of moral responsibility as 'just following orders' as the Nazi war criminals did.

Dworkin argues that in nation states like Ireland, Algeria, France, Israel (and Palestine) and many others, where women support liberation movements, in the aftermath of conflict, when insurgent or other groups assume power, women are immediately resubordinated and their suffering of women (on both sides) is devalued and ignored. While their complicity in 'armed struggle' is typically lionized and women are promised the world during active resistance, when the fight is over, these promises tend to come to nothing and women and girls are simply told to get back into the home and back to their unpaid and/or sexual work. Dworkin paraphrasing Paul Breines (Dworkin, 2000: 71) insists that nationalism breeds conformity, an ideology of toughness, paranoia in the face of difference and violence. These are feelings and a political ethos toward other nations and peoples that she considers highly dangerous and deeply hypocritical.

For women, the family is the ideological manifestation of the state. 'All power and authority traditionally reside in the head of the family, male; and religion, culture, art, and money delineate and reinforce his sovereignty over women and children' (Dworkin, 2000: 73). In the family, women are accorded the affective and private domain of 'love' as the source of meaning (not real love which is reciprocal but the 'love' of subordination and servitude); her work is unpaid and usually undervalued. Her other main duty is to reproduce and to socialize her daughters to fulfil similarly subordinate and sometimes exploitative roles. In many cultures, the woman of the family is even subordinate and subservient to her own sons.

The family is the physical and social site of women's captivity. Betty Friedan, another Jewish feminist intellectual of the time, controversially called it the 'comfortable concentration camp' [1963] (1992). On the other hand, the family epitomizes the private realism, is the site of men's absence, as they occupy other and more powerful places in the public sphere. In the aftermath of WWII where everyone, women included, was promised so many freedoms, the modern nuclear family was immediately constructed as the central carceral institution delimiting the power, freedom and influence of women for participation in the public sphere and also the possibility of self-realization in the private or individual domain. Dworkin reiterates the fact that women (and children for that matter) are more likely to be violently abused in the home than they are on the street; a criminological fact that is still the case to this day. This division between the public and private spheres where violence against women and children remains largely hidden and unaddressed is a major issue for Dworkin, and reflects the intrinsic imbalance of gender power relations in the institutional organization of the modern nation state. This is the real truth behind the 'freedoms' of the state, one built upon conflict, violence and the widespread toleration of victimization and crime.

Dworkin goes on to link the systematic correlation between relations characterized by conflict and violence in the home and at the level of the state on the international stage. Like their patriarchal male counterparts, states as actors are able to manifest their will in the global arena by adversarial politics backed up by the threat of military force, which constantly generates fear and aggression and then seeks to remedy this through the actual use of coercion, often violently. This is the real history of the modern age, and it seems to get more violent and atrocity-ridden as it goes on. There is little or no real effort or confidence invested in more consensual and collaborative means of conflict resolution which Dworkin associates with the (social) aspects of femininity, or the divestment of power from the top-to-bottom hierarchical structures of modern social institutions. In other words, it's a man's world at the public and private, family and state levels, and it operates according to very masculine principles of 'power over', rationality and conflict. This is rooted in a Hegelian political 'politics of Right' that views history, philosophy and consciousness (both individual and collective) as formed by an active yet 'monstrous' egotism whereby spirit/mind/*Geist*, thought and language are collapsed into what is propounded to be a transparent, rational and universal process of signification that benefits all (Gallagher, 1997; Ferguson, 1993). As such phenomena reliant upon presumptions of the universality, homogeny and self-evidenced legitimacy of rational hegemony encountered previously have demonstrated, on this idealized model of history and the state, evil often ensues.

Evil and 'the chosen'

Dworkin develops her thesis implicating the state in the systematic abuse and suffering of women, children and disenfranchised 'others' by drawing attention to the link between the historical and mythical suffering of the Jewish people and their status as God's 'Chosen people'. This, she says, provides a strong cultural and narrative model legitimating the infliction of sometimes great and even undeserved suffering on the ones you love (with you in the role of God/sovereign)—remember Job (Chapter 2)? The wielding of great power is accompanied by emotions of desire jealousy and anger, in both the relationship between God and His people and also between man and his 'chosen' woman on the paradigm of romantic love. This spiritual paradigm, theological principle, lends itself to sadomasochism and the equivalence between being 'chosen' and suffering. Both are extremely influential in the experience of women in the state.

The Jews as 'the Chosen' have had to endure jealousy and envy among modern men. Dworkin claims that Hitler was in part motivated by his coveting of this chosenness and, like other anti-Semitic leaders, sought to appropriate it from the jewish people as the property of the new 'Master Race', hence the need to destroy the Jews. This leads to even more suffering by the Jewish people. A mark of this 'chosenness' and the Covenant among Jews is the practice of circumcising their men. Even though it has become a widespread practice among some non-Jewish populations in the interests of 'hygiene' (again, notably in the US), for Jewish men, circumcision still carries a specific symbolic meaning. Dworkin argues that this particular practice marks Jewish men in a very special way, on the body, and as such it gives rise to huge if latent castration anxiety among other men (the excision of the penis) thus symbolically linking them with women (as penis-less and bleeding beings). Chosenness equates to the strong ethnic, racial (and by extension national) sense of identity and superiority, but also leads to the Jewish identification as the 'Other' for those who are not among the chosen. This is a very potent and dangerous status in a political context dominated by volatile masculinity, aggression, conflict and violence. George Steiner has similarly argued that the symbol of the 'Chosen' race served Hitler as a model for Aryan racial superiority. But in the context of evil and the state, Dworkin is more interested in the cultural and political phenomenon of linking chosenness with femininity.

Here, we encounter the symbolic construction of what Dworkin terms the 'menstruating male'; the bleeding and emasculated man as a symbol of the evils of both chosenness and submission, phenomenal qualities linked by atrocious and undeserved suffering. 'The chosenness antagonizes; the submission feminizes' (Dworkin, 2000: 115). Both are extremely sinister and the source of overwhelming anxiety and fear among men. It has generated massive amounts of hostility and resentment against the Jews as 'feminized' men. Counter-intuitively, Dworkin offers the example of the iconic menstruating male in relation to the state as the figure of the crucified Jesus. Symbolically, for Dworkin, one of the central strengths of this New Testament Christian storn of the scourging and crucifixion of Christ is its power to supplant the Hebrew God with a new figure of the divine that similarly links chosenness and suffering in a new covenantal relationship. But take away the narrative conclusion of resurrection contained in the Christian narrative, and what you have, Dworkin contends, is a paradigm case of the historical suffering of the Jewish people in the figure of the crucified Christ. There is the brutal and violent attack on an innocent and defenceless person, feminized by the piercing of Jesus's body by the centurion (a symbolic act of rape foretold by prophesy). Dworkin asks her readers to consider an alternative version of the Christ story, or 'the good news' as it is termed in Christian theology, as a possible source of reflection on the residual Jewishness of the Christian Saviour King and God, and a way of perceiving the great historical suffering of blameless and nameless peoples (men, women and children) at the hands of the state. True to the radical and polemical character of Dworkin's thought, her use of the story of the crucified Christ as a model for Jewish suffering and chosenness and its symbolism as a narrative for the suffering of women and children in relation to the state is deeply counter-intuitive but astonishing in its perspicacity as a way of reflecting afresh on the politics of evil and the state, and the complicity of institutions and norms converging around nationalism, identity, the family, gender and the erotic ideologies of chosenness and romantic love.

Summary and conclusion of section

In this and the previous two chapters, we have considered evil from the point of view of the social sciences, e.g. social psychology, anthropology, cultural/film/media studies, political science, sociology and feminist theory. While the emphasis has not surprisingly focused on context—whether history, social structures, politics, narrative, gender and/or sexual norms, culture, language—nevertheless, concepts derived from some of the theological and philosophical theories considered in the early chapters of this book remain relevant. In this chapter, as we have seen, even the most recent efforts to make sense of one of the most current and contemporaneous of modern manifestations of evil, i.e. terrorism and state violence, still require a knowledge of some theories from the ancient world, such as Manicheanism, the Augustinian concept of evil as privation and narrative respresentations of evil in ancient Greek tragedy and Judeo-Christian myth. Each of these in their own way help illuminate new dimensions of recent political discourses and rhetorics converging in the 'axis of evil', the 'war on terror' and the 'enemy within'. In addition, other more modern concepts of evil such as those contained in the rationalist philosophy of Descartes, and more recent theories put forward by thinkers such as Jean Baudrillard and Andrea Dworkin, demonstrate the usefulness of interdisciplinary theories of evil from philosophy and feminist theory for criminological research. What we have seen over the last three chapters is a reconsideration of traditional understandings of evil (Manicheanism, myth, symbol, narrative), and in the social sciences a putative rejection of metaphysical notions of evil; an embracing of evil as a human and historical-political (and collective) phenomenon.

At the same time, in this chapter, we have seen this so-called rejection metaphysics, onto-theology and myth dissipate with the return of metaphysical evil in the age of terrorism. As Baudrillard has strongly argued, the war on terror requires us to pursue a more critical and informed 'intelligence of evil'; that is, a true knowledge about evil that incorporates philosophical insight into its actual 'duality and reversibility' (Baudrillard, 2005: 159). Evil is not a metaphysical or objective reality; it has no real substance; it is not to be confused with the 'crude Manicheanism' (Chan, 2005) the Bush administration considers it to be. Evil isn't 'reversible' in that it is the opposite of the good, rather it is 'reversible' in the sense that it is always 'turning about, as a reversible form of becoming' (ibid.: 159). It is 'automatic': a part of existence that is constantly returning in our lives, re-emerging as a form in our present existence. Evil is 'radical' (in the Kantian sense) in that it is 'implied automatically in every one of our acts' (ibid.: 160). According to Baudrillard, evil doesn't exist as such as a substantial ontological reality, but it is a 'form' that shapes our (increasingly virtual-material) existence.

But to then consider it as merely non-existent and therefore empty or vacuous is to be too naïve about evil and its influence in the world. It knows and shapes us, so we must do what we can to know and shape it as it really is.

Finally, with evil as the 'enemy within' we have in the work of Andrea Dworkin observed the proximity and intimacy of evil in public and private life, the gendering of organized and state violence in global modernity and the disproportionate impact on women and children of nationalism and the ideology of romantic love. In the words of the philosopher Alain Badiou: 'I might also have pointed out that the most intense subjective sufferings—those that really highlight what is involved in "hurting someone", and often lead to suicide or murder—have as their horizon the existence of a process of love' (2001: 66).

In the next and final chapter, we will explore all of the previous in terms of influencing and informing criminological research into just such types of suffering and harm.

10
Conclusion: Touching the Void or Looking Through a Glass Darkly? Evil and Criminology

This final chapter comprises a summary of the main themes covered in the previous chapters in respect of the three main categorical theories of evil (at least as I have mapped them; certainly there would be alternative ways): onto-theological and philosophical, narrative and psychoanalytic, and social scientific. This summary is conducted with a view to the relevance (or otherwise) of evil to the study of crime, criminality, deviance and/or social control—the traditional domains of criminology as an academic subject discipline. We will briefly look at how each disciplinary area has dealt with the 'problem' of evil vis-à-vis concepts, epistemologies, ontologies, sense-making processes and partial (re)solutions. I will conclude by reflecting on what these different approaches offer to the understanding of evil and its potential for use as a concept for understanding crime, or for criminology.

Theodicy and philosophy

This book began with a consideration of what Paul Ricoeur called the 'onto-theological' conception of evil, particularly as it is represented in the theodicy, or the 'problem of evil', in a world created by an absolutely good God. How can evil exist when God has made the world, and us, who are imperfect creatures who do evil? What we encountered there were a number of resolutions of this more or less syllogistic conundrum, based on mythic, Gnostic and/or rationalist lines of reasoning. These resolutions of the problem of evil verged widely from what Susan Neiman (2002) identified as the 'best of all possible worlds' (e.g. Leibniz) variants that focus on this world and making the best we can with what we've got of an occasionally bad lot (a kind of communitarian approach as depicted, for example, in the stories of the Hebrew

Bible) or alternatively on the 'it's all good' versions that tend to gloss over or seek to explain away what appear to be grave consequences of evil as unfortunate yet necessary milestones on the road to perfection (e.g. in the infamous Malthusian theodicy). While the moral and ethical connotations of these theodicies vary wildly, to say the least, the justifications, rationales and impact of socio-economic factors such as global capitalism would tend to suggest that they would be, or should be, of interest to a social scientific discipline like criminology that seeks to deal with the commission, consequences and/or regulation of such inbuilt, systematic violations and harms.

What does theodicy have to do with criminology? In his book *The Trouble With Evil* (1997), the sociologist of deviance and frequent contributor to the theoretical literature on criminology Edwin Lemert is fairly forthright in his denunciation of theodicy as capable of contributing in any especially meaningful way to sociology (and by extension other cognate social sciences such as criminology). Neither, he contends, are disciplines like anthropology or sociology able to offer anything to contribute to the understanding of evil as represented by theodicy. In the face of such a declaration, arrived at after his rather fruitless journey into the domain of evil recounted in the Preface, Lemert devotes a short paragraph in the first chapter of his book to his thesis that there is nothing to see here, and that we criminologists should basically move along to direct our critical gaze at something else which holds out the prospect of being more promising (in his case, concentrating on the anthropological study of witchcraft and sorcery, and the sociological phenomenon of the witch hunt).

But is this really a fair conclusion of the matter? Is Lemert justified in his conclusion about evil/theodicy and its utility (or not) for criminology?

In my view, the answer to this question is no, not necessarily because I disagree with Lemert on what he does say (which sometimes I do) but because I think he has given it too little serious consideration, despite his prefatory remarks decrying the amount of time he has already spent on this vexed topic. And to be fair to him, he is not the only one to have had this experience and come out of it feeling 'best not'.

But, given the range, diversity and complexity of approaches and issues considered in this book, is it really such a surprise that evil has proven to be so elusive, even after years of study and to the likes of a mind like Lemert's? I don't think that the admittedly frustrating lack of clear and decisive conclusions about evil should have surprised Lemert if he had really thought about it, as it has eluded some of the greatest minds of centuries past. Maybe it smacks of hubris to consider that if it hasn't yielded itself up to years of study by any individual scholar, then it is best dismissed as a lost cause. Perhaps the days of searching for theories and concepts that are less 'ambiguous' have passed. Maybe the best we can offer is a series of tiny insights gained through arduous study over a long time and among a great number of contributors, taken together and across each other. And perhaps paradoxically, we see more and more of those who are accused or convicted of heinous acts in the public and popular press denounced as 'evil' as if we all know what this means. For criminologists, is it sustainable or desirable to continue to ignore this recursion to evil as a designator of criminality, deviance, and regulation. Maybe a better question is this: is it legitimate or advisable for us as academic criminologists to ignore an explanatory concept that has such enduring public appeal? Probably not, as this in itself seems to distance us from public debate more and more.

So let us then reconsider, as our first example, the uses of theodicy for a discipline like criminology:

> There is a kind of tautology or circular argument implicit in the policeman's view. People do evil things because they are evil. Some people are evil in the way that some things are coloured indigo. They commit their evil deeds not to achieve some goal, but just because of the sort of people they are. But might this not mean that they can't help doing what they do? For the policeman, the idea of evil is an alternative to such determinism. But it seems that we have thrown out a determinism of environment only to replace it with one of character. It is now your character, not your social conditions which drives you to unspeakable deeds. And though it is easy enough to imagine an environment being changed—slums demolished, youth clubs set up, crack dealers driven out—it is harder to imagine such a total transformation which it comes to the question of human character. Yet if I happen to be evil, only such a deep-seated change will do. So policemen are really pessimists ...
>
> Eagleton (2010: 4)

If nothing else, from what we have seen, the theodicy—among other religious and theological treatments of evil—serves a useful and, in many ways, cautionary purpose. It exposes at once the deeply human and also ineffable nature of evil as something which has affected all people at all times and can thus be counted as part of the human condition, like deviance and crime (as well as the socio-economic need and ideological mechanisms through which to operationalize methods of social control). Theodicy emphasizes the dualistic nature of good and evil, that these are regarded according to the conventions of theodicy to two mutually exclusive categories, primarily human but nonetheless conditioned by the presence of God. This modelling and syllogistic logic of evil is in many respects enshrined in the legal-juridical system, emphasizing blameworthiness and guilt on the part of the perpetrator as opposed to the suffering of the victims, and the need—if not the longing—for lament on the part of wrongdoers. As Ricoeur noted, theodicy as a way of representing and resolving the problem of evil exposes our strange passivity in the face of the evil we suffer and commit; that despite the dualistic and formal structures we erect around evil (e.g. formal systems such as religious institutions, the criminal justice system and informal ones like gossip and ostracism), we still feel ourselves to be victims even when we are guilty of doing evil, that somehow we have been compelled or seduced by some stronger, outside influence that we as mere mortals are simply too weak to resist. It's that God is testing us, a demon is tricking us or that we are just not up to obeying the prevailing moral code because of a weakness that is not our fault.

Is God—or the devil—the problem with theodicy? Even more overtly secular-humanist attempts to rationalize and manage evil based on a theology model carry their own perils. That is because what theodicy does is expose the often horrific dangers inherent in trying to totally 'rationalize', explain or even solve the problem of evil within what are the limited terms of human reason. This should act as a warning about the hubris of expectation and denial with respect to what are our imperfect powers of understanding and remedy when it comes to the evils that we do and suffer. As Lemert himself alludes, theodicy offers a valuable insight into the origins of humanist theories like functionalism; that is, a recurrent and occasionally highly influential (or deeply disparaged, depending on your point of view) sociological theory based on a hard science/biology model that takes the view that social phenomena should be understood in terms of the 'organic' whole, not any particular part. But, as the contributions of theologians and philosophers like Ricoeur have argued, this way of studying evil and the human condition is fraught with hazards, not least of which is the 'rationalization' (i.e. dismissal) of the sometimes dire suffering of one or more groups of (usually powerless, excluded or marginalized) people for the greater common good. Morally and ethically, from a contemporary human rights-oriented point of view, this is unacceptable, and it can be argued even warrants the label of 'evil' in its fullest sense in its ethical consequences and connotations. In addition, the inauguration of the victims' rights movement also in many ways casts light on the conventions of the criminal justice system based on the theodicy, exposing the fragility and limitations of the real-life suffering and trauma of being a victim and its true impact on the lived experiences of (in)justice. What is more, the neatness and objectivity of theodicy occludes what are the very messy realities of remorse, rehabilitation, healing and/or reoffending that are intrinsically embodied, emotional, cyclical, ritualistic and collective, not objective, measured, individualized and developmentally linear.

Notwithstanding these criticisms, the argument has been made that theodicy casts valuable light on the recently revived 'problem of suffering' or as it has been termed 'sociodicy' (Morgan and Wilkinson, 2001; Wilkinson, 2005). In this respect, even with its faults, theodicy provides the social sciences and other disciplines with a framework for critiquing the normative ideals of modernity (e.g. freedom, equality, fraternity, justice) with the realities with which we live (e.g. any number of varieties of previously unimaginable levels of human suffering, atrocities, inequalities and injustices on an apparently increasingly extreme, endemic and/or grand scale). From this point of view, it is not enough for social scientists to simply document the suffering that takes place in the modern world or identify random causes, but they must also reassess the origins of this suffering as among the consequences of or even implicit within the very notion of progress and power that constitute what we call the whole of the modern Enlightenment project, and how many of these 'evils' are caused by the multi-faceted and relentless drive toward 'progress' that capitalist modernity entails. Again, the theodicy exemplifies this slipperiness and irony of good and evil in the presence of attempts to objectify and eliminate it, where the most black and white binaries collapse into a single, ambivalent moral morass when we try to 'sort them out' in ways that don't take account of the whole picture. As Neiman (2002) states in her assessment of theodicy-type arguments, there is a notable difference between the position adopted by a philosopher like Leibniz that promotes the view that while not perfect this is the 'best of all possible worlds' and that of someone like Calvin, Al Gazali, Thomas Malthus or Bayle (in her example) that defend the hyper optimistic motto that 'it's all good' regardless of who gets hurt or gets the short end of the stick. Ricoeur detects similar foundational principles in the mythic versus the onto-theological versions of theodicy, whereby in the former God exists in and among His creation and deports Himself as a loving father, while in the latter, God is a distant, judgemental and ever-vigilant force of surveillance, noting our shortcomings and calculating our eternal punishments for the Day of Judgement. While each of these arguments has its advantages (sometimes), the trouble is that none of these calls to acceptance or sanguinity are especially comforting in the long run, at least not during the acute phase of pain when evil befalls us.

It is not just the fear generated by the conceptualization of the theodicy on this model as a mechanism for a rather crude rendering of knowledge as surveillance and related brutal mechanisms of social control (as noted by Foucault, with its emphasis on the subject formation and the need for the continuous monitoring of the self) that are difficult to take. It is also the implied hiatus or break it creates between guilt and punishment, as when innocent people suffer evils in this world for which they bear no direct or personal responsibility; a conundrum of evil that is by no means limited to us moderns. This rupture between guilt and punishment manifest by the widespread suffering of evil by 'innocents', as reiterated in the story of Job, threatens to destroy the very substance of any organized social system or institution to be able to explain and deal with evil vis-à-vis human rationality and moral agency. These are indicative of the sorts of frustrations, paradoxes, reversals and ironies of philosophical-theological attempts to rationalize evil for centuries.

And as numerous Jewish scholars and philosophers like Derrida and Dworkin have insisted, not only do such highly dualistic, reductive and abstract philosophical-theological efforts to rationalize and explain evil ultimately fail; more to the point, they often result in the proliferation of evil actors who then commit acts of even more indiscriminate and pernicious evil on ever more undeserving and defenceless victims. Political scientists like Jervis and Chan, in their analysis of the 'axis of evil', would exemplify this view, furthermore pointing out that the expansion and increase of such evils on a global scale is further exacerbated by the underlying sense of righteousness in the cause that such political actors, often those with great military power and self-belief in their moral probity, frequently claim. We might also refer to theories from the criminological canon such as that developed by Katz (1988) to argue that the state in its role as victim in the age of terrorism is every bit as much vulnerable to the strident emotions of humiliation, anger and vengeance as any street-gang member, and prone to act with disproportionate violence as a remedy to such deeply felt public shame and loss of international status. This can be observed not just in the pre-emptive and disproportionate military attacks upon and among the populations of other sovereign nations beyond the remit of international law and criminal justice systems as seen during the war on terror and before (e.g. the kidnapping of Adolf Eichmann by the Israeli secret service, the Iraq War and the assassination of Osama bin Laden), but also in the rolling back of civil and human rights for all citizens and suspects and the rise of extrajudicial mechanisms within and across national jurisdictions in the name of 'security' as a preventative to the evils of the 'enemy within'.

Turning to metaphysical theories of evil, the fable of the Evil Genius proffered by Descartes and reinvigorated by Derrida and Foucault presents us with the opportunity to reassess the moral and ethical value of the rationality we have ourselves placed at the centre of our modern world. This is to act as the touchstone for future progress and to protect us from the evil of error shaped by our overwhelming desire for *certainty*, with the transparency of glass and the mirror at its metaphorical core. But as philosophers such as Derrida and Baudrillard have argued, while the confidence and utility of such 'specular' and fundamentally reflexive systems of knowledge about entities like God, the world, the subject and 'the other' generated by modern science and rationalism may be in evidence, in reality, in the face of evil, these are often of extremely limited use, to put it mildly. In an age that is so dominated by what are increasingly mediated images and virtual realities, the proliferation of the demonic, horrific, terrifying and monstrous, without any discernible or proportionate motivation or restraint for being horrid and inflicting evil are clearly in evidence. This proliferation of evil exposes the frailty of personal and social morality based on codes of civility as opposed to the restraints of tradition and more interpersonal, informal mechanisms of control (as in premodern times). On the contrary, the rise and enmity of villainous evil in the form of the Internet 'troll' (for example) makes modern manifestations of and mechanisms for controlling evil all the more challenging and pressing. It would seem that the fable of the Evil Genius retains its dimensions of moral, as well as epistemological if not also ontological (i.e. relating to new and emergent worlds), meaning, revealing an evolving and challenging problem of evil.

Radical evil—Kant

We recall from our study of Kant that radical evil ' ... refers to our propensity knowingly to choose maxims contrary to the moral law' (Louden, 2000: 138). Radical evil is the (occasional) deviation from the moral law, even though we know what it is and what we should do. It is about our weakness or moral frailty, and sometimes even our wicked and perverse enjoyment, of doing bad things in order to satisfy what are essentially selfish desires. Basically, at our worst, we use people and other living beings as means to an end, and this end is our own base gratification. We all do it, or are prone to it. That's what is and all that is 'radical' about evil: it's essentially human quality, not something diabolical or to do with gods or demons.

Kant rejected theodicy as a failed experiment in the attempt to explain evil. His main problem with theodicy was that in its representation of transcendent/metaphysical realities and/or entities (e.g. God, the devil, other world(s), demons, evil geniuses etc.) it was too speculative, regardless of how obscure or sketchy its renderings of such beings, spirits or domains. Speculation in such an important area of moral philosophy, he argued, is simply unacceptable; we must concentrate our efforts as moderns on what we can and do know, not on what can never be fully comprehended or what might be. Such speculative approaches based on the evidence of superstition, tradition or hearsay are unfit for a modern scientific age and, more to the point, give moral actors an excuse to shift the blame for their evildoing onto other non- or extra-human causes. For Kant, this abdication of moral responsibility simply would not do. Is it dishonest and disempowering, and prevents us from grasping the moral nettle, as it were, and taking responsibility for our own actions, thereby enhancing the prospects for our character development and moral maturation. Basically, the problem with theodicy is that it tells us nothing, allows us to wiggle off the hook for the evil we do and ultimately holds us back from making any real progress (moral, personal or social).

Kant's rejection of theodicy and religion in favour of modern philosophy as a method of construing and dealing with evil extends to his refusal to accept that human beings could be diabolically evil. This is because he thought it was impossible for human agents to be sufficiently unself-interested in their motivations or perverse enough in their understanding of and relationship to the moral law to satisfy the conditions for this type of transcendental evil. He also thought it was impossible for the human subject to lose the degree of common sense, compassion, empathy and humanity in general for this conversion to take place and still be human. Such a diabolical stance was for Kant irreconcilable with his understanding of human nature, knowledge and being. I hope I am not unfairly paraphrasing Kant here, but what we can be certain of, as a starting and end point, is that we are not gods. While that might be the bad news, the good news is that we're not devils either. Our evil—and by implication the *only* evil we can actually do something about—lies somewhere in-between, in the realm of human being and understanding. Hence, Kant considered evil a problem for modern moral philosophers, not for theologians or religious leaders, because that kind of evil is basically beyond us, as a notion that is rationally comprehensible to a sufficient degree. Kant was, in terms of ethics, quite the pragmatist, and indeed he assigned ethics to what he called 'practical' (as opposed to 'pure') reason.

Was Kant right? Has history since born this out? Are we as open to good, or at least as (relatively benignly) selfish in our badness, as Kant's view of radical evil would seem to suggest? While Kant's work was decisive in removing the study of evil from its context in religious, theological and metaphysical thought, we may ask if its reconstitution as a problem for moral philosophy has really yielded the level of benefits that its subjection to human cogitation would have appeared to Kant to offer. Are we, for instance, less evil as people, members of communities, citizens or planet-dwellers than 'religious' premodern people were? Hmmm. Overall, the outcomes wouldn't appear to be particularly good.

At least it would seem that Kant's faith in things like common sense and human empathy and compassion might have been a bit optimistic as a prophylactic against evil in the context of what a global capitalism the likes of which he probably wouldn't have envisaged. Even the great Kant couldn't have predicted the depths and depravity of evil that were yet to be carried out intentionally by people who were very rational and even progressive in their use of modern technologies and scientific knowledge to do so, a theme that would present itself again in a most inauspicious way in the mid-twentieth century and beyond, and not just in his native land.

Narrative and evil—Ricoeur's symbolism of evil

In *The Trouble With Evil* (Lemert, 1997), Lemert is similarly critical of the potential of the study of the 'rhetoric' of evil, language or even the specific work on symbolism by Paul Ricoeur. He considers it just too ambiguous for the needs of social scientists. He also unfairly, in my view, represents Ricoeur's phenomenological hermeneutics as presenting a 'universal' or 'unilinear' historical account of the narratives of evil devised in the past. Rather, what we get from Ricoeur's work on the symbolism and historical narratives of evil is the (continuing) power of these symbols and narratives as ways of (in Ricoeur's own memorable phrase) 'bringing to language' the disruptive, ineffable, acutely raw and painful experiences of suffering we experience as an intrinsic part of our lives and as a constant of the human condition, the same as happened to all people in the past and to all those in the future. So rather than tracing a unilinear history, Ricoeur's hermeneutic and phenomenological concepts and typologies help us to decipher or 'decode' the types of stories we tell—and have always told and are yet to tell—ourselves and others about evil, so that we may gain some kind of insight into the world view implicated in these different and recurring narratives. As demonstrated in Chapter 4, Ricoeur's typologies can be analysed with respect to the use of symbolic language about evil, and in the utilization and development of the 'great narrative cycles' he found in cultural myths concerning the problem of evil. Hence, we see, again in the groundbreaking but as yet still developing work of those studying a range of social evils such as, for example, Katz's analysis of the stories told by and about serial killers and their reiteration of the primal narrative of the 'wicked god' and evil as chaos, to the evils of police violence and institutional racism represented in the symbolic language of evil in newspaper accounts of the beating of Rodney King by Jacobs (1996), the use and media representations of these hermeneutic and phenomenological renderings of evil are key to our reflexive understandings of the social harms that persistently 'bedevil' society.

As a recent commentator on policymaking in parole hearings quoted below indicates, the symbolism of evil is still a very live concept in the criminal justice system and beyond, whether we as social scientists like to admit it or not, in spite of criminological discomfort with such a value-laden, archaic and emotional word. For example, in his article 'Assessing Evil: Decision Behaviour and Parole Board Justice' (Hawkins, 1983) published in the *British Journal of Criminology*, the author makes this statement about the realities of the process of deciding on parole, emphasizing the elements of symbolism and evil, and that in many ways the parole decision is itself of symbolic importance in the public imagination:

> In analyzing the exercise of discretion by parole boards in reaching decisions about the release or continued incarceration of prisoners, one point in particular should be kept in mind. In making judgments about release or restraint, a parole board is engaged in the appearance of condoning or condemning criminal behaviour; it is making statements about good and evil, desert and punishment, to the prisoner, the institution, and the wider community. The parole decision, in short, is symbolically significant.
>
> Hawkins (1983: 102)

Here, again, the translation of the rationalism of theodicy to the institutional structures and principles of the criminal justice system that have placed the focus so forcefully on the accused individual and the establishment of his or her guilt, punishment and lament has as its legacy the reviving of narrative. For instance, the narrative perspective on evil and storytelling in relation to crime and criminality very much reasserts the legitimacy and primacy of *victims* and their experiences of suffering, trauma and harm, if only through its long absence in institutional/official judicial narrative. This is manifested in the rise of the victims movement specifically, and also in the reassertion of evil as a generic explanatory term in public/popular/ordinary discourses of crime and victimization. Hence, we see, in various media, that 'evil' is often used as a label but also a remedial and corrective term, rendering a critical edge to what many see as the intrinsic limitations or failures of the criminal justice system to produce what people consider to be justice. Again, in this respect, it is vital (albeit uncomfortable) for criminologists to take a more nuanced and serious view of evil and its theories, rhetorics and critiques in relation to the designations of good and evil, right and wrong, normal and deviant, and how these are understood and dealt with in what is an increasingly media-dominated age where public and popular perspectives are more vocal and potentially powerful than ever before. Regardless of its 'ambiguity', this is of paramount significance in many if not most people's understanding of and feelings about crime, deviance and social control. If nothing else, evil reveals that we are irredeemably 'ambiguous' creatures. Ricoeur and others state, this is where evil and its symbolic and narrative language exposes what are fundamentally basic dimensions of what is the human condition, what it is to be human. This has deeply philosophical ramifications vis-à-vis the 'problem of evil', as we have seen, but also very practical impacts on popular and everyday cultures, as Silverstone astutely recognizes:

> ... I want to explore the problem of evil as a singularly important one for an understanding of the contemporary moral order and the media's place within, and indeed responsibility for, that order. I want to suggest that the identification of evil is a problem for practical morality, in the capacity to make the singular judgements of absolute right and wrong that humanity must make if it is to survive. It is a problem for ethics and politics, in the rhetoricization of those judgements, judgements which in their convenient direction towards the status of the other, say a great deal about ourselves. And it is a problem for the media who, in their willingness to collude with such appellations, in that collusion both legitimate and amplify them.
>
> Silverstone (2007: 56)

I would argue that this increasingly hysterical space for the type of 'collusion' Silverstone identifies is expanded and exacerbated by the absence of critical and informed dialogue about evil and a theoretical and conceptual referent amplified by the silence of the academic community. It is the role of social scientists and criminologists to bring the necessary reflexive and critical traction to such public spaces to make these dialogues and debates about such evils more inclusive, informative and productive, not to simply opt out or otherwise recoil in disgust or horror. This does nothing to advance the profile or usefulness of criminology as a subject discipline in the public imagination, or to inform public debate about crime.

Evil and psychoanalysis

Psychoanalysis is a kind of hermeneutics (Ricoeur, 1970): the 'talking cure'. As in the work of reflection and interpretation, psychoanalysis relates our own individual experiences of evil to the symbols and narratives of our cultural and mythical histories. So interpretation and storytelling based on the use of symbol and myth are vital here, as is the process of self-reflection, subject formation and knowledge creation in the interactive process of communication. It is through articulating our experiences that we can gain a greater understanding of our world and ourselves, and thereby a better acceptance of the human condition, including the evils that we do and suffer. In relation to the trauma, inevitability and ineffability of evil, the need for articulation is, from a psychoanalytic perspective, often driven by neuroses and psychoses as the result of a deep psychic disruption between our conscious understanding and actions in relation to unresolved unconscious drives (often related to sexual and aggressive urges). Fear of the unknown propels our inscrutable, compulsive or addictive behaviour, specifically the urgency of deep-seated sexual and aggressive drives. According to Julia Kristeva (1982), Oedipal and pre-Oedipal sexual urges are key to making sense of evil as the dread and horror of abjection, the fear that is especially acute and endemic in modern individualistic societies of being isolated and alone, and prone to evil acts and epidemic levels of mental illness such as anxiety and depression. But there is a compelling, imaginative and even joyous dimension to evil exposed here too, as a possible moment of creativity, a revolutionary departure from convention and restraint. We are invited to consider the chaotic and sometimes even generative aspects of evil and the challenges and even opportunities for difference and development it poses. Creativity is not always positive (think of the atom bomb) and destruction is not always negative (think of student or other political protests). Neither are our loves and desires always 'good', let alone 'politically correct'; more often than not, just the opposite (e.g. the need and fear of what Kristeva called the 'archaic mother'). Dread, abjection, loss, fear and the neuroses and compulsive/addictive behaviours that accompany them are rife if not epidemic in modern societies, according to Kristeva; and there is ample evidence to indicate that these are significant contributing factors to crime, deviance and suffering as among the prevalent social evils of our times. Among other things, what such psychoanalytic theories offer is the opportunity to revisit or instigate new debates over the role of sexuality, desire and the feminine/maternal in crime and deviance irrespective of gender identity (e.g. male or female). The experience and grotesque nature of the body and embodied subjectivity in relation to such evils are key starting points for reflection here (as opposed to mind/spirit/ideas/*Geist*), being as they are the real and real-imagined site of ethics and subject formation, as a purely disembodied being would not be in need of either ethics or identity (or at least not as we know them) (Shabot, 2005).

Evil, literature and romanticism

In this chapter, we encountered the fullest and most wanton embracing of evil as something that wilfully and recklessly eludes rationality and laws (even the laws of genre). Here, we traced the cultural influence of romanticism in its celebration, fascination and obsession with evil as the basis of experiences of the sublime, horror, corruption and decrepitude; how it wallows in the moral relativism of our age, and takes joy from the lack of certainty about the world and the human condition. Evil in romanticism in art/literature was prevalent in the nineteenth century. This cultural phenomenon was intimately linked to the rise of the individual in modern Western industrial societies. In contrast to Cartesian rationalism and Enlightenment thought, romanticism comprised a resurgence and obstreperous celebration of the unruly: emotion, the body, spirituality, the paranormal and personal experience as basis of knowledge. Henceforth, nature and spirit, not reason, became the 'mirror' of humanity through which experience and feeling as the new source of reflection were refracted—another instance of that potent spec(tac)ular metaphor of evil in modernity. Romanticism was also intrinsically linked to the rise of industrial capitalism and the nation state, as manifest in the decline of religious orthodoxy, burgeoning of moral relativism and the immiseration of multitudes of people during the industrial era and urbanization. This, combined with a tendency to slip into sentimentality and nostalgia about the past and the future, led to naïve and often brutal political realities in the nineteenth century, and beyond. It is by no means coincidental that this was the age of experimentation and excess with respect to revolution, the terrors and numerous acts of anarchy in the realm of global politics.

Such a disavowal of the dispassionately rational and stoically intellectual extended to all areas of existence and philosophy, including creativity itself. The insistence on the 'artistic' nature of evil as both generative and destructive inspired by romanticism has endured, resulting in a widespread acceptance/expectation/tolerance even demand for artists to plumb the depths of human depravity, violate codes of decency, transgress and exceed taboos and other social norms on others' behalf and for the benefit of art (as argued and illustrated in the challenging works of De Quincey, Lord Byron, Bataille and Sade, among others). But does this legitimate the 'enjoyment' of the dire evils of our age, e.g. violence, atrocity, depravity, misogyny and war? Is it morally defensible to (re)claim evil (remember Ricoeur's typology and the myth of the wicked god, transforming evil via the cathartic beauty of the drama) as the domain of art? Is there, as Susan Sontag (1983) posited, an aesthetically and critically legitimate 'pornographic imagination'? And how do we in criminology construe such cultural products and ethics of deviance?

Evil and the social sciences—doing evil

In this third and final section of the book, we considered this fascination with the feelings associated with actually *doing* evil, the corporeal and emotional aspects of the evil deed, (finally) seeping into the social scientific discourse on evil in general and crime, in particular. It is not that Katz (1988) is celebrating evil (as opposed to some of the thinkers in the previous chapter), but rather that he is recognizing its influence as a causal factor in the committing of crime and other forms of deviance. This might not be quantifiable vis-à-vis the conventional theoretical frameworks or concepts of criminology as a science, but it would be utterly foolhardy to ignore it as a significant variable.

We also saw in this chapter how Katz drew on other theories, notably Ricoeur's *Symbolism of Evil*, as resources for developing his symbolic interactionist/ethnographic/phenomenological/hermeneutic analysis. Evil has a sensual and emotional quality that influences some people to want to, or feel compelled to, do it, and also impacts on our reception of it in the public domain. To make sense of evil and, indeed, crime as social scientists, we must look outside of our disciplinary comfort zone for help and answers, and in this regard, Katz (1988) has provided a useful example.

In this section, we also focused on some landmark research in the history of the social sciences, specifically the infamous obedience and Stanford Prison Experiments conducted respectively by Stanley Milgram and Philip Zimbardo. Both of these milestones in social psychology focused on the importance of social situations (as opposed to individual dispositions) when it comes to evil. They also emphasized the influential role of cultural norms of politeness, civility and self-identity to the phenomenon of evil in a modern and rational age dominated by bureaucracies and institutions which, in many ways, make the proliferation and damage of evil greater than ever due to the technological capacity and organizational reach. This is enabled and reinforced by a propensity for individuals to divest themselves of individual moral responsibility for their actions by assigning such responsibility to figures of authority or alternatively to roles or 'the system' itself. Such a divestment of moral agency and responsibility is, as is witnessed again and again, extremely dangerous and harmful, and represents a major challenge to the whole of the social sciences, particularly those with an interest in crimes of or involving the regulation and policing of bureaucratic organizations and/or the state.

Collective evil and genocide

Evil in the twentieth and twenty-first centuries emblematized as organized and horrific suffering was the subject of this section, and how this goes against but is in some ways the legacy of modern Enlightenment discourses of progress, tolerance and humanism, and the use of technology and science to make more people's lives better. The critiques presented pointed out that, to some extent, the rationality and efficient working of organizational systems, rather than (only) contributing to the common good, have all too often been implicated in the intentional and systematic suffering of greater numbers of people, to the point of the extermination of whole populations. Repeatedly in the 'long' twentieth century, we see the horror of genocide unfolding, but apparently we can do little to stop it. As Wole Soyinka testifies in his autobiography *The Man Died*, there is a widespread and comforting myth that these events happen spontaneously, but as in the Biafra situation, the reality is that they are ruthlessly planned and carefully orchestrated; in other words, they take time, preparation and effort, which is somehow allowed them in current international politics.

In the wake of the atrocities of the twentieth century, the question is, are those who perpetrate or engage in genocide evil monsters? This manifestation of evil resurrected the now familiar question of whether or not evil is dispositional or situational, and if they are monsters, are they born or made? Are the instigators of genocide villains, demons, ordinary people, or pathetic/sadistic/hateful/thoughtless 'clowns'? We saw in Hannah Arendt's work the transformation of the idea of the evil people behind such atrocities as monsters to the reconsideration of them as frighteningly ordinary. This thesis has attracted so much controversy that the topic of evil has remained largely undeveloped among scholars, at least until recent years. Arendt's thesis on the banality of evil has many echoes and similarities to the other approaches we have investigated which focus on the relative nature of evil and the fact that we are all capable of great good and also great evil (Kant) in the course of our everyday lives and activities. What is more, it is our 'progress' and the ethos of ambition and self-actualization within highly individualistic, morally relativistic, diverse and consumer-oriented societies that can contribute to the commission of atrocious evil on the scale of the Holocaust. This is the evil of our times, and the challenge to our ways of living, acting and being.

This section also focused on the notion of collective evil and the convergence of a number of elements in the manifestation of genocide drawing on the theories and concepts developed by thinkers such as Milgram, Zimbardo, Vetlesen and Staub on the convergence of a number of external (and to a more variable extent, internal) factors to make great collective acts of evil (e.g. genocide, slavery, war) possible. These include what would be categorized as a constellation of dispositional as well as situational, individual and collective factors, which Vetlesen breaks down into the three elements of character, situation and social structure, which are all dialogically related. Among other issues for a subject discipline like criminology is, in a culture that valorizes the individual, how are we to integrate into our legal, ethical and regulatory systems such notions of collective evil? How do we act to prevent and protect each and every global citizen from such vile and catastrophic evil using the tools and remedies we have to hand, and/or inventing others? And how do we face the manifold complexity of collective evil in the suffering, abuse and harm experienced by the non-human animals, nature and the environment in the wake of global warming etc.?

Evil and the state

This led us to consider finally the role and potential regulation of evil in relation to the state, the arbiter of the criminal justice system. Here, we encountered three very different but not necessarily unrelated treatments of evil specifically to do with the modern nation state. We began with the interesting arguments put forward by political scientists Jervis and Chan that the so-called 'war on terror' and the 'axis of evil' were based on a reductive and deterministic Manichean conception of evil as totally distinct from and in combat with the 'good'. Hence, the prominence of political discourses justifying pre-emptive and/or the unleashing of indiscriminate, disproportionate, frenzied, abandoned violence based on the forces of darkness and light, etc. which we spoke about in the opening chapters on theological and narrative theories of evil. On this analysis, the use of 'terror' and 'shock and awe' are deeply emotive and performative in nature, and their effects are profoundly and, indeed, emotionally traumatic and deeply felt, and this is just as much the case when a government sees itself as a victim of crime as when an individual citizen does. What is more, the lack of preparation for the aftermath of the military invasion of Iraq was not so much an oversight as it was the natural conclusion of a faith-based policy founded on the understanding of the 'good' filling the vacuum created by the excision of evil: this being aligned exclusively to the person and administration of Saddam Hussein.

We also explored Terry Eagleton's deconstruction of the war on terror, and his turning to the narratives of ancient Greek drama as vital resources in understanding the fear and anxiety of contemporary terrorism produced on the modern political stage. Eagleton advocated a reconsideration of notions from dramaturgical narratives of ancient and early modern societies such as evil (along with sacrifice, death and the sublime) as crucial to making sense of our own modern world. While this is not to try to go back and recreate a mythic or metaphysical world we no longer share with the past, it is rather to try to learn the lessons our ancestors taught through the stories they told about what are timeless human experiences. We would do well to listen and to respond to these stories, which reaffirm the non-dualistic, intimate and proximate nature of evil.

Finally, we explored Andrea Dworkin's thesis on evil, the family and the state. Like Eagleton, Dworkin found a close link between gender, the family, intimacy and the evil of great suffering. She also linked this to an ancient historical mythic tradition (in this case, Judaism) and traced this influence through the gender politics of the ancient to the modern world. Like many other theorists considered in the book and beyond, she closely scrutinized the myths and symbols surrounding the stories of evil and drew parallels to our own current political situation in which being 'chosen' often produces great suffering.

Criminologists on evil

What have criminologists and also commentators on crime made of evil in the past, including the not-so-distant past? Let's consider some of the different opinions on the matter in the authors' own words:

> The fallacious notion is that evil consequences (crime) must have evil precedents (biological pathologies, low IQ, pathological mental states, sordid living conditions).
> (Hugh Barlow, *Introduction to Criminology*, 1981: 36)

> 'Any theory based on personality traits must recognize and explain the fact that the delinquent often is, or may be, as attractive and as socially acceptable a sort of person as the nondelinquent' (Vold and Bernard, 1986: 199). Once again we observe a handy knowledge destruction technique: personality-criminality correlations may be discounted through judgments that the predictor variables are either 'too evil' or 'insufficiently evil.' More general still, of course, any personality finding may be discounted insofar as it is not rooted in the evils of capitalism.
> (Maclean, 1986)

(D.A. Andrews and J. Stephen Wormith, 'Personality and Crime: Knowledge Destruction and Construction in Criminology', *Justice Quarterly* 1989, 6: 3, p. 298)

History forms no structured 'whole' yet is made to appear as if it does by those with the power to do so; in this way and as such both they and history are empowered with seemingly 'natural' authority. It is through these processes that the meanings of crime become lost, buried deep in the histories of the powerful where crime becomes reprocessed into the discourse of evil acts and evil people.

(Mike Presdee, *Cultural Criminology and the Carnival of Crime*, 2000: 21–22, London: Routledge)

Given the data I find I conclude that the media study of 'evil' brings evidence to both an ongoing conception of 'crime' as socially constructed and an accompanying conception of 'crime' and 'criminal' as other than socially constructed. These findings support existent literature, which already argues that modern criminology is in part built on top of a model that rejects the social construction of crime.

(M.J. Coyle (sociologist), 'The Discourse of Crime as "Evil" in Media' (2005), unpublished manuscript)

It seems as if criminology has had something of a long-standing problem with, and also brushes with, evil. From an epistemological point of view, evil is problematic because it violates one of criminology's most cherished foundational principles of being 'scientific', rather than a discipline based on speculation or ideology (religious ideology included). As a modern science, it should be able to relate itself quite objectively and rationally to the designation crime and the dispensing of punishment on behalf of an impersonal bureaucratic state apparatus (i.e. the criminal justice system). Criminology should be positivistic in that it is not only devoted to observing the law, but should likewise develop and use its theories, concepts and logics to discover the laws of law-breaking and the causes of deviancy and functional praxes of rehabilitation. It should base itself on the principles of the Enlightenment, that insist on the basic goodness and perfectability of each and every individual. It should also retain its presumption that crime is a socially constructed phenomenon, so things like evil that emanate or imply metaphysical, religious or individual pathologies should not be recognized from a disciplinary academic perspective.

But while this is consistent, or even in many ways laudable, is it justified? Has it advanced our understanding of crime and punishment or raised the profile and increased the impact of academic research in public and policy discourses to the fullest possible extent? Or has ignoring evil and leaving it to the 'true crime' merchants to bandy about more or less without criticism or complaint further polarized public and popular understandings of crime, deviance, punishment and social control, and made scholarship in these areas appear even more elitist and irrelevant?

It is pretty clear when you get to the reality, that the aspirations listed above as to what criminology should be are not much more than that. Evil is ever present and indeed rife in the doing of crime, the suffering of victims and the impact on society, and (perhaps more importantly) the ways in which ordinary people are able to make sense of this whole mix.

Maybe this is what some of these criminologists are getting at when they point to the divergence between crime as something that is socially constructed and the foundations of criminological logic which suggest that something else is at work (which is in essence evil). Pretending it is not an issue is to be in complete denial of the facts. Dealing with it theoretically as a 'construction' of social reality as opposed to a 'positive' fact of reality also would appear to be an insufficiently stable dichotomy. As is the designation of the source(s) of evil: is crime generated by wicked people, or are there perfectly explainable social circumstances to blame? Is it really the case that the criminal justice system distinguishes systematically and consistently between the two options (see Hawkins, 1983)?

Could evil help reinvigorate criminology for the public?

So what should we do?

Perhaps a first step is to acknowledge, as the disciplines we have discussed throughout this book have done, that evil is not a dead or dumb concept, consigned to history along with the other superstitions of premodern times. Perhaps it is time to admit that it is time for criminologists to finally face evil.

Second, we might begin by taking on board some of the lessons offered by the thinkers we have discussed throughout this book among others, and begin (or in some cases continue) the painstaking work of relating these interdisciplinary conceptual and theoretical frameworks to the existing epistemologies of criminology.

Consider the thoughts on crime and criminality suggested by Eagleton, Kristeva and Ricoeur and their concentration on narratives of violence, desire and punishment:

> If the word 'evil' is not to be found in the dictionary of political correctness, it is because it is thought to imply a particular theory of wrongdoing, one which regards it as springing from metaphysical rather than historical causes. It is not poor housing and lack of prospects which led you to steal the car, but the eating of an apple long ago. The business of changing the world so as to diminish the causes of crime accordingly gives way to right-wing talk of the obduracy of human nature and the darkness of the human heart. Talk of evil can be left to the neo-Gothic, vampire-crazed young, for whom the word figures as a compliment.
>
> (Eagleton, 2005: 115–116)

> It is thus not lack of cleanliness or health that causes abjection but what disturbs identity, system, order. What does not respect borders, positions, rules. The in-between, the ambiguous, the composite. The traitor, the liar, the criminal with a good conscience, the shameless

rapist, the killer who claims he is a saviour... Any crime, because it draws attention to the fragility of the law, is abject, but premeditated crime, cunning murder, hypocritical revenge are even more so because they heighten the display of such fragility. He who denies morality is not abject; there can be grandeur in amorality and even in crime that flaunts its disrespect for the law—rebellious, liberating, and suicidal crime. Abjection, on the other hand, is immoral, sinister, scheming, and shady: a terror that dissembles, a hatred that smiles, a passion that uses the body for barter instead of inflaming it, a debtor who sells you up, a friend who stabs you...

(Julia Kristeva, *The Powers of Horror* (1982: 4))

As these two quotes suggest, evil is something that is always subject to our cultural will to divest ourselves of such 'essentialist' and metaphysical baggage from the past, but at the same time it still exerts the same irresistible epistemological pull that it has for millennia. In the search for the science of crime, where do we go from here? I don't have the answers for you as this is very much a live issue in the discipline. I hope this book will give rise to thoughts and debates about evil that will take these discussion and debate further. These are my choices and impressions, as a criminologist and a human being. I am interested in what my academic colleagues, but just as importantly, what my students and any other readers have to say on these matters.

What do you think?

References

Alexander, Jon (1990) 'Job Considered as a Conversion Account'. *Spirituality Today*. Vol. 42, No. 2., pp. 126–140.

Alford, C. Fred (1997) *What Evil Means to Us*. Ithaca and London: Cornell University Press.

Andrews, D.A. and Wormith, Stephen J. (1989) 'Personality and Crime: Knowledge Destruction and Construction in Criminology'. *Justice Quarterly*. Vol. 6, No. 3, September 1989. pp. 289–309.

Arendt, Hannah (1977) *Eichmann in Jerusalem: A Report on the Banality of Evil*. Harmondsworth: Penguin.

Arnolds-Ratliff, Katie (2012) '(At Least) Fifty Shades of Erotica'. *Time Magazine*. 9 July 2012. Available online at http://content.time.com/time/magazine/article/0,9171,2118283,00.html (accessed 16 September 2013).

Aukerman, Miriam (2002) *Extraordinary Evil, Ordinary Crime: A Framework for Understanding Transitional Justice*. Section IIIB 'Picking Paradigms'. *Harvard Human Rights Journal*. Vol. 15, Spring 2002. Available online at http://www.law.harvard.edu/students/orgs/hrj/iss15/aukerman.shtml#Heading560.

Badiou, Alain (2001) *Ethics: An Essay on the Understanding of Evil*. London: Verso.

Baldick, Chris (2008) *The Concise Oxford Dictionary of Literary Terms (Third Edition)*. Oxford and New York: Oxford University Press.

Barlow, Hugh (1981) *Introduction to Criminology*. Boston, MA: Little, Brown.

Baron Cohen, Simon (2013) 'The Science of Evil'. *The Huffington Post*. 15 October 2013. Available online at http://www.huffingtonpost.com/simon-baroncohen/science-of-evil_b_2831311.html (accessed 15 October 2013).

Bataille, Georges (2006) *Literature and Evil*. Translated by Alaister Hamilton.

Baudrillard, Jean (1993) *The Transparency of Evil*. Translated by James Benedict. London: Verso.

Baudrillard, Jean (2005) 'The Intelligence of Evil' in *The Intelligence of Evil or The Lucidity Pact*. Translated by Chris Turner. Oxford: Berg.

Bauman, Zygmunt (1989) *Modernity and the Holocaust*. Cambridge: Polity.

Becker-Leckrone, Megan (1995) 'Salome: The Fetishization of a Textual Corpus'. *New Literary History*. Vol. 26, No. 2, pp. 239–260.

Beker, Sonia Pauline (2007) *Symphony on Fire: A Story of Music and Spiritual Resistance During the Holocaust* (First edition). Wordsmithy.

Bergen, Doris L. (1996) 'Music and the Holocaust' in David Scrase and Wolfgang Mieder (eds), *The Holocaust: Introductory Essays*. Burlington, VT: The Center for Holocaust Studies at the University of Vermont, pp. 133–147.

Bernstein, Richard J. (1996) *Hannah Arendt and the Jewish Question*. Cambridge, MA: MIT Press.

Bernstein, Richard J. (2001) 'Radical Evil: Kant at War With Himself' in Pia Lara (ed), *Rethinking Evil: Contemporary Perspectives*. London: University of California Press, pp. 55–85.

Bernstein, Richard J. (2002) *Radical Evil: A Philosophical Interrogation*. Cambridge: Polity.

Birmingham, Peg (2003) 'Holes of Oblivion: The Banality of Radical Evil'. *Hypatia*. Vol. 18, No. 1 (Winter 2003), pp. 80–103.

Browder, Laura (2006) 'Dystopian Romance: True Crime and the Female Reader'. *Journal of Popular Culture*. Vol. 39, No. 6, pp. 928–953.

Buonaventura, Wendy (2010) *Serpent of the Nile: Women and Dance in the Arab World*. London: Saqi Books.

Bush, George W. (2002) *The National Security Strategy for the United States of America*. September 2002. Available online at http://www.whitehouse.gov/nsc/nss.pdf (accessed 7 June 2007).

Card, Claudia (2002) *The Atrocity Paradigm: A Theory of Evil*. Oxford: Oxford University Press.

Carter, Angela (1979) *The Sadeian Woman: An Exercise in Cultural History*. London: Virago.

Chan, Stephen (2005) *Out of Evil: International Politics and Old Doctrines of War*. London: I.B. Taurus.

Christie, Nils (2001) 'Answers to Atrocities: From Amnesia to Amnesty'. Available online at http://home.online.no/~ivajoha/nato/answers.html (accessed 6 January 2014).

Clarke, R.V.G. and Felson, Marcus (eds) (2004) *Routine Activity and Rational Choice (Advances in Criminological Theory Vol. 5)*. Transaction Publishers: New Brunswick, NJ.

Cohen, Stanley (1985) *Visions of Social Control: Crime, Punishment and Classification*. Cambridge: Polity.

Cohen, Stanley (2001) *States of Denial: Knowing About Atrocities and Suffering*. Cambridge: Polity.

Cohen-Rottenberg, Rachel (2012) 'Representing Difference as Pathology: An Example From Simon Baron-Cohen's *The Science of Evil*'. Available online at http://www.autismandempathy.com/?page_id=1583 (accessed 15 October 2013).

Copjec, Joan (ed) (1993) *Radical Evil*. London: Verso.

Copjec, Joan (ed) (1996) *Radical Evil*. London: Verso Booles.

Coyle, M.J. (2005) 'The Discourse of Crime as "Evil" in Media'. Available online at http://citation.allacademic.com/meta/p_mla_apa_research_citation/0/2/2/1/0/pages22109/p22109-8.php (accessed 16 September 2013).

Creed, Barbara (1993) *The Monstrous-Feminine: Film, Feminism, Psychoanalysis*. London: Routledge.

Cropley, David H., Cropley, Arthur J., Kaufman, James C. and Runco, Mark A. (eds) (2010) *The Dark Side of Creativity*. Cambridge: Cambridge University Press.

Davies, Paul (1998) 'Sincerik and the End of Theodicy: Three Remarks on Levinas and Kant'. *Research in Phenomenology*. 28(1): 126–151.

Dearey, Melissa (2012) 'Dealing With Metaphysical Evil: The Banker as Evil Genius in the British Television Show *Deal or No Deal*'. *Journal of British Cinema and Television*. Vol. 9, pp. 262–282.

Derrida, Jacques (2002) *Writing and Difference*. London and New York: Routledge.

Descartes, Rene [1641] (1996) *Meditations on First Philosophy*. Translated and edited by John Cottingham. Cambridge: Cambridge University Press.

Dobash, R.E., Dobash, R.P., Schlesinger, P. and Weaver, C. (1998) ' "Crimewatch UK": Women's Interpretations on Televised Violence' in M. Fishman and G. Cavendish (eds), *Real Crime*. pp. 37–58. New York: Aldine de Gruyter, 1998.

Donahue, Deirdre (2012) '10 Reasons "Fifty Shades of Grey" Has Shackled Readers'. *USA Today*. 7 October 2010.

Duncan, Sam (2012) 'Moral Evil, Freedom and the Goodness of God: Why Kant Abandoned Theodicy'. *British Journal for the History of Philosophy*. Vol. 20, No. 5, pp. 973–991.

Du Plessix Gray, Francine (2000) *At Home With the Marquis de Sade*. London: Pimlico.

Dworkin, Andrea (2000) *Scapegoat: The Jews, Israel, and Women's Liberation*. London: Free Press.

Eagleton, Terry (2005) *Holy Terror*. Oxford: Oxford University Press.

Eagleton, Terry (2010) *On Evil*. New Haven and London: Yale University Press.

Easton, Dossie and Hardy, Janet W. (2004) *Radical Ecstasy: SM Journeys to Transcendence*. Oakland, California: Greenery Press.

Eliade, Mircea (1958) *Patterns in Comparative Religion*. Translated by Rosemary Sheed. Lincoln: University of Nebraska Press.

Fackenheim, Emil L. (1992) 'Kant and Radical Evil' in Ruth Chadwick (ed), *Immanuel Kant: Critical Assessments*. Vol. 3. London: Routledge, pp. 259–273.

Ferguson, Kathy E. (1993) *The Man Question: Visions of Subjectivity in Feminist Theory*. Berkeley and Los Angeles: University of California Press.

Fine, Robert (2001) 'Understanding Evil: Arendt and the Final Solution' in Mara Pia Lara (ed), *Rethinking Evil: Contemporary Perspectives*. Berkeley and London: University of California Press, pp. 131–150.

Foucault, Michel (2006) *History of Madness*. Edited by Jean Khalfa, translated by Jonathan Murphy and Jean Khalfa. London: Routledge.

Franzosi, Roberto (1998) 'Narrative Analysis—Or Why (and How) Sociologists Should Be Interested in Narrative'. *Annual Review of Sociology*. August 1998. Vol. 24, pp. 517–554.

Friedan, Betty [1963] (1992) *The Feminine Mystique*. Harmondsworth: Penguin.

Frost, Laura (2000) ' "Every Woman Adores a Fascist": Feminist Visions of Fascism From *Three Guineas* to *Fear of Flying*'. *Women's Studies: An Interdisciplinary Journal*. Vol. 29, No. 1, pp. 37–69.

Fuller, Steve (2011) 'Theodicy Sociologised: Suffering Smart in the Twenty-first Century'. *Irish Journal of Sociology*. Vol. 19, No. 1, pp. 93–115.

Fukuyama, Francis [1992] (2012) *The End of History and the Last Man*. London: Penguin.

Gallagher, Shaun (ed) (1997) *Hegel, History and Interpretation*. Albany: SUNY Press.

Gasché, Rodolphe (1986) *The Tain of the Mirror: Derrida and the Philosophy of Reflection*. Cambridge, MA and London: Harvard University Press.

Gaukroger, Stephen (1997) *Rene Descartes: An Intellectual Biography*. Oxford: Oxford University Press.

Geddes, Jennifer L. (ed) (2001) *Evil After Postmodernism: Histories, Narratives and Ethics*. London: Routledge.

Gino, Francesca and Ariely, Dan (2011) 'The Dark Side of Creativity: Original Thinkers Can Be More Dishonest'. Working Paper 11–064. Harvard Business School. Available online at http://www.hbs.edu/faculty/Publication%20Files/11-064.pdf (accessed 20 June 2013).

Greenspan, Henry (1998) *On Listening to Holocaust Survivors: Recounting and Life History*. Westport, CT: Praeger.

Greer, Germaine (1991) *The Change: Women, Ageing and the Menopause*. London: Penguin Books.

Grindstaff, Laura (2002) *The Money Shot: Trash, Class and the Making of TV Talk Shows*. Chicago and London: University of Chicago Press.

Grosz, Elizabeth (1989) *Sexual Subversions: Three French Feminists*. St Leonards, NSW, Australia: Allen & Unwin.

Halbersham, Judith (2001) 'Oh Behave! Austin Powers and the Drag Kings'. *GLQ A Journal of Lesbian and Gay Studies*. Vol. 7, No. 3, pp. 425–452.

Halbersham, Judith (2005) *In a Queer Time and Place: Transgender Bodies, Subcultural Lives (Sexual Cultures)*. New York: NYU Press.

Hanson, Erik M. (2012) 'Immanuel Kant: Radical Evil'. *Internet Encyclopedia of Philosophy*. Available online at http://www.iep.utm.edu/rad-evil/ (accessed 21 February 2013).

Haraway, Donna (1991) *Simians, Cyborgs and Women: The Reinvention of Nature*. New York: Routledge.

Hawkins, Keith (1983) 'Assessing Evil: Decision Behaviour and Parole Board Justice'. *British Journal of Criminology*. Vol. 23, No. 2. April 1983. p. 102.

Hibbert, Christopher (1963) *The Roots of Evil: A Social History of Crime and Punishment*. London: Weidenfield & Nicholson.

Hill, Lesley (2001) *Bataille, Klossowski, Blanchot: Writing at the Limit*. Oxford: Oxford University Press.

Huang, Hsuan (undated) 'Kant's Concept of Radical Evil'. Available online at http://inter-disciplinary.net/ati/Evil/Evil%209/huang%20paper1.pdf (accessed 22 February 2013).

Ian, Marcia (1993) *Remembering the Phallic Mother: Psychoanalysis, Modernism and the Fetish*. Ithaca and New York: Cornell University Press.

Icoz, Nursel (2006) 'The Un-Dead: To Be Feared and/or Pitied' in Peter Day (ed), *Vampires: Myths and Metaphors of Enduring Evil*. New York: Rodopi, pp. 209–226.

Interview With the Vampire: The Vampire Chronicles (1994) [film] Directed by Neil Jordan. Geffen Pictures.

Jacobs, Ronald N. (1996) 'Civil Society and Crisis: Culture, Discourse, and the Rodney King Beating'. *The American Journal of Sociology*. Vol. 101, No. 5 (March 1996), pp. 1238–1272.

James, E.L. (2012) *Fifty Shades of Grey*. London: Vintage.

Janowski, Zbigniew (2002) 'Cartesian Theodicy: Descartes' Quest for Certitude' [book review]. *Project Muse*. Available online at http://muse.jhu.edu/journals/journal_of_the_history_of_philosophy/v041/41.2watson.pdf (accessed 20 August 2007).

Jervis, Robert (2003) 'Understanding the Bush Doctrine'. *Political Science Quarterly*. Vol. 118, No. 3, pp. 365–388.

Jong, Erica [1973] (1974) *Fear of Flying*. London: Secker & Warburg.

Katz, Jack (1988) *Seductions of Crime: Moral and Sensual Attractions in Doing Evil*. New York: Basic Books.

Kristeva, Julia (1982) *Powers of Horror: An Essay in Abjection*. New York: Columbia University Press.

Kristeva, Julia (1992) *Black Sun: Depression and Melancholia*. New York and Oxford: Columbia University Press.

Kristeva, Julia (2008) 'The Impenetrable Power of the Phallic Matron'. First published in *Libération*, 25 September 2008. Available online at http://www.kristeva.fr/palin_en.html (accessed 4 April 2013).

Langdridge, Darren (2007) 'Speaking the Unspeakable: S/M and the Eroticisation of Pain' in Darren Langdridge and Meg Barker (eds), *Sane, Safe and Consensual: Contemporary Perspectives on Sadomasochism*. Basingstoke: Palgrave Macmillan.

Lara, Mara Pia (ed) (2001) *Rethinking Evil: Contemporary Perspectives*. Berkeley and London: University of California Press.

LeMahieu, D.L. (1979) 'Malthus and the Theology of Scarcity'. *Journal of the History of Ideas*. Vol. 40, No. 3 (July–September 1979), pp. 467–474.

Lemert, Edwin M. (1997) *The Trouble With Evil: Social Control at the Edge of Morality*. New York: SUNY Press.

Lessing, Doris (2002) *The Summer Before the Dark*. London: Flamingo.

Let the Right One In (2008) [film] Directed by Tomas Alfredson. EFTI.

Lewis, Helen (2012) 'Leather Bound'. *New Statesman*. 23 July 2012, pp. 48–49.

Louden, Robert B. (2000) 'On the Radical Evil in Human Nature' in *Kant's Impure Ethics: From Rational Beings to Human Beings*. New York: Oxford University Press.

Lowen, Linda (undated) 'What is a milf? What does milf stand for?'. *About.Com Women's Issues*. Available online at http://womensissues.about.com/od/femalesexuality/f/whatismilf.htm (accessed 22/14/2013).

Lukacher, Maryline (1994) *Maternal Fictions: Stendahl, Sand, Rachilde, and Bataille*. Durham, North Carolina: Duke University Press.

Lye, John (1996) 'Some Principles of Phenomenological Hermeneutics'. Available online at http://www.brocku.ca/english/courses/4F70/ph.php (accessed 5 March 2013).

Macfarlane, Alan (1985) 'The Root of All Evil' in David Parkin (ed), *The Anthropology of Evil*. Oxford: Basil Blackwell, pp. 57–76.

Maritain, Jacques (1969) *The Dream of Descartes Together With Some Other Essays*. Port Washington: Kennikat Press.

Maruna, Shadd (2001) *Making Good: How Ex-Convicts Reform and Rebuild Their Lives*. Washington, DC: American Psychological Association.

Melehy, Hassan (1997) *Writing Cogito: Montaigne, Descartes, and the Institution of the Modern Subject*. New York: State University of New York Press.

Memmott, Carol (2012) 'E.L. James Basks in "Fifty Shades" of Sudden Success'. *USA Today*. 5 May 2012. Available online at http://usatoday30.usatoday.com/life/books/news/story/2012-05-07/el-james-fifty-shades-of-grey-books/54813990/1 (accessed 16 September 2013).

Merrin, William (2001) 'To Play With Phantoms: Jean Baudrillard and the Evil Demon of the Simulacrum'. *Economy and Society*. Vol. 30, No. 1. February 2001, pp. 85–111.

Miles, Donna (2003) 'Rumsfeld Dispels "Quagmire" Label for Operation Iraqi Freedom'. *American Forces Press Service*. 8 October 2003. US Department of Defense. Available online at http://www.defense.gov/News/NewsArticle.aspx?ID=28354 (accessed 17 July 2013).

Milgram, Stanley (1968) *The Compulsion to Do Evil: Obedience to Criminal Orders*. Corinth, VT: Black Mountain Press.

Miller, Arthur G. (ed) (2005) *The Social Psychology of Good and Evil*. Hove: Guilford Press.

Mittleman, Alan (2009) 'The Job of Judaism and the Job of Kant'. *Harvard Theological Review*. Vol. 102, No. 1. January 2009, pp. 25–50.

Morgan, David and Wilkinson, Iain (2001) 'The Problem of Suffering and the Sociological Task of Theodicy'. *European Journal of Social Theory*. Vol. 4, No. 2. pp. 199–214.

Murray, Michael (2005) 'Leibniz on the Problem of Evil'. Stanford Encyclopedia of Philosophy Online. Available online at http://plato.stanford.edu/entries/leibniz-evil/#Hol (accessed 31 January 2013).

Naughton, Julie (2012) 'Anything Goes: Focus on Romance: Fall 2012'. *Publishers Weekly*. 14 November 2012. Available online at http://www.publishersweekly.com/pw/by-topic/new-titles/adult-announcements/article/54762-anything-goes-focus-on-romance-fall-2012.html (accessed 16 September 2013).

Natural Born Killers (1994) [film] Directed by Oliver Stone. Warner Brothers.

Neiman, Susan (2002) *Evil in Modern Thought: An Alternative History of Philosophy*. Princeton, NJ: University of Princeton Press.

Nemo, Phillipe (1998) *Job and the Excess of Evil*. Pittsburgh, PA: Duquesne University Press.

Neuman, Lex (2010) 'Descartes' Epistemology'. Stanford Encyclopedia of Philosophy. Available online at http://plato.stanford.edu/entries/descartes-epistemology/#2.2 (accessed 17 August 2013).

Oliver, Kelly (2008) 'Julia Kristeva's Maternal Passions'. *Journal of French and Francophone Philosophy—Revue de la philosophie française et de langue française*, Vol. XVIII, No. 1. (2008–2010), pp. 1–8.

Parker, James (2012) 'Bad Romance: What the *Fifty Shades of Grey* Phenomenon Says About the Modern Sexual Condition'. *The Atlantic*. 19 September 2012. Available online at http://www.theatlantic.com/magazine/archive/2012/10/bad-romance/309082/ (accessed 4 September 2013).

PBS online (undated) 'The Trial of Adolf Eichmann'. Available online at http://www.remember.org/eichmann/intro.htm (accessed 6 September 2013).

Phillips, John (2005) *The Marquis de Sade: A Very Short Introduction*. Oxford and New York: Oxford University Press.

Presdee, Mike (2000) *Cultural Criminology and the Carnival of Crime*. London: Routledge.

Rangelov, Iavor (2003) 'Ideology Between Radical and Diabolical Evil: Kant's "Ethics of the Real"'. *Facta Universitatis*. No. 10, pp. 759–768.

Rendell, Matt (2011) *Salsa for People who Probably Shouldn't*. Edinburgh: Mainstream Publishing Company.

Ricoeur, Paul (1967) *The Symbolism of Evil*. London: Beacon Press.

Ricoeur, Paul (1970) *Freud and Philosophy: An Essay on Interpretation*. Translated by Denis Savage. New Haven and London: Yale University Press.

Ricoeur, Paul (1977) *Freud and Philosophy: Essay on Interpretation*. New Haven, CT: Yale University Press.

Ricoeur, Paul (1984) 'Evil, a Challenge to Philosophy and Theology'. *Journal of the American Academy of Religion*. LIII, Vol. 3. Available online at http://jaar.oxfordjournals.org/cgi/reprint/LIII/4/635.

Roberts, L., Lafta, R., Garfield, R., Khudhairi, J. and Burnham, G. (2004) 'Mortality Before and After the 2003 Invasion of Iraq: Cluster Sample Survey'. *Lancet*. Vol. 364, pp. 1857–1864.

Roche, Geoffrey (2006) 'Black Sun: Bataille on Sade'. *Janus Head*. Vol. 9, No. 1, pp. 157–180.

Rogozinski, Jacob (1993) 'It Makes Us Wrong: Kant and Radical Evil' in Joan Copjec (ed), *Radical Evil (S)*. London: Verso, pp. 30–45.

Rorty, Amelie (2001) *The Many Faces of Evil: Historical Perspectives*. London: Routledge.

Scarry, Elaine (1985) *The Body in Pain: The Making and Unmaking of the World*. Oxford: Oxford University Press.

Schaap, Andrew (2001) 'Guilty Subjects and Political Responsibility: Arendt, Jaspers and the Resonance of the "German Question" in Politics of Reconciliation'. *Political Studies*. Vol. 49, pp. 749–766.

Schott, Robin May (2003) 'Introduction: Special Issue on "Feminist Philosophy and the Problem of Evil"'. *Hypatia*. Vol. 18, No. 1.

Shabot, Sara Cohen (2005) 'The Grotesque? On Fleshing Out the Subject of Ethics' in Anna Fahraeus and Ann Katrin Jonsson (eds), *Critical Studies 26*, Textual Ethos Studies or Locating Ethics, pp. 67–84(18). Amsterdam: Rodopi.

Shafer-Landau, Russ (2004) 'Chapter 17: Values in a Scientific World'. *Whatever Happened to Good and Evil*, pp. 91–101. New York: Oxford University Press.

Shermer, M. (2004) *The Science of Good & Evil: Why People Cheat, Gossip, Care, Share and Follow the Golden Rule*. New York: Henry Holt.

Silverstone, Roger (2007) *Media and Morality: On the Rise of the Mediapolis*. Cambridge: Polity Press.

Skyfall (2012) [film] Directed by Sam Mendes. Eon Productions.

Sia, Santiago (1985) 'Reflections on Job's Question'. *Spirituality Today*. Fall 1985. Vol. 37, pp. 234–242.

Smith, David Woodruff (2011) 'Phenomenology', *The Stanford Encyclopedia of Philosophy* (Fall 2011 Edition), Edward N. Zalta (ed). Available online at http://plato.stanford.edu/archives/fall2011/entries/phenomenology (accessed 20 February 2013).

Smith, Karl E. (2004) 'Further Towards a Sociology of Evil'. *Thesis Eleven*. November 2004. No. 79, pp. 65–74.

Sonnet, Esther (1999) ' "Erotic Fiction by Women for Women": The Pleasures of Post-Feminist Heterosexuality'. *Sexualities*. Vol. 2, No. 2, pp. 167–187.

Sontag, Susan (1983) 'The Pornographic Imagination' in *A Susan Sontag Reader*. New York: Vintage Books, pp. 205–233.

Speak, Gill (1990) 'An Odd Kind of Melancholy: Reflections on the Glass Delusion in Europe (1440–1680)'. *History of Psychiatry*. June 1990. Vol. 1, No. 2, pp. 191–206.

Staub, Ervin (1989) *The Roots of Evil: The Origins of Genocide and Other Group Violence*. Cambridge: Cambridge University Press.

Stein, Ruth (2002) 'Evil as Love and as Liberation'. *Psychoanalytic Dialogues: The International Journal of Relational Perspectives*. Vol. 12, No. 3, pp. 393–420.

Sullivan, Roger J. (1989) 'The "Radical Evil" in Human Nature' in *Immanuel Kant's Moral Theory*. Cambridge: Cambridge University Press, pp. 124–126.

Swinburne, Richard (1996) 'Some Major Strands in Theodicy' in Daniel Howard-Snyder (ed), *The Evidential Argument From Evil*. Bloomington and Indianapolis: Indiana University Press, pp. 30–48.

The Hunger. (1983). [film] Directed by Tony Scott. MGM/United Artists.

The Matrix (1999) [film] Written and directed by Andy and Lana Wachowski. Warner Brothers Pictures.

Tremblay, Pierre (2004) 'Searching for Suitable Co-Offenders' in R.V.G. Clarke and Marcus Felson (eds), *Routine Activity and Rational Choice (Advances in Criminological Theory Vol. 5)*. Transaction Publishers: New Brunswick, NJ. Chapter 1, pp. 17–36.

Turner, J.G. (2002) *Libertines and Radicals in Early Modern London: Sexuality, Politics, and Literary Culture, 1630–1685*. Cambridge: Cambridge University Press.

TV Tropes (undated) 'Evil Twin'. Available online at http://tvtropes.org/pmwiki/pmwiki.php/Main/EvilTwin (accessed 19 August 2013).

Ussher, Jane M. (2006) *Managing the Monstrous Feminine: Regulating the Reproductive Body*. London: Routledge.

Vaaranen, Heli and Presdee, Mike (2004) 'Stories From the Streets: Some Fieldwork Notes on the Seduction of Speed' in J. Ferrel, K. Hayward, W. Morrison and M. Presdee (eds), *Cultural Criminology Unleashed*. Norfolk: Biddles Ltd.

Vetlesen, Arne Johan (2005) *Evil and Human Agency: Understanding Collective Evildoing*. Cambridge: Cambridge University Press.

Wall, John (2005) 'Phronesis as Poetic: Moral Creativity in Contemporary Aristotelianism'. *The Review of Metaphysics*. Vol. 59, No. 2. December 2005, pp. 313–331.

Weedon, Chris (1987) *Feminist Practice & Poststructuralist Theory*. Cambridge: Blackwell, pp. 63–73.

Weinstein, Deena (2000) *Heavy Metal: The Music and Its Culture*. Cambridge, MA: Da Capo Press.

Welzer, Harald (2002) 'On the Rationality of Evil: An Interview with Zygmunt Bauman'. *Thesis Eleven*. No. 70. August 2002, pp. 100–112.

White, R.W. (1993) *Provisional Irish Republicans: An Oral and Interpretive History*. London: Greenwood Press.

Wilkinson, Iain (2005) *Suffering: A Sociological Introduction*. Cambridge: Polity Press.

Young, Jock (2011) *The Criminological Imagination*. London: Polity Press.

Zimbardo, Philip (2007) *The Lucifer Effect: How Good People Turn Evil*. London: Rider Books.

Index

Printed and bound by CPI Group (UK) Ltd, Croydon, CR0 4YY